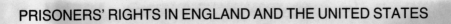

PRISONERS' RIGHTS IN ENGLAND AND THE UNITED STATES

Prisoners' Rights in England and the United States

A. J. FOWLES
Lecturer in Social Policy and Social Work
University of York

Avebury

Aldershot · Brookfield USA · Hong Kong · Singapore · Sydney

Published by

Avebury

Gower Publishing Company Limited
Gower House, Croft Road, Aldershot,
Hants, GU11 3HR, England

Gower Publishing Company
Old Post Road, Brookfield, Vermont 05036
USA

ISBN 0-566-07083-9

Printed and Bound in Great Britain by
Athenaeum Press Ltd., Newcastle upon Tyne.

Contents

Acknowledgements

I would like to take this opportunity to thank all of the people who have given their time and help so freely in the preparation of this study. It is not invidious to mention some for particular thanks.

Special thanks should go to Ira Kirschbaum of the General Counsel's Office of the Federal Bureau of Prisons, Richard Groskin of the General Accounting Office, and Alan Chaset of the Federal Judicial Center, for their time and patience in explaining the activities of the federal courts in American prisoners' rights litigation.

I would like to thank Kay Jones, John Martin, Graham Zellick and David Cornwell for their many helpful comments which have been used in the revisions of this study. Members of the Department of Social Policy and Social Work who are rightfully to be thanked are Liz Wilson and Alison Holdsworth, the latter deserves special thanks, not only for coping with the manuscript, but also for overcoming the new technology.

Table of cases

Williams v. Home office (No. 2) (1982) 2 All ER 564 CA: 60
Yorke v. Chapman (1839) 10 Ad. and El. 207: 42

European Convention on Human Rights

Boyle and Rice v. United Kingdom Judgment 27 April 1988: 90
Brady v. United Kingdom 3 EHRR 297: 71, 81
Campbell and Fell v. United Kingdom 5 EHRR 207: 28, 65, 74-6, 80, 82, 83
Golder v. United Kingdom 1 EHRR 524: 40, 65, 72-3, 77-8, 83, 84, 91, 92, 93, 97, 99
Hamer v. United Kingdom 4 EHRR 139: 81-2, 84
Hilton v. United Kingdom 3 EHRR 104: 69-70, 74, 94, 150
Kiss v. United Kingdom 1977 Yearbook pp. 156-80: 69, 73-4
Knechtl v. United Kingdom 1970 Yearbook pp. 730-60: 72, 84, 92, 97
Reed v. United Kingdom 3 EHRR 136: 70-1, 83
Silver and Others v. United Kingdom 3 EHRR 475: 76
Silver and Others v. United Kingdom 5 EHRR 347: 30, 78-80, 82, 83, 91, 92, 93, 97, 99
Tyrer v. United Kingdom 2 EHRR 1: 93
X v. United Kingdom 5 EHRR 162: 80
X v. United Kingdom 5 EHRR 192: 80
X v. United Kingdom 5 EHRR 260: 80

United States

Argon v. Montayne 392 F. Supp. 454 (1975): 130
Banning v. Looney 213 F. 2d 771 (1954): 109
Barnett v. Rodgers 410 F. 2d 995 (1969): 131
Baxter v. Palmigiano 47 L. Ed 2d 810 (1976): 116
Bell v. Wolfish 60 L. Ed 2d 447 (1978): 114, 126
Bounds v. Smith 52 L. Ed 2d 72 (1977): 112
Bribson v. Lane 554 F. Supp. 426 (1983): 130
Brown v. Peyton 437 F. 2d 1228 (1971): 131
Butler v. Preiser 380 F. Supp. 612 (1974): 129, 135, 154
Chavis v. Rowe 643 F. 2d 1281 (1981): 117
Clonce v. Richardson 379 F. Supp. 338 (1974): 118
Cooper v. Pate 324 F. 2d 165 (1963): 111, 138
Cruz v. Beto 31 L. Ed 2d 263 (1972): 131
Finney v. Mabry 485 F. Supp. 720 (1978): 133
Fortune Society v. McGinnis 319 F. Supp 901 (1970): 128
Freeman v. Lockhart 503 F. 2d 1016 (1974): 132
Gates v. Coolier 390 F. Supp. 482 (1975): 140-1, 143
Grummett v. Rushen 779 F. 2d 491 (1985): 134
Hewitt v. Helms 74 L. Ed 2d 675 (1982): 119
Holt v. Sarver 309 F. Supp.362 (1970): 122-3, 127, 132, 155
Hudson v. palmer 82 L. Ed 2d 393 (1984): 121, 134, 153
Hughes v. Rowe 66 L. Ed 2d 163 (1980): 116
Hutto v. Finney 57 L. Ed 2d 522 (1978): 125-6
Johnson v. Anderson 370 F. Supp. 1373 (1974): 116, 125, 128,
Johnson v. Avery 21 L. Ed 2d 718 (1969): 111
Jones v. North Carolina Prisoners' Labour Union Inc. 53 L. Ed 629 (1977): 129-30, 154
Kahane v. Carlton 527 F. 2d 492 (1975): 132
Lawrence v. Davis 401 F. Supp. 1203 (1975): 129

Long v. Parker 390 F. Supp. 816 (1968): 131
Meachum v. Fano 49 L. Ed 2d 451 (1976): 118
Monroe v. Pape 365 US 167 (1961): 110, 120, 136
Montayne v. Haymes 49 L. Ed 2d 466 (1976): 119
Newman v. Alabama 559 F. 2d 283 (1977): 124, 132-5
Olim v. Wakinekona 75 L. Ed 2d 813 (1982): 119
Palmigiano v. Garrahy 443 F. Supp. 956 (1977): 124-5
Parratt v. Taylor 68 L. Ed 2d 420, (1981): 120, 121, 153
Peek v. Ciccone 288 F. Supp. 329 (1969): 133
Pell v. Procunier 41 L. Ed 2d 495 (1974): 128
Pepperling v. Crist 678 F. 2d 787 (1982): 117
Ponte v. Real 85 L. Ed 2d 553 (1985): 118
Procunier v. Martinez 40 L. Ed 2d 224 (1974): 129
Prushinowski v. Hambrich 570 F. Supp. 863 (1983): 132
Pugh v. Locke 406 F. Supp. 318 (1977): 123-4, 125, 126, 127, 132, 133
Rhodes v. Chapman 69 L. Ed 59 (1981): 125, 127, 143
Ruiz v. Estelle 679 F. 2d 1115 (1982): 126-7
Saxbe v. Washington Post Co. 41 L. Ed 2d 514 (1974): 128
Siegel v. Ragen 180 F. 2d 785 (1950): 110
Trop v. Dulles 356 US 86 (1958): 121
United States v. Gouveia 81 L. Ed 2d 146 (1984): 114
Venus v. Goodman 556 F. Supp. 514 (1983): 133
Vitek v. Jones 63 L. Ed 2d 552 (1979): 119
Walker v. Blackwell 411 F. 2d 23 (1969): 131
Weems v. United States 217 US 349 (1910): 122
Wolff v. McDonnell 41 L. Ed 2d 935 (1974): 111, 115-6, 118
Wyatt v. Stickney 325 F. Supp. 781 (1971): 133

Canada

R v. Miller and Cockriell (1975) 63 DLR 3d 193:47
Solosky v. The Queen (1980) 105 DLR 3d 745: 99

Introduction

> Let it be roundly said, there is no such thing as prisoners' rights
> – such cant can safely be left to....ubiquitous prison reformers....

This statement was made in a <u>Times</u> leader shortly after the capital punishment debate in the House of Commons in 1983. It is disquieting for three reasons: first, the domestic law of England establishes that all citizens, whether they are at liberty or not, have fundamental rights recognised by the courts. Second, Britain is a signatory to a number of international Human Rights conventions, including the European Convention on Human Rights which established a Court of Human Rights at Strasbourg. The Court of Human Rights has found Britain to be in breach of its international obligations, and has led to changes in prison policy. Third, British readers expect <u>The Times</u> to get its facts right. In this case, the leader writer seems to be motivated by a simple determination to put the clock back.

In recent years, there has been an increasing interest in prisoners' rights among penologists, lawyers, and critics of the penal system. One of the features common to much of the writing produced by these individuals and groups has been the habit of alluding explicitly or implicitly to the development of prisoners' rights in the US. In the mid 1970s, the American federal courts were actively supporting the claims brought by prisoners. The English courts by contrast were almost totally uninterested in the fate of prisoners after conviction. [1] At the same time, the prisoners held in American prisons were undergoing a fierce process of politicisation which led to confrontations with the prison authorities in the prisons themselves and in those bastiors of the establishment – the courts. The prisoners were fighting back, and winning important victories.

The example of the American prisoners' movement and the legal approach to prisoners' rights provided useful ammunition for some of the more radical critics of the penal system in England. Important points could be won by holding up the American experience as a contrast to the lethargy and backwardness of the English system. Stan Cohen used the American prison experience as a signpost for Britain's prisons. (Basaglia, 1975) Cohen stresses the common Anglo-American experience of prison building and the uses of imprisonment. The paper is clearly a product of the 1970s and it concentrates on the contemporary fears of indeterminate sentencing and the threat this was thought to pose to the personal integrity of the prisoner.

In 1977, Fitzgerald published his study of the origins and development of PROP (Preservation of the Rights of Prisoners), Prisoners in Revolt. Fitzgerald recounts the histories of PROP in England and various prisoners' unions in the US. Although he does not say explicitly that an English prisoners' union would take precisely the same form as those in America, he provides a series of instances of what has happened in the US and contrasts the situation with that in England.

More recently, Martin Wright, a former Director of the Howard League, in Making Good uses American prisoners' grievance mechanisms as a demonstration of what would be possible in England. Wright's approach is one of silent reproach of the English system which he regards as unimaginative by comparison. (Wright, 1982)

Genevra Richardson discussed the apparent convergence of the legal systems of late capitalist societies and raised the question whether British experience in this field of prisoners' rights would necessarily mirror the American. Richardson suggests that this will probably not happen, as the cultural and legal contexts differ significantly. (Richardson, 1984)

To date, there has been very little comparative research on prisoners' rights. The major work is Marin's study of prison discipline. (Marin, 1983) This study covers developments in this field up to 1979. Marin's study is concerned primarily with procedural issues. Though it broke some new ground, and provides an excellent background to problems of prison discipline its significance is gradually diminishing since there has been a flood of decisions since the last case reported. Gillian Douglas's brief comparative study compares the methods provided for prisoners to complain against decisions taken by prison administrators in England and Wales, Sweden and Denmark. (Douglas, 1984)

The present study is broader, it is concerned with prisoners' rights, a topic of which prison discipline and grievance procedures are sub-sets. Since it is necessary to draw a clear finishing line in an area of study where cases are often protracted, and major changes are taking place, it ends with the Leech decision made by the House of Lords in November 1988.

A problem faced in any comparative analysis is whether the cultural, political and legal contexts differ so greatly that fair comparisons are impossible. At first sight, a comparison between England and Wales and the US looks straightforward: there was a common heritage in political philosophy and jurisprudence up to the last quarter of the eighteenth century. But there are now many differences between the legal procedures and legal assumptions (e.g. judicial review of the constitutionality of legislation versus Parliamentary supremacy) of the two countries, resulting from two hundred years of separate development.

The Constitutions of the two countries, which may be thought of as providing the rules of the game, are different. The US has a written constitution which provides a constant frame of reference against which the constitutionality of new legislation may be tested. In England, there is nothing like this degree of constancy as statute law, the assumed content of common law, and judicial views of public policy are all liable to change over time. In recent years accession to the European Community has brought a new locus of decision making. Since Britain became a signatory to the European Convention on Human Rights, there is now a written and potentially enforceable list of rights which apply to everyone living in the country; but realisation that this is so develops slowly, even in the courts.

The legal professions differ in a number of important ways. The English legal profession is divided into two branches while the American legal profession is unitary. The social backgrounds and methods of professional training of lawyers in England and America differ significantly, and there has always been a strong tradition of some American lawyers taking an interest in the legal problems of socially disadvantaged groups. Many American law firms have used the opportunities for pro bono publico work to attract the best candidates to their practices. (Taylor, 1981) There is also strong evidence that lawyers recruited into the federal Department of Justice are younger, better qualified and more interested in civil rights issues than lawyers in other government departments. (Horowitz, 1977)

The opportunities to raise prisoners' rights issues in the two countries differ. England and Wales form a unitary legal system, and precedent usually closes down the causes which may be brought before the courts. Rejection of a line of argument basically means that the issue is closed. In the US, the only nationally binding precedent is that provided by the Supreme Court. A decision made by one of the courts of appeals is binding only on the inferior courts in its circuit, and there are eleven circuits. Until precedent is established, the district courts may make different decisions on similar facts and submissions. By contrast with the forty-plus cases reported in England and Wales since 1822, there were 15,629 prisoners' rights cases brought before the federal courts in America in 1981 alone. (Powell, 1982)

There are significant differences between the major symbols to which the two political and legal systems respond. The idea of the 'the state' is important in the context of prisoners' rights because of the concern with the relationship between the citizen and the state. Dyson has argued in The State Tradition in Western Europe that the idea of the state has been neglected in the English-speaking world as both the traditional British empiricist and the American pragmatist viewpoints define concepts as useful only if they are grounded in experience. Historically, both England and the US have shared a 'stateless' quality, neither has developed notions of permanent structures of power and authority beyond government. Until recently, there was no such thing in English law as a body of 'public law' designed to cope with the power available to government in its dealings with individual citizens. Slowly, public law has become more highly developed in theory and teaching, and there has been greater acceptance of its ideas among the legal professions and the judiciary. The situation in the US is different in that while the state does not play a very great part in American political theory, Americans are deeply distrustful of governmental power; the American system of government is proclaimed to be one of 'laws not men'. There is another strand in American society which has introduced a much stronger attack on the state: the presence of groups who emigrated from the 'state-societies' of Europe. Both of these strands have combined to produce a view which is highly sceptical of state power and official direction.

British and American societies have taken different views on equality and the related problem of how to cope with minorities. The British view of equality has been generally one of individual freedom rather than of group progress and social mobility. In the US, on the other hand, since the 1950s and the beginning of the movement to increase racial equality, there has been an increasing emphasis on equality of outcome rather than simple equality of opportunity. This approach has been traced to the view that the Constitution itself establishes the limits of government (majoritarian) power in relation to small and helpless minorities; and there is the widely-held view that the courts exist to remedy defects in the legislative process.

This book is concerned with five main questions:

1. what is the general philosophical context of prisoners' rights within the general human rights debate?
2. what protections and safeguards exist for prisoners in English domestic law?
3. what rights have been established, or are currently being claimed, under the European Convention?
4. what rights exist for prisoners in the US?
5. what are the similarities and differences between the two systems?

The leader writer in The Times argues that the state has only minimal obligations to prisoners, the provision of accommodation and discipline:

> There is nothing wrong with slopping-out or any of the other personal indignities so vividly described by penal reformers - provided that these are willed by the state as part of the punishment....There is a strong case - now even stronger - for the consistent application of an uncomfortable regime to Category A prisoners: who need shed a tear at their confinement in solitary for long periods? For a strictly defined class of convict, rehabilitation is now a loose idea of the 1960s: the hour is retribution.

While it is conceded that 'our present array of overcrowded jails, Victorian sanitation and arbitrary lock-ups' makes it difficult to meet even the minimal obligations of accommodation and discipline, the argument is that imprisonment means not only liberty lost - it means the abrogation of all rights in order to provide additional elements of punishment. Prisoners have broken the law, and may therefore lose all the rights and privileges of the law-abiding. Imprisonment by its nature gives the body of the prisoner into the total power of the state.

This is an argument which has to be taken seriously, because the question of prisoners' rights is not only of importance to prisoners, prison administrators and penal reformers. It is a central issue in political and social theory. The question of what limits can be placed on the power of the state over people whom the state has deprived of their liberty provides a significant test case of more general arguments about rights; and a test of the moral standing of the state.

Note

[1] This study is concerned with developments in England and Wales. England and English are used as shorthand although the discussions apply equally to Wales.

1 Rights for prisoners

The civil rights movement in the US in the 1960s brought about the end of many forms of overt racial discrimination. President Jimmy Carter tried to base US foreign policy on human rights considerations. A variety of International Covenants originating with the United Nations in the same decade were designed to tackle economic, social and cultural issues. (Brownlie, 1971, p. vii)

In Britain, lawyers and politicians have called for a Bill of Rights to provide individual citizens with a defence against the evils of 'elective dictatorship', to use Lord Hailsham's phrase. (Hailsham, 1983) Professor Frank Stacey saw a New Bill of Rights as a way to 'provide a yardstick for central and local government services, and for the standards of fairness and humanity which they achieve in their dealings with the individual'. (Stacey, 1973, Preface)

The whole question of rights has become both a political battleground and the source of great intellectual confusion. The political arguments have tended to concentrate on whether various groups should have rights and if so, which rights. Intellectual arguments, mainly from philosophers and lawyers, have concentrated on the question of whether rights can be said to exist and if so, how they can be legitimated.

The nature of human rights

Any discussion of rights tends to look alien in the British context. Britain has an unwritten constitution and rights have traditionally been defined in negative rather than positive terms, i.e. in terms of what the state may not do rather than what the citizen can claim. When asked in 1975 by Norman Tebbitt MP to list the basic rights of the citizen

1

throughout the UK together with the statutes under which they were guaranteed, Dr Shirley Summerskill, then Minister of State at the Home Office, replied in a brief and unedifying way:

> There is no distinction in the law of this country between 'basic' and other rights, and many rights of the citizen are derived from common law rather than statute. (House of Commons Debate, 15 January 1976, col 196 WA)

This lacks a degree of precision. No one can say with certainty what actual rights citizens possess, or whether the rights they ought to possess in theory can be claimed in practice. Further confusion is added by the conflation of legal and moral issues. Political and moral philosophers have distinguished two main kinds of rights: human or natural, and legal.

Because of the importance of the United Nations' Universal Declaration of Human Rights of 1948, there is a tendency to see human rights theory as a recent development; but, as Cranston puts it

> Human Rights is a twentieth century name for what has been traditionally known as natural rights or, in a more exhilarating phrase, the rights of man. (Cranston, 1973, p. 1)

Locke argued in Of Civil Government, published in 1690, that in the state of nature, there was perfect freedom for men to order their actions. This state of nature was one of equality, where power and jurisdiction over others were reciprocal. It was also a state of liberty where men were free to enjoy life, health and possessions. Men were restrained from invading the rights of others and 'from doing hurt to one another'. Locke argued that man retained these rights from the state of nature even when other forms of civil and political organisation developed.

These ideas of liberty deriving from the state of nature were influential in the development of the theories of government of the American colonists. The Bill of Rights which was adopted by the Virginia constitutional convention in 1776 was greatly influenced by Locke and in turn provided a basis for the Bill of Rights adopted in 1791 by the US. Jefferson added the right of the pursuit of happiness to those of life and liberty. The Constituent Assembly in France after the Revolution adopted the Declaration of the Rights of Man and of the Citizen. The Declaration states that 'men are born and remain free and equal in rights' and asserts that political organisation exists to protect these rights. Both the American and French models assert that these rights are both natural and inalienable.

The developments in human rights doctrine since the Second World War have been in response to government actions which deprived people of their rights by making rights dependent on citizenship, and then by stripping some people of their citizenship. Modern human rights doctrine has gone back to Locke and the presupposition of a concept of equal and universal human worth. Rights are not based on merit or fulfilment of duty. In respect of human worth, all persons are graded equally. Rights are held by all human beings because they are human, and as Joel Feinberg argues that in a society based on rights, at least some rights will belong irrevocably to fools and rogues as well as everyone else. (Feinberg, 1973, p. 90)

In the last 40 years, the concept of positive rights has been added to the older idea of negative rights. Both the US Bill of Rights and the

French Declaration of the Rights of Man and the Citizen were essentially libertarian documents, designed to put limits on the powers of governments. The change to positive rights has been commented on by Professor Sir Norman Anderson in his Hamlyn Lectures, Liberty, Law and Justice. Anderson suggested that these new positive rights represent aspirations 'which are designed to set goals and establish principles rather than define provisions which could be incorporated in legislative enactments'. (Anderson, 1978, p. 41)

There is a certain amount of overlap between negative human rights and legal rights in Anglo-American legal systems. The establishment of legal rights involves either the incorporation of particular freedoms and/or the recognition of the existence of rights. The recognition that certain persons have a particular right has two immediate consequences: it imposes corresponding duties on other persons and it enlists the state's aid in the protection of those rights. In Kleinig's telling phrase

The coercive possibilities of legal rights have provided political muscle for moral rights. (Kleinig, 1978, p. 36)

Jenkins has argued that once the ideas of Locke had roused the American colonists against what they saw as arbitrary and oppressive government, the attention of the newly independent Americans shifted to establishing an apparatus to secure the rights that had been won. (Jenkins, 1980, p. 246) In America, the Bill of Rights and its subsequent Amendments has been the main vehicle for establishing individual rights. The traditional rights are protective in the sense that they guarantee basic freedoms, e.g. 'excessive bail shall not be required, nor excessive fines imposed', or 'no soldier shall, in time of peace be quartered in any house'. Legal rights of this kind do not confer positive benefits on people. These rights are enforceable. Disputes about their nature and scope can be assessed by judges in court.

Legal rights also have correlative duties which usually fall upon the state. These duties usually take the form of prohibitions. They demand that the state refrains from interfering with the lawful activities of the citizenry and from discriminating arbitrarily among them. (Jenkins, 1980, p. 247)

Legal philosophers have traditionally required four elements to be present before any claim can be recognised as a legal right: (i) there is the holder, or subject of the right - the person, real or legal, in whom the right inheres; (ii) there is the res that the right governs - the object (in the widest sense of the term) of the right; (iii) there is the act or forbearance commended by the right; and (iv) there are persons on whom specific duties are imposed. More recently, the school of legal realists has added a fifth element: (v) the legal procedures and remedies by which the right is protected and sanctioned. (Jenkins, 1980, p. 247)

It is possible to see the first four elements as the definition of primary rights while the fifth is a remedial right, to use Lloyd's term. (Lloyd, 1979, p. 312) The remedial right is procedural law which comes into play when a breach of a right has occurred and the injured party seeks to obtain a remedy. Until the legal system has been activated and the claim of injury has been recognised and accepted, the action for the breach of a right remains only a claim. There may well be instances where the rules of legal procedure prevent the establishment of an otherwise viable right - e.g. a time limit.

There is a further point to be made here which stems from the existence of a court. In this context it is argued that for most purposes a 'claim-right', to use Hohfield's concept, remains such until a court recognises it as a right. The court has the task of deciding whether the procedural rules have been followed and applied properly, but it also has to decide whether the right being claimed is one that already exists or that should exist. This consideration is important because judicial law-making or constitutional interpretation has usually been anathema to legal positivists. Judicial behaviour varies considerably between England and America. In the latter the US Supreme Court is concerned with constitutional issues and has established new rights which could not have been envisaged by those who drafted the Constitution in the late eighteenth century.

The American federal courts have played a significant part in determining the content of rights. Rights which began as broad claims without any highly formalised view of potential holders or of the acts demanded have been elaborated within a body of doctrine surrounding each right. Jenkins argues that eventually the body of doctrine becomes the right, in much the same way that a piece of grit becomes a pearl. (Jenkins, 1980, p. 248) Discussions surrounding the substance and protection of rights tend to be based entirely on legal arguments with little or no regard to the social, physical, or moral environment. Constitutional law and interpretation respond to their own inner logic, and the individual consciences of the judges. There is no guarantee as to the quality of the logic, nor to the representativeness or contemporaneousness of the consciences.

The English legal system of interpretation is different in that there is a hierarchy of courts which decide arguments on the basis of decontextualised instances, and avoid hypothetical issues of principle. Also the English courts are bound by the precedents of those above them in the hierarchy. Until 1966, the House of Lords was bound by its own precedents. Another significant contrast lies in the judicial protection of rights. English judges are not asked to rule on the constitutionality of legislation, but they may apply arguments about citizens' rights to a particular case. The opportunity available to the judges to consider issues of rights may be limited by the wording of legislation which prevents this kind of issue from emerging, or the judges may choose not to consider arguments about rights. The English judges are frequently less than willing to deal with issues of principle, irrespective of their place in the judicial hierarchy. (Stevens, 1979, pp. 269-70) Questions of public policy may have a greater impact than individual rights.

These relatively clear waters have been muddied in several different ways. First, there is the matter of the status of the European Convention on Human Rights (discussed in chapters 4 and 5). The words 'Human Rights' are clearly stated in the title of the Convention, to which Britain is a signatory. While the title gives the impression that it is concerned with the moral claims to rights derived from the human rights doctrine, this is in reality misleading. The European Convention on Human Rights fulfills all of the criteria listed above to be considered a convention on legal rights. The Convention is a set of legal rights backed by legal procedures and institutions which carry considerable legal force. The High Contracting Parties accept the binding nature of the Court of Human Rights decisions, and are committed to enforcing those decisions.

Second, in the US there have been important examples of the transition of claim-rights into legal rights. The Fourteenth Amendment to the Bill of Rights adopted in 1868, providing equal protection to all regardless of race and colour, developed notions of equality contained in the Declaration of Independence. But the rights guaranteed by the Fourteenth Amendment were effectively denied to blacks until the Civil Rights Act 1965. This statute law reinforced and gave procedural reality to what had previously been a moral right. The Civil Rights Act allowed cases involving constitutional issues to proceed directly to the federal courts without having previously exhausted state remedies.

The application to prisoners' rights

The general debate about the existence and nature of rights has always been heated, but opinions are as divided when the question 'Do prisoners have rights?' is posed. There seem to be five basic positions taken on the issue.

No one has rights

The argument that prisoners have rights is a logical absurdity. This view of rights can be traced back to Thomas Hobbes. The Hobbesian position is basically that the loss of natural rights was the price each man paid to join a larger social group, the common good necessitates the loss of individual autonomy. It is an argument for absolutist government.

Rights are only to be taken seriously if they exist in law

This is the view of Sir Norman Anderson

> So it has been suggested that the term 'rights' should be used exclusively to describe those rights which are, or at least could be, formally recognised and enforceable by legal standards, so that 'a right to equal pay' would, for example, only exist when a legal requirement on employers to provide equal pay for equal work existed. (Anderson, 1978, p. 43)

Rights exist, but may be lost as a consequence of individual actions

This view, the moral correlation of rights and duties, holds that 'the acquisition or possession of rights is the ability and willingness to shoulder duties and responsibilities'. (Feinberg, 1973, p. 61) The argument is based on morality rather than logic. In this view, it is acceptable to send a man to prison and deprive him of his liberty because he has not respected the rights of others. The linking of duties with rights does not mean that an offender will be deprived of all his rights on a permanent basis: rights may be restored when he shows that he can once again be considered trustworthy.

Rights are inalienable even if the individual breaks the law

Obviously this view creates a problem: what punishment, if any, can be imposed which will not diminish the offenders' rights? The reply provided by Lord Kilbrandon, then a Lord of Appeal, was that the sentence of imprisonment was 'no more than the deprivation of liberty'. (British Institute of Human Rights, 1975, p. xiii) The circumstances in which liberty may be constrained are limited in the sense that the offender can only be punished for an actual offence, and not for

5

individual or general deterrence. In custody, the state is expected to respect all of the individual's normal social, political and civil rights. All of the rights applying to a citizen survive conviction and follow him into the prison which should only be concerned with limiting liberty of movement. David Fogel provides the most substantial version of this view

> The prison sentence should merely represent a deprivation of liberty. All the rights accorded free citizens consistent with mass living and the execution of a sentence restricting the freedom of movement should follow a prisoner into prison. (Fogel, 1975, p. 202 emphasis in original.)

Rights can be used to attack the prison system as a whole

This might be called the agitational use of rights, where rights are cited as a means to other ends. As Cohen and Taylor put it

> Prisoners' rights have become a major concern of radicals in the United States in recent years. This is not because sensitive revolutionaries have decided to turn to the problem of imprisonment, but because direct confrontational tactics by inmates have forced the problem into public consciousness....
> Direct confrontation becomes the most appropriate style of fighting back for those groups which can unite under an anti-authoritarian ideological banner, and who can manifest sufficient solidarity to counteract the inevitably harsh retaliation by the authorities. (Cohen and Taylor, 1972, p. 145)

Social research in prisons

Few commentators have looked at the issue of offenders' rights in a consistent manner, and it is remarkable that major studies of the prison on both sides of the Atlantic generally treat the issue as one of only minor interest. Studies are predominantly concerned with three issues: descriptions of the prison world, analyses of the dynamics of prison life (usually defined as the official problem of how to maintain order), and the social organisation of inmates.

Descriptions of the prison world

There is a fairly high degree of continuity in the research conducted by social scientists on prisons. Donald Clemmer's The Prison Community, first published in 1940, was the first modern social science report on the prison, and has been seminal to much later research. Clemmer's approach is concerned with the creation of order in the prison. Clemmer argued that his study centred on the structure of social relationships in the prison community

> The point of view of this study may be said to be a sociological one, since its chief concern has been the making of an analysis of social patterns of the determinants of behaviour. (Clemmer, 1940, p. xvi)

After the publication of The Prison Community there was quite a long gap in the development of social research on prisons. There was a revival of interest in the 1950s and one of the new generation of sociologists, Donald Cressey, not only produced his own research but also provided a Foreword to the new edition of The Prison Community. Cressey suggested that although American sociology had moved on since the 1930s, most of the basic concepts and principles had remained unchanged. Cressey makes the important point that Clemmer's study implicitly deals with the prison as a social microcosm in which the conditions and processes in the broader society are observable. (Clemmer, 1940, ibid)

Cressey states in the Foreword that Clemmer cannot be expected to use the language of contemporary social science, or to make certain kinds of observation, and he then goes on to refer to Erving Goffman's recent essays on 'total institutions'. Cressey says that

> Clemmer could not make a comparison of his prison and, say, mental hospitals for the simple reason that the idea of comparing them was not part of the sociological culture of the 1930s. (Clemmer, 1940, p. viii)

This seems a little unfair, since Cressey was not to develop the comparative method himself. Clemmer's collection of essays published in 1961 as The Prison: studies in institutional organization and change. New large-scale studies of institutions and institutional life were now available and it was thought possible to supplement Clemmer's work: The Prison was to be regarded as a companion volume. (Cressey, 1961, p. v) The Prison was also to be concerned with the new preoccupation with effectiveness and efficiency, and material is presented from a range of organisations, for example, factories, military etablishments, governmental bureaux, and hospitals.

The orientation of the essays is towards discovering the processes by which prisoners are either reformed or are confirmed as hardened criminals. It is generally assumed that the effects of imprisonment ought to be therapeutic, and while other aims such as the protection of offenders from each other, from members of the community, and the imposition of punishment are also put forward. The collection of essays was intended to describe ways in which existing power structures might be changed.

The contributors to The Prison are for the most part academics, only one, Johan Galtung, had any experience of imprisonment at first hand. Galtung had served a six-month sentence in connection with conscientious objection to military service in Norway. Galtung states that the dilemma of judicially imposed punishment is not that goods etc are restored to the victim, but that the offender is to be deprived. Galtung argues that this consequence of imprisonment will lead to institutionalised defence mechanisms which conflict with the aim of the resocialisation of offenders. (Galtung, 1961, pp. 111-2)

Other essays, such as Stanton Wheeler's 'Role Conflict in Correctional Communities' and Glaser and Stratton's 'Measuring Inmate Change in Prison' are concerned with the effects of prison and the prison culture on the individual. (Wheeler, 1961; Glaser and Stratton, 1961) They stress the rehabilitative potential of the prison which was certainly a frequently stated justification of penal systems in the 1950s and 1960s. There is no attempt to question the assumption that this should be a legitimate goal of the penal system. One of the more remarkable essays in The Prison is Richard McCleery's 'Authoritarianism and the Belief System of Incorrigibles'. (McCleery, 1961) McCleery compares the effectiveness of an authoritarian versus a liberal regime in changing the attitudes of people classified as incorrigible trouble-makers. In one of the two units, McCleery reports that 'The system of government is geared to compel a vegetable-like level of existence'. (McCleery, 1961, p. 267)

McCleery's position is based on efficiency rather than ethics. He does not ask whether prisoners should be kept in such grim conditions for an indefinite period. McCleery simply asks which system reduces the prison system's problems most efficaciously. The regime which uses group therapy is seen as acceptable because it is more efficient, rather than for any reason of greater humanity. The question of whether the prison authorities have the right to change the prisoner's personality is not considered.

At this point the rehabilitative ideal and the dominant type of research on prisoners interact. The rehabilitative ideal involves the assumption that the aim of treatment is to bring about the individual's adjustment to society, the prison authorities taking the view that their views and society's are the same - adjustment in prison is the first step to adjustment outside. A feature common to much of this research is the view that the prison is a closed system which effectively re-moulds the prisoner's personality or self. The adaptations to prison life are conceptualised as being independent of either external or prison influences.

Clarence Schrag and his students from the University of Washington helped to create a series of stereotyped views of prison adaptations. (Schrag, 1961) A rigid methodology confirmed these stereotypes in the prisons where it was applied. The possibility that these typologies could have been an artefact of the method does not seem to have been considered. But the real significance of these typologies was the ready connection that could be made with the beliefs about diagnosis in the rehabilitative ideal. At no point in their work did the people working on typologies of adaptation ask about the rightness of the circumstances leading to such adaptations. The adaptations were regarded almost as facts of nature whose existence was to be described but not questioned.

There is only one major English study in the descriptive tradition: the Morrises' Pentonville, published in 1963. (Morris and Morris, 1963) Terence and Pauline Morris stated that their research was to provide not only factual observation, but also to include the processes of perception of those individuals involved in the formal and informal social structures - that is, the prison culture. But at a number of points in the book the Morrises stand back from the material and take a more critical stance than that found in the American studies. They mention the Prison Rules, question the justice of a system which leaves a large number of prisoners' claims to the discretion of the prison authorities. The system for hearing grievances is seen through the eyes of prisoners whose views are regarded as cynical. The term 'rights, legal, prisoners" merits only one entry in the Index, and the Morrises describe legal rights as 'a narrow field' and 'a complicated one'. (Morris and Morris, 1963, p. 41)

Although Pentonville is important as the first major sociological study of a British prison, the study is written with little reference to other sociological research apart from that of Gresham Sykes (see below) and passing references to one or two other American writers. Ideas are transported across the Atlantic, but little attention is paid to their transportability.

Studies of prison dynamics

From this perspective the main problem faced by the prison authorities is thought to be the maintenance of order (or the prevention of disorder). The most important starting point for this approach is the work of Gresham Sykes, The Society of Captives. (Sykes, 1958) This study of a maximum security prison was written in response to a wave of riots which affected over a hundred American prisons in the early 1950s. In Sykes' view, the basic problem facing prison staff is the prevention of escapes and disorder. The staff appear to have 'total power' in the shape of the courts and firearms. The reality of the prison is quite different. According to Sykes, there are major defects in the structure of total power

> The lack of a sense of duty among those who are held captive, the obvious fallacies of coercion, the pathetic collection of rewards and punishments to induce compliance, the strong pressures towards the corruption of the guard in the form of friendship, reciprocity and transfer of duties into the hands of trusted inmates – all are structural defects in the prison's system of power rather than individual inadequacies. (Sykes, 1958, p. 61)

Sykes goes on to look at the problems which confront the prisoner, 'the pains of imprisonment', e.g. the deprivation of liberty, the deprivation of goods and services, the deprivation of heterosexual relationships, the deprivation of autonomy.
    Consequently for Sykes it is only possible to run an apparently orderly and quiet institution by allowing inmate leaders to run the institution for their own benefit and advantage. This study is explicitly managerial in the sense that the intention behind the inquiry is to find the means of preventing disorder. But at the same time there is the recognition of the importance of the relative deprivation of the prison world. The prison is treated as a closed system, separate from the outside world; but the outside world is also a point of comparison.
    King and Elliott's study of Albany was conducted over ten years later and is also concerned with the breakdown of order. In Albany: birth of a prison – end of an era, they describe how an English maximum security prison went within a period of six years, from being a showplace prison run on therapeutic community lines with great emphasis on industrial training, to a trouble-prone, riot-torn prison. (King and Elliott, 1977) King and Elliott describe the problem of prison discipline offences, the discipline machinery and the mechanisms for airing prisoners' grievances. These contributed to, and were affected by, the changes in the prison regime. The few references made to prisoners' rights refer almost exclusively to the activities of PROP during the various disturbances. King and Elliott were more concerned with the problems of prison discipline and the practices of reporting offences. The activities of prison governors and the board of visitors are seen in the light of how they contributed to the disintegration of social order as the prison became the 'electronic coffin'. (King and Elliott, 1977, pp. 287-8)
    Essentially ideas and arguments about prisoners' rights are peripheral in a therapeutic system. The assumption underlying the model is that what is being done is for the prisoner's own good and requires no other justification. The precise limits of what may be done for the prisoner's own good are not explored, but it is generally assumed that

the prison system cannot abuse the prisoner because it is designed to be benevolent. Arguments about rights began to emerge at the same time as the rehabilitative ideal went into decline.

Radical criminology

It is difficult to give a precise date for the beginning of the movements generally called radical criminology, but influences can be seen in the prison literature in the 1960s. Some mention must be made of Erving Goffman whose writing on the inmate world and the similarities of 'total institutions', were circulating in the field from the end of the 1950s. While Goffman was principally concerned with mental hospitals, his ideas provided a new perspective on the prison. The traditional view had been managerially oriented, from the top downwards, based on the view that institutional activity was directed toward therapy or improvement in the inmates. Goffman was critical, radical and inmate-oriented. (Goffman, 1961)

One of the first empirical studies to adopt the new approach to prisons was Thomas Mathiesen's Norwegian study The Defences of the Weak. Mathiesen was influenced by both Sykes and Goffman, and his study still has an interest in treatment, but as he says in the Preface

> But my personal attitude towards prisons is not only guided by the criterion of efficacy. I have to state also that in many cases I find imprisonment unjust, in the sense that I find the penalty unnecessarily hard in relation to the offence. In other words, I often do not find a criminal offence important or dangerous enough to warrant mobilization of all the deprivation of imprisonment. (Mathiesen, 1965, p. vii)

Mathiesen uses 'censoriousness' to describe one of the principal modes of reaction by prisoners. This response is designed to make the staff members feel that the distribution of benefits and burdens is illegitimate, in the hope that changes in decision-making will be made in a way desirable to the prisoner. Prisoners use norms relating to justice and efficiency as the basis of this strategy; and justice is the more relevant in this context. The prisoners studied by Mathiesen were being held in the Ila Institution for Preventive Detention in Oslo. The distinctive feature of preventive detention in Norway was long-term custody to protect society and to rehabilitate the offender. The prisoners regarded this type of sentence as being unjust, as the sentence was in addition to punishment for a particular offence.

'Censoriousness' served a similar function for these prisoners that peer solidarity served for prisoners in other kinds of institutions. Mathiesen concludes that 'reliance on the rules of justice may have the same conflict-solving function as in outside society'. (Mathiesen, 1965, p. 186)

Cohen and Taylor in Psychological Survival, a study of the experience of long-term imprisonment, argue that prisoners facing long sentences may resist the conditions imposed upon them rather than simply adapting to them. Cohen and Taylor rejected earlier sociological accounts of adaptations to prison life.

Cohen and Taylor discuss the five types of resistance that they found in the 'E' Wing of Durham prison. The type of resistance of special interest is that known as 'campaigning'. Cohen and Taylor argue that 'campaigning' is allied to Mathiesen's notion of 'censoriousness', but it differs in that it is not a substitute for peer solidarity. 'Campaigning' can take two forms: some campaigns are concerned exclusively with individual grievances; others refer to collective complaints about prison conditions. It is suggested by Cohen and Taylor that while the former are rarely successful, the latter type of campaign has a cumulative success in changing conditions for the better. Campaigns are principally designed to annoy those in authority – especially the campaigns directed at the Home Office. The Durham prisoners argued that the Home Office was not a rational decision-making organisation so there was no point in wasting time in presenting a rational argument. On the other hand, it was possible that occasionally the harassed bureaucrats might make a decision in a prisoner's favour.

There have been no other systematic attempts by radical criminologists to study prisoners, and prisoners are rarely mentioned in the radical criminology literature. For radical criminologists two problems prevented discussion of the topic. First, there was the general problem for some radical criminologists, especially in the early 1960s, that they tended to confuse criminality with the attack on capitalism. This form of 'left-idealism' has been challenged more recently since the recognition by radical criminologists such as Jock Young that the victims of most crimes are often members of the working class. (Young, 1979, pp. 12–9) Second, arguments about rights also posed problems for radical criminologists. The dilemma is well stated by Pat Carlen

> The practical question concerns the grounds upon which it could be argued that struggles to maintain and increase civil rights may be progressive rather than reformist. (Carlen, 1980, p. 7)

Many radical criminologists are really more concerned with liberty than with rights. They are not interested in reforming prisons through the establishment of prisoners' rights because they are committed to abolition of the prison system. Cohen and Taylor never made this clear, but Thomas Mathiesen has written at length on strategies to be used to bring about the abolition of imprisonment. (Mathiesen, 1974)

Studies of prisoners' rights

Studies of the rights of those involved in the penal system have fallen into two general categories: writings on rights of offenders generally; and second, studies of prisoners' rights in particular.

General discussions of offenders' rights has been important because these writings contributed to re-assessment of the penal system in general and the purposes of imprisonment in particular. Since the publication in 1971 of the Report of the American Friends Service Committee, Struggle for Justice, there has been a steady flow of material challenging accepted views about the purposes of the law and the justifications of punishment. The Report of the Committee for the Study of Incarceration, Doing Justice, was concerned with limiting the scope of the criminal law by concentrating on offences rather than the offender. (von Hirsch, 1976) Punishments should be the same for all those committing the same offence, as discretion in sentencing had become discrimination. Neither of these reports actually refer to prisoners' rights, presumably because it is assumed that specific rights are unnecessary once general principles are established. The Committee which signed the Report included Erving Goffman, Stanton Wheeler and Leslie Wilkins from the social sciences. The lawyers on the Committee included Alan Dershowitz and Herman Schwartz, who have been concerned with offenders' rights and prisoners' rights respectively. The historian David Rothman was also a member. The Report was written by Andrew von Hirsch who had been the staff Director; David Greenberg, the Senior Fellow, had been one of the principal authors of Struggle for Justice.

Leslie Wilkins was rather more explicit in his discussion of rights in the context of sentencing violence-prone offenders. (Wilkins, 1974) He suggested that a first offender had an absolute right to be given a sentence for the offence committed (a deserts-based sentence). As offenders commit more offences, and especially violent ones, they would lose their right to be treated as a non-violent person and could then be given a preventive sentence. A strategy of this kind would, Wilkins hoped, not only protect the offender from long sentences and intrusion into his life and personality, but it would also protect society.

The conference proceedings, The Coming Penal Crisis, provide a number of attempts to put forward new ideas leading to substantive justice within the penal system rather than a simpler procedural justice. (Bottoms and Preston, 1980) Fairness has been re-emphasised as has been the idea that involvement in educational or vocational programmes should be voluntary. Prisoners should be treated as persons with the clear implication that this would inevitably lead to a restructuring of relationships within the prison.

There are three studies by social scientists in which prisoners' rights are either central, or at least play an important part in the analysis: A Taste of Prison, Stateville and The Future of the Prison System. The first to be published was King and Morgan's A Taste of Prison: custodial conditions for trial and remand prisoners compared the regimes in the remand wing of a local prison, and a remand centre designed exclusively to deal with prisoners awaiting trial or sentence. (King and Morgan, 1976) The special provisions for prisoners on remand stem from the presumption of innocence. King and Morgan argue that the fact that the rights are enshrined in the Prison Rules does not mean that they are respected, and one of the tasks they set is to discover how far these rules were respected. They conclude that in the remand wing of the local prison the special protections for the unconvicted meant very little in practice. The reality was a very restrictive regime for these prisoners.

James Jacobs' study, Stateville: the penitentiary in mass society, cannot be easily categorised as it combines a wide range of traditional social science concerns with the development of prisoners' rights and the place of the prison in mass society. (Jacobs, 1977) Jacobs reports on the history of Stateville penitentiary in Illinois from its construction in 1925 to 1975. The early history of the prison was typified by a high degree of social instability, the staff of the prison changed with party political fortunes, and the prison staff 'contributed' to party funds in return for their jobs. The period 1936-61 was marked by the establishment of an authoritarian regime under the control of Warden Joseph Ragen. The Warden imposed an unassailable order on the prison and gained a large measure of political, economic and moral autonomy. Ragen's control was based on patriarchal authority - 'his life (was devoted) to perfecting the world's most orderly prison. He exercised personal control over every detail, no matter how insignificant'. (Jacobs, 1977, p. 29)

In the 1950s and 1960s, the racial composition of the prison population changed to a black majority, and this coincided with the emergence and growth of the civil rights movement outside. The inmates of Stateville were politicised by the civil rights movement and the organisation of the Black Muslims, whose activities directly challenged the traditional relationship between prisoners and their keepers. Allowing Muslims to have copies of the Koran did not appear to threaten prison security, but the recognition of the Muslims as a bona fide religious group, entitled to the deference and legitimacy of the traditional religions, was seen by the prison hierarchy as a grave threat to the moral order of the prison. The Muslims called the prison racist, discriminatory and repressive; they linked the defects of the prison to the illegitimacy of the white government that ruled America.

The argument used by the prison authorities, that any concession to the Black Muslims would lead to chaos within the prison, gave the impression that the staff were capricious and arbitrary. The appearance in court of prisoners as equals in litigation to the prison director intensified the challenge to the traditional status of prisoners. Complaints to the courts mobilised support the liberal establishment outside the prison.

The prison authorities regarded the courts as the greatest obstacle to the proper organisation of the prison, despite the fact that the courts actually showed great deference to prison administrators. The courts could not be regarded as requiring revolutionary, or even radical changes. What would satisfy the courts was the demonstration of rational decision-making. (Jacobs, 1977, p. 113)

Although King and Morgan, and Jacobs spend considerable time discussing prisoners' rights, the central concern in each study is the prison and its regime. Issues relating to rights are discussed because they are part of the dynamic processes that are the authors' real interest. If their researches had thrown up some other driving force then prisoners' rights would have been consigned to the periphery.

Social scientists also write books and articles which are more concerned with what is wrong with the system. These publications use empirical research to evaluate the claims made by prison administrators, from a moral or ethical basis rather than one based on effectiveness. This evaluative material falls into two main types, reformist or abolitionist, and as a result evaluations tend to fall into two corresponding groups - criticism on the one hand and indictment on the other.

In Britain, the reformist oriented evaluations have been produced by R.D. King, R. Morgan and J.P. Martin who were concerned with the Prison Regimes Project financed by the Home Office. Some of the research from this Project has been quoted previously, and it also provided the basic criticisms to be found in the same authors' The Future of the Prison System. (King and Morgan, 1980)

In the US social scientists have played a similar role to that of their British counterparts. But two features are quickly apparent, first there is an American tradition of citizens' committees of inquiry which seem always to include at least one social scientist; second, American penologists have placed far more importance on notions of rights. Gordon Hawkins wrote The Prison: policy and practice within an American context, and he devoted a chapter to prisoners' rights. (Hawkins, 1976) Hawkins argues that the real importance of judicial intervention in prison life has been to reduce the amount of human suffering caused by poor conditions. Hawkins concludes by saying

> what it comes to is this: convicted offenders must remain within
> the constitutional and legislative protection of the legal system.
> It is foolish to treat those who have broken the law other than by

13

processes which sedulously adhere to the law. (Hawkins, 1976, p. 159)

There is a new idea here - that prisons may be 'lawless'. The idea had been put forward a few years previously and given wide publicity by Jessica Mitford in Kind and Usual Punishment. (Mitford, 1971 and 1974) She opened a chapter entitled 'The Lawlessness of Corrections' with a quotation from a federal Appeal Court judge's evidence to a US Congressional committee

> I would like to say one thing, this Committee should consider: that one of the astounding facts about prisons is this, that they are probably the most lawless places in our society.. this is a dominating factor in every place, that they are lawless. (Mitford, 1974, p. 247)

The view that prisons are lawless led to the production of David Fogel's '...We are the Living Proof...'. (Fogel, 1975) The book's subtitle is a clear indication of its focus - the justice model for corrections. At the time of writing, Fogel was the Executive Director of the Illinois Law Enforcement Commission. Fogel argues that the correctional model of justice must focus on the consumers, rather than the official possessors of justice. The basic value underlying all prison administration should be justice-as-fairness. This would provide both the keeper and the kept with a rationale and morality for their shared lives in a prison organisation. Fogel also wants to bring prison administration into main stream public administration and bring an end to the isolation of the prison world. The prisons must also learn to be lawful.

Nigel Walker is an important exception to the tendency to favour prisoners' rights. (Walker, 1980, chapter 8) Walker criticises the notion of offenders' rights generally on the classical grounds that rights have to be recognised in law in order to exist, and that rights may be lost if the individual breaks the law. Walker adds criticisms of his own, suggesting that many of the deprivations of imprisonment are simply consequences of living in a large-scale, closed institution, and are not part of the sentence of the court. Walker suggests that while the state may legitimately curtail the rights of some, it is not entitled to discriminate against categories of people, e.g. blacks or whites, men or women. He suggests that instead of talking about 'offenders' rights', it might be more useful to talk about 'discrimination against offenders'.

Comparative studies of prisons and prisoners' rights

A distinctive features of the literature is that ideas are frequently handled without much attention to their origins. Ideas, concepts and models have been swopped backwards and forwards across the Atlantic as if that barrier was of no significance. Some authors convey little sense of the differences of constitution and government, differences in the legal systems and legal practices. These differences were less important while the dominant view of the prison was that the prison was separate from society, or that it could be treated as if it were separate. The notion of the prison as a microcosm of society has already been mentioned. Comparative studies of prisons have been rare, and there have been few attempts to study the same prison at different points in time. Jacobs' work is important because he explicitly

recognises the issue of the integration of the prison with the larger
society and he was concerned to demonstrate how the changing
relationship of the prison to the society is reflected in changes in the
patterns of authority within the prison. (Jacobs, 1977, p. 2)   This
shift to macrosociology brings with it a new contextual awareness and
the understanding that it is no longer legitimate to ignore such
differences.

Another exception is Fitzgerald's Prisoners in Revolt. (Fitzgerald,
1977) This study is essentially a critique of British penal policy, but
it also provides a history of the organisation PROP. Fitzgerald also
devotes a chapter to the origins and development of prisoners' unions in
the US.   He uses the American experience to provide models of
development for the prisoners' rights movement in Britain.   The history
and experience of prisoners in the two countries is treated as
comparable information with little or no attempt to evaluate the
similarities and differences which might affect the substance of the
argument.   Indeed, the arguments for future activity cross and re-cross
the Atlantic with ease.

Once social scientists do begin to look at the legal and
constitutional context of prisons for ideas and standards they are
immediately confronted by the vast legal literature on prisoners'
rights.   In the US the field of prisoners' rights has been the subject
of detailed study since the 1960s.   The growth of the civil rights
movement and the successes of court-based challenges to violations of
citizens' constitutional rights beginning with Brown v. Board
of Education in 1958 stimulated interest in the rights of many social
groups.   Cases and issues have been chronicled and discussed in great
detail in law journals, books and handbooks.   Literally hundreds of
articles followed the initial publication of 'Beyond the Ken of the
Courts: a critique of judicial refusal to review the complaints of
convicts'. (Anon, 1963)

In Britain, lawyers have paid less attention to these issues for a
number of reasons.   Until recently there was relatively little to write
about.   The exception to this is Graham Zellick who has become the
leading contributor to the legal discussion of prisoners' rights in
Britain. The topic has begun to attract a little more attention in the
last ten years, and more British lawyers have been drawn into the
debate. (English, 1973; Beaven, 1980; Tettenborn, 1980; Birkinshaw,
1981; and, Richardson, 1984)

But this still does not deal with the problem of comparison.   There is
only one existing direct comparison of Britain and the US, Bayard
Marin's Inside Justice which is concerned with prison discipline
systems. (Marin, 1983)   Marin's choice of the US and Britain for
comparison is that the former had experienced considerable legal
intervention while Britain has not.   Marin's goal was 'thoroughly to
explore practices and procedures in each country'. (Marin, 1983, p. 19)

Marin concludes by looking at the original question of the need for
legal involvement.   He argues that his study has clearly demonstrated
the need for access to the courts and to counsel.   Marin suggests that
the lengths to which some prison authorities will go to prevent access
mean that they have something to hide.   As far as Britain is concerned,
Marin argues that the existence of constitutional safeguards alone is
not very much help - there have to be means of enforcement and the
judiciary has to recognise the applicability of such rights to
prisoners.

The description of Marin's study leads directly to the rationale for
the present inquiry.   There are three basic reasons for this

comparative study of prisoners' rights. First, rights go much wider. A study of prisoners' rights may help to locate some of the problems and issues Marin noted in their proper context. Second, Marin's inquiry begins with the prison, and avoids issues of the socal and political context of the prison and the awkward question of the comparative method. But these issues have to be dealt with to assess the relevance of the American experience for the British prisoners' rights movement. Third, Marin writes as a lawyer. As noted above, social research on prisons and legal research on prisoners' rights have developed almost independently and with little interaction. There has been little social research dealing directly with the sorts of issues raised by arguments about prisoners' rights, although grievance mechanisms have attracted some attention.

Towards a justification of prisoners' rights

The arguments about whether there are rights, and whether prisoners can be said to possess rights, have largely taken place in isolation from what is actually happening in British prisons.

Prisoners' rights are important in a context where prison conditions are bad. How bad conditions in British prisons are is a matter of some dispute but the reports of successive HM Chief Inspectors of Prisons are not encouraging. The most basic problems stem from the population crisis; many of the prisons were built in the nineteenth century for small numbers of prisoners. The then Chief Inspector wrote in his 1981 Report

> Overcrowding... also places an intolerable burden on the essential services of the prison. Drainage systems become blocked so that sewage washes back upon the wings; the water supply is no longer sufficient and runs out in some parts of the prison for a few hours each day; the recesses and baths available, not provided on a generous scale by Victorian architects, become wholly inadequate... But the problems of overcrowding do not end there. It must be remembered that the shared facilities installed in local prisons were provided on a scale consistent with the original population... There is rarely room within the perimeter to add modern facilities to cope with modern numbers... There is no pretence of an organised regime. (Home Office, 1982, p. 18)

The issue of prisoners' rights is important as it directly affects sentencing policy. It is widely accepted that imprisonment is liable to result in severe personal deterioration. The lowering of conditions either because of overcrowding or security measures is not part of the sentence of the court. The other, related problem of the connection between the conditions of imprisonment and the intentions of the court is one of equity. At the moment, the conditions in which prisoners serve their sentences depend to a large extent on luck.

The criticisms of prison conditions that can and have been made, do not come simply from the 'ubiquitous penal reformers' mentioned by The Times. Prison conditions have been criticised in a number of official reports, and criticisms have been made by senior officials of the Prison Service. The Chief Inspector of Prisons was unequivocal

> By no stretch of the imagination can these conditions be regarded as humane or proper. They are unacceptable. (Home Office, 1982, p. 19)

Prison governors have spoken out independently and collectively about their conditions of work. The remedy they suggest is a code of minimum standards, and the governors are not alone in this. The Chief Inspectors have referred frequently to the Council of Europe's Standard Minimum Rules for the Treatment of Prisoners. Would sets of standards provide adequate safeguards, given what is already known about prison conditions?

Britain already accepts the European Standard Minimum Rules for the Treatment of Prisoners but their precise status is open to doubt. They may be held to be mere expressions of good intentions. What happens if (when) prison conditions do not meet the European standards? It is quite clear from the Chief Inspector's reports and the answers to Parliamentary Questions that British prisons frequently fall below the standards. The Home Office has said that the acceptance of a set of standards would produce problems as its ability to carry out repairs and renovations was restricted by financial limitations.

Prison administrators in the US have tried a somewhat similar approach. The American Correctional Association sponsors the Commission on Accreditation for Corrections, which has produced comprehensive manuals of standards for correctional institutions. In August 1982, Circuit Judge David Bazelon resigned from the Commission and attacked its methods, motives and integrity. He said that many correctional officials were manipulating the Commission to deflect public criticism and scrutiny of their own management. Some of the conditions had been waived to allow the accreditation of Florida's State Prisons where standards were particularly bad. (New York Times, 8 August 1982, p. 20) Even if the integrity and probity of British officials protected a similar scheme from the worst defects of the US Commission on Accreditation for Corrections, there would still be the problems of self-policing; and if that approach really worked we would not now be discussing the bad conditions found in British prisons.

Respect for prisoners' rights may also be especially important now that the prevailing penal policy is 'humane containment', which could so easily degenerate into punitive warehousing for the majority and explicit punitiveness for the few as demanded by The Times. Rights should be a matter of moral consensus by the whole of society, not a matter of administrative expediency and political fashion. John Locke saw the dangers in the seventeenth century, when he wrote

one man comes by power over another, but yet no absolute or arbitrary power to use a criminal, when he has got him in his hands, according to the passionate heats or boundless extravagancy of his own will. (Locke, 1690, p. 120)

2 Protections and safeguards for prisoners in England and Wales

The history of imprisonment in England since the end of the eighteenth century is a chronology of attempts to control prisons conditions and to supervise the conduct of prison staff.   Acts of Parliament were passed to extend central government's control over those prisons which until 1877 were under local administration;   there have been the continuing assumptions in English prison legislation that the enactment of law will provide an example for those who behave in a fair and lawful manner towards prisoners in any event, and a means of condemning the behaviour of those who would mistreat prisoners.   In the second half of the twentieth century there has been a growing tendency towards external oversight over many forms of administration and varieties of 'ombudsmen' have been established.   The courts have been involved intermittently in the control of prisons, although most of their involvement has been since 1979.   In addition to the protections and safeguards provided by administrative and domestic legal mechanisms, there are the opportunities and institutions provided by the European Convention on Human Rights to which Britain is a signatory.

The ensuing discussion of prisoners' rights in England histories of these control mechanisms and the interactions between them.   The structure of domestic and international legal institutions has meant that there is some overlap between developments in each.

This study is limited to the rights of adult prisoners who have been convicted and sentenced to immediate imprisonment.   This is a significant point in that people held in custody awaiting trial are treated differently in England and America;   conditions surrounding youth custody on each side of the Atlantic are governed by a mixture of legislation which involves a new set of special considerations depending on the status, as young people, of those in detention.   It might seem obvious, but the study is also restricted to those held in prisons. The practice of holding people in police cells while awaiting trial has become widespread in England in the 1980s. Generally, this study of prisoners' rights will be concerned with the conditions of those serving longer terms of imprisonment in purpose-built institutions.

The administrative protections and safeguards available to prisoners in England fall into three major categories: those which are internal to the prison sytem, those which are semi-independent, and those which are independent of the system.

Internal protections and safeguards

Since the late eighteenth century, prison administration in England has placed great importance on the power of the prison governor. There has been a strong and continuing belief in the need for firm supervision of both staff and inmates by the governor. Legislation in the nineteenth century required the governor to visit each cell once every 24 hours; the primary task under common law was to maintain the safe custody of the prison. The safety of the prison consisted not only of preventing abuses by inmates, e.g. fighting or intimidation, and abuses by members of staff, but also included the mangement of 'a poorly paid, hard-worked subordinate staff of low status and ill-educated, in social conditions which favoured a climate of corruption'. (McConville, 1981, chapter 9) McConville lists nearly 100 Acts which dealt either wholly or in part with prison administration between 1758 and 1879. (McConville, 1981, pp. 485-7)

The Prison Act 1952 is the main legislative basis for contemporary prisons. This Act of 25 pages and four schedules was designed to consolidate a number of changes in policy in legislation passed after the Second World War in relation to those sentenced. A more detailed set of rules is provided by the Prison Rules 1964 (as amended).

The significance of this delegated legislation to prison administrators was made clear by Sir Lionel Fox, who wrote

> Not the least important provisions of the Act of 1898 were those which repealed the statutory regulations of 1865, and left the whole of the detailed regulation of the system to the Secretary of State, who was given power to make all rules necessary for the government of both local and convict prisons. The code of rules made in 1899, with such amendments as from time to time proved necessary, remained in force until 1933, when a more consolidated and simplified code was substituted with certain revisions of details to bring it into line with more recent developments. This code, with occasional amendments, remained in force until 1949. The value of this more elastic procedure, which made it possible for changes to be effected without fresh legislation on each occasion, is indicated by the fact that under it the natural development of fifty years was able to proceed without further intervention by Parliament. (Fox, 1952, pp. 57-8)

An application to the prison governor is the most basic and most frequently used means of making a complaint within the prison system. The logic behind the provision is that the governor is the person responsible for the management of the institution. He has the power to investigate complaints, and may remedy the grievance if he thinks it proper to do so. The kinds of complaints which make up the governor's applications are usually concerned with obtaining discretionary variations in the Prison Rules, e.g. extra letters or visits, but prisoners may also wish to complain about other matters such as the calculation of the date of release, security classification, or allocation to a particular prison.

The effectiveness of the governor as the first level of the grievance mechanism within the prison is open to question. The governor may be the person to whom complaints may be made, but he is at the same time responsible for the order and discipline of the prison. As JUSTICE recognised in its report on prisoners' rights, the governor is not, and cannot appear to be an independent tribunal. (JUSTICE, 1983, p. 26) This problem is made worse when the substance of the complaint is the conduct of his subordinate officers. If the governor should dismiss the complaint, he may be suspected of taking sides unquestioningly with his officers; on the other hand, upholding a prisoner's complaint may lead the officers to believe that the governor is undermining their authority. An unsubstantiated complaint against the staff will render the prisoner liable to the charge under rule 47 (12) of 'making any false and malicious allegation against an officer'.

If a prisoner is charged with any of the 21 offences against discipline, he will usually be segregated from the other prisoners pending adjudication. The prisoner will be brought before the governor, who inquires into the charge, and unless the alleged offence is grave, the governor will hear the case. If the governor finds that the charges have been proved, there is a range of punishments he may inflict. The maximum penalties he may give are

Caution	
Forfeiture of privileges	28 days
Exclusion from associated work	14 days
Stoppage of earnings	28 days
Cellular confinement	3 days
Forfeiture of remission	28 days

Throughout the prison system there is this combination of functions: those who are responsible for hearing complaints are also responsible for hearing disciplinary charges and punishing those who have been convicted.

The staff from the regional offices of the Prison Department are also part of the complaints mechanism. Under the same rule as that concerning applications to the prison governor, prisoners may apply to see the regional directors or their deputies whenever these officials visit a prison.

The third and final part of the internal complaints procedure in English prisons is the right to petition the Home Secretary. JUSTICE suggests that the right of petition seems to stem from the subject's right at common law to petition the Crown to remedy an injustice. This right can be traced back to mediaeval times and is referred to in the Bill of Rights of 1689. (JUSTICE, 1983, p. 27) The system of petitioning involves the submission of a petition through the governor, who attaches a report adding whatever information he considers relevant and states his recommendations. The sorts of issues dealt with include allegations against officers, compensation for injury in prison, legal proceedings and complaints against punishments for offences against discipline. (Home Office, 1979, p. 97)

There have been a number of criticisms raised about the petition system

1. The information used is limited to that supplied by the petitioner and the governor. A new investigation is not normally mounted but this can be done.
2. The procedure is completely internal without any independent element.
3. The system is slow, taking between six and nine months before a reply is received.
4. The procedure was criticised in the Fifteenth Report of the Select Committee on Expenditure on two grounds. First, the Select Committee endorsed the evidence presented by Charles Irving MP who stated that thousands of prisoners had written to him complaining that petitioning the Home Secretary 'is an absolute waste of time'. Second, the Select Committee also endorsed evidence from the Howard League which argued that while the petition should be an exceptional and serious safeguard, it was in fact being devalued through excessive use. (Select Committee on Expenditure, 1978, para 177) The JUSTICE Committee reported that about 12,000 petitions are presented annually, of which about 18% are granted. (JUSTICE, 1983, p. 28)

Recent Home Office research on prisoners' confidence in grievance procedures shows that satisfaction is related to the type of prison. Those in local prisons (where pressure is greatest) were the least satisfied and these prisons showed the greatest scope for improvement. In training and dispersal prisons problems were both less pressing and prisoners had informal contacts with the staff. Prisoners attach great importance to applications to the governor. The time taken to respond to petitions was not regarded as excessive but both staff and prisoners felt that insufficient detail was given for the decisions reached. (Ditchfield and Austin, 1986)

Semi-independent grievance mechanisms

The semi-independent bodies concerned with prisoners' complaints and prison conditions generally are the boards of visitors and the Prison Inspectorate. The activities and approaches of these organisations to the problems of prison life are different. The board of visitors is designed to allow for an element of local, non-professional involvement in prison administration while the Inspectorate can be thought of as an example of professional, expert oversight.

The Prison Act 1952 requires the Home Secretary to appoint a board of visitors for every prison. Between 1898 and 1971, only certain prisons had boards of visitors appointed by the Home Secretary. The local prisons which received people committed directly from the courts had visiting committees. Originally boards of visitors were concerned with the convict prisons, i.e. establishments administered by central government holding the long-term prison population. The boards had to have some magistrates among their membership, the minimum number was two. The distinction was abolished in 1972 and all are now called boards of visitors. The duties of boards of visitors are set out in the rules 94 and 95 of the Prison Rules
1. they shall satisfy themselves as to the state of the prison premises, the administration of the prison and the treatment of prisoners;
2. they shall inquire into and report on any matter into which the Home Secretary asks them to inquire;
3. they shall direct the attention of the governor to any matter which

calls for his attention and report to the Home Secretary any matter they consider expedient;

4. they shall inform the Home Secretary of any abuse which comes to their knowledge and shall have the power to suspend any officer;
5. they, as a group or individually, shall hear any complaint or request, which a prisoner wishes to make;
6. they shall arrange for the inspection of the prisoners' food at frequent intervals;
7. they shall inquire into any report made to them that a prisoner's health, mental or physical, is likely to be injured by the conditions of his imprisonment.

Each board is required to submit an annual report to the Home Secretary on the state of the prison and its administration together with any appropriate advice and suggestions. There is now a growing trend among boards of visitors for them to publish their own annual reports.

The Prison Rules also empower members of the boards of visitors to visit any part of the prison at any time and to see every prisoner. Members of the board may interview any prisoner out of the sight and hearing of the officers. Board members also have a right of access to the records of the prison, though the Rules do not specify whether medical records are included. This oversight and supervision is expected to be frequent, and the Rules specify that a rota must be arranged so that at least one member visits the prison between board meetings. The board is normally required to meet in the prison once a month unless it resolves to meet less frequently.

There has been a longstanding conflict over how the boards are seen officially and how they see themselves. The Committee established under H.W. Franklin to review punishments in prisons and other custodial establishments reports that in the period after the 1877 Prison Act, visiting committees were mainly concerned with the maintenance of discipline. The 'forceful new commissioners' overpowered the visiting committees to such an extent that few took any interest in the running of the prisons. (Home Office, 1951, p. 86) The Prison Act of 1898 developed the more positive, but potentially conflicting, combination of activities that exists today.

The official view of boards of visitors has always stressed the way in which boards are part of the management of the prison system. For example, the Annual Report of the Prison Department for 1972 states that the boards have to be kept properly informed of policy developments generally and in their particular prison for them to be able to work effectively. The Annual Report added that boards are responsible for the work of organisations which are not only geographically remote, but are socially isolated and consequently the work is extremely demanding on the staff.

The division of the prison into two opposing groups means that there is no middle ground. When offences against discipline are being dealt with, some prisoners may well plead not guilty simply in order to make life difficult for the staff who will have the extra task of proving the offence. It is open to question how far this use of the right to plead 'not guilty' accounts for the high rate of findings of guilt by boards of visitors and how far this stems from the perceived need to support the staff. Smith and his colleagues reported in their study of adjudications in four prisons that between 91 and 100 per cent of charges were found proven. (Smith, Austin and Ditchfield, 1981, p. 11)

The current Home Office view of the boards of visitors is that they provide an independent element in the running of each prison. In their evidence to the Committee of Inquiry into the UK Prison Service (the May Committee), the Home Office said that the boards 'remain an independent body whose role is that of "watchdog" rather than 'Board of Governors". (Home Office, 1979, p. 223)

The Home Secretary was reported in 1972 as having four objects in mind when selecting members of boards

> first, to provide members who have the personal qualities, the interest and the time to make a useful contribution to the establishment; second, to ensure as far as possible that the membership contains a good cross-section of the local community, and that particular occupations are not over-represented; third, to obtain a suitable mixture of experienced and younger members; and ultimately to achieve a numerical balance on all boards between those members who are magistrates and those who are not. (Home Office, 1973, para 185)

They may not necessarily see themselves in this way; nor is it the way they are seen by the prisoners. Important issues surround the membership of the boards. The Home Office has stated that there are about 1,400 members of boards, and appointments are for three years at a time. About 230 new appointments are made each year, and about 450 members were re-appointed each year. (Home Office, 1973, ibid) These simple figures do not however give any clues as to the composition of the boards' membership. There have been two studies of the membership of boards of visitors. (Borrie, 1976; Maguire and Vagg, 1983) Both have commented on the distinctive social class and age distributions of the boards, which are predominantly middle class and elderly. A significant recent change is the decline in the proportion who are justices of the peace. The Prison Rules require that each board shall have a minimum number of justices. Before 1972, the majority of members were justices, especially in the local prisons. Maguire and Vagg report that the overall proportion of magistrates had fallen to 43% in 1981. (Maguire and Vagg, 1983, p. 241)

The boards have been thought of as bringing some of the standards of the outside world into the prison. The importance of this independent supervisory activity of the boards has been stressed by all of the bodies which have inquired into their work. The report of the joint Committee set up by JUSTICE, the Howard League, and NACRO under the Chairmanship of the Earl Jellicoe, and the more recent report by JUSTICE, have tried to elaborate what is meant by independence in this context. (JUSTICE, 1975; JUSTICE, 1983)

But how successful are the boards in achieving these goals? It has been suggested by Maguire and Vagg that the selection of members who are neither elected nor professionally trained depends on the expectation that they will work as fair and open-minded outsiders who will not be partisan either in relation to the prison or in their bringing of the outside world into the prison. Members of boards of visitors come from the public service tradition of the British business and professional classes. (Maguire and Vagg, 1983, p. 246)

The appearance of independence is reduced in the view of the Jellicoe Report simply through the secrecy of the selection process. The names of potential members are frequently submitted via the governor and the chairman of the board, both of whom are thought likely to have a considerable influence on selection. (JUSTICE, 1975, p. 44) Membership can be terminated by the Home Secretary at will. The process of selecting the first chairman of a board is appointment by the Home

Secretary. The Jellicoe Report stressed the importance of the chairman of each board, taking the view that this individual has a disproportionate influence on how the board operates and in the selection of new members. In the survey of chairmen for that report, some chairmen were reported as seeing the maintenance of staff morale as being an important function of the board, while one chairman went so far as to place it first in their order of priorities, subordinating the welfare of inmates. (JUSTICE, 1975, p. 54) It is interesting to juxtapose this view with the Home Office's argument that the boards have an equal duty to both staff and inmates, and must never appear to take sides. (JUSTICE, 1983, p. 26)

The actual working methods are more significant to inmates and less visible to outside observers. The JUSTICE report stated that practices vary greatly from one prison to another. Some members hear complaints while making their periodic visits, others hold regular clinics so that a member of the board is available at a specified time and place to see any one who so wishes. (JUSTICE, 1983, p. 26) Maguire and Vagg report that prisoners may not be able to distinguish between board members and other visitors being conducted round the prison. (Maguire and Vagg, 1984, p. 152) Prisoners said that they did not make their presence felt. Members do not seem to be active investigators. A further criticism raised by JUSTICE concerns the usual practice of asking for an official response from either the governor or another officer. This may simply be the appearance of independent investigation without the reality.

Additional evidence as to the variability in the behaviour of boards, and their limitations, has been provided by J.P. Martin, who has compared and contrasted the activities of three boards of visitors after rioting or other incidents in their prisons. (Martin, 1980a) After the Hull riot of 1976, the Chairman and Deputy Chairman were present when the prisoners surrendered, and stayed for over seven hours to check the condition of each man. Some time after they left, prisoners were assaulted, and eight prison officers were later charged and convicted of conspiracy to assault the prisoners. In October 1978 there was a brief riot at Gartree. Members of the board were present, and provided supervision for the surrender of prisoners. Both staff and prisoners appreciated the presence of members of the board as independent observers. On 31 August 1979, there was an 'incident' in Wormwood Scrubs which involved use of prison officers as an anti-riot squad. A large but unspecified number of prisoners were injured, and personal property was damaged. The board of visitors was not involved even though the incident lasted up to five hours, nor were they involved after the incident had been concluded.

What is important is the range of responses to the three sets of events. At Hull, the board tried to supervise the surrender but was not successful. Martin points out that the board had warned that trouble was brewing and wrote directly to the Home Secretary, but also makes the point that the board was somewhat out of touch with events. The board also seems to have been dominated by its more senior and more conservative members. The Gartree board seems to have been completely successful in restoring peace to the prison, and acted throughout as an independent watchdog. At Wormwood Scrubs, the board of visitors seems either to have been ignored by the prison administration or to have had no wish to become involved.

Now it is necessary to turn to the other side of the board of visitors' duties, as a discipline board. The Prison Rules state that if a prisoner is charged with a grave offence (e.g. escape or violence) or an especially grave offence (e.g. mutiny or gross personal violence to an officer) and the governor does not dismiss the charge, the offence is referred to the board of visitors. A panel is chosen from the main board of not less than two and not more than five members. In especially grave offences, the minimum is raised to three, and at least two of the panel have to be magistrates. The panel has to inquire into the alleged offences, and the accused prisoner has to be given the opportunity of presenting his own case. If the allegation is proved, a number of penalties are available of which the maxima are:

Caution	
Forfeiture of privileges	No limit
Exclusion from associated work	56 days
Stoppage of earnings	56 days
Cellular confinement	56 days
Forfeiture of remission	180 days (but no limit in the especially grave offences)

There have been considerable criticisms of particular decisions and punishments awarded by boards of visitors. These will be discussed in chapter 3. The intention here is to discuss some of the issues of principle which arise from adjudications. The first issue relates to the nature of the adjudication process. When dealing with discipline offences, the boards employ an inquisitorial system. The charges are formulated and presented by officers. The accused is allowed to present his case, but there are problems in preparing and presenting a defence. First, the accused will usually have been held in segregation since the incident which led to the charge. In some instances, the accused may even have been removed to another prison. Second, witnesses may be reluctant to appear on the accused's behalf, and it is highly unlikely that independent disinterested witnesses will be available. Third, the accused has no assistance in preparing a defence. Boards of visitors are forced to rely on their own judgements more than would be the case in any other kind of court. Martin has pointed that it might be thought that experience as a magistrate could be useful, but this is not necessarily the case. The nature of proceedings is quite different from that of the courts, for three reasons. First, magistrates do not usually have any responsibility towards those appearing before them, but boards of visitors are also part of the prison management. Second, in the magistrates' courts there is a prosecuting counsel, and the accused is usually legally represented; these conditions do not apply in prison adjudications. Third, the accusatorial system of the magistrates' court also has a number of procedural safeguards to protect the defendant, while in the prison adjudication the same assumptions apply but without the safeguards. (Martin, 1974) The outcome of these difficulties is that there is often an element of rough justice in these proceedings, and it may be very difficult for the board to avoid appearing to be merely a tool of the governor. (JUSTICE, 1975, p. 26) These criticisms are more damaging when it is remembered that the loss of 180 days' remission is in fact the equivalent of a nine month prison sentence.

In 1974, the Home Office set up a Working Party, under the chairmanship of T.G. Weiler, a senior member of the Prison Department, to review 'the arrangements for the hearing by Governors and Boards of Visitors of disciplinary charges against inmates... and to make recommendations'. (Home Office, 1975, p. 11) The Working Party's chief recommendations were

1. governors should conduct their inquiries into alleged offences not later than the following day;
2. governors should consider whether it is necessary to keep the prisoner in isolation if he has been segregated, if the prisoner should be kept in isolation this may be kept in mind when deciding the punishment;
3. the prisoner should be given sufficient time to prepare his defence, and be asked to nominate any witnesses;
4. there should be experiments in representative establishments to test the effect of assistance by an officer or assistant governor in preparing the prisoner's defence;
5. the governor should be present throughout the adjudication, but be seated apart from the board, and he should withdraw while the board is considering the punishment;
6. boards should try to be consistent in the punishments they give;
7. members of boards should be given training, as should members of the governor grades. (Home Office, 1975, pp. 36-40)

The Weiler Report tends to play down the importance of adjudications in the work of boards of visitors, and figures are quoted to show that applications greatly outnumber adjudications. (Home Office, 1975, Annex B) Some of the proposals were given effect fairly quickly, the proposal to set up experiments in providing assistance proved more difficult. The Home Office Research Unit was asked evaluate the experiments and also took the opportunity to provide information on how the adjudication process is seen by prisoners. (Smith, Austin and Ditchfield, 1981) Only one of the four prisons originally chosen was available as both the Prison Officers Association (POA) and the Governors' Branch of the Society of Civil and Public Servants decided they did not wish their members to assist prisoners even for the purposes of an experiment. A modified experiment using board members to help prisoners prepare their defence was objected to, and in the end only one prison was used, where a member of the board was available to explain the procedures to the prisoner before the hearing.

The research carried out by the Home Office team involved the observation of prisoners appearing before adjudication panels. Many prisoners were considered to be ineffective in their own defence because they did not understand the procedures and hence could not use them. They noted that various parts of the procedure had not been followed, e.g. prisoners were not given a written list of charges at least two hours before the hearing. Some prisoners had not been able to call witnesses, either because they did not know names or they had been in segregation before the hearing. (Smith, Austin and Ditchfield, 1981, pp. 5-6)

These observations are echoed in Maguire and Vagg's study of boards of visitors carried out in the early 1980s. (Maguire and Vagg, 1984, pp. 159-61). Boards of visitors have subsequently changed their procedures significantly to comply with the legal decisions discussed in chapter 3.

The innovation of a board member explaining the procedures was not thought to have led to any great improvement in performance. In some instances, the governor had forgotten to ask the prisoner if he wished to be advised by a board member. When interviewed, those board members who had the task of explaining the procedures said that it was difficult to stick to this brief rather than helping to prepare a defence. The boundary line is blurred in practice. (Smith, Austin and Ditchfield, 1981, p. 27)

Suggestions have been made to improve the protection of prisoners before boads of visitors of which most frequent is that of legal representation. The Royal Commission on Legal Services of 1979 recommended setting up a rota of solicitors in each prison to provide legal advice to prisoners, paid out of the legal aid fund. Additionally, prisoners charged with discipline offences would be represented legally in cases where the board could impose a penalty involving the loss of remission of more than seven days. (Royal Commission on Legal Services, 1979, chapter 9) The idea of legal representation received a considerable rebuff in the May Committee's report in 1979 which accepted the Home Office view of the activities of boards of visitors.

Both the Jellicoe report and the JUSTICE report recommended that the adjudication functions of the boards of visitors should be removed in order to allow the board to act as watchdogs. In order for this new body, to be called a 'Council', to be effective, the Committee argued that it should both enjoy and display what the Committee called 'conspicuous independence'. Independence of this kind would involve a divorce from all executive functions and responsibilities. Responsibility for running the prisons would lie with the political head of the prison service, i.e. the Home Secretary.

The Jellicoe Committee recommended the establishment of a discipline body in the form of a panel of adjudicators to be appointed by the Lord Chancellor, and drawn from lawyers of the standing required for appointment as either circuit judges or recorders. But the Committee argued that power of this kind should not be exercised by a single individual and it was suggested that the professional chairman should sit with one or two lay members. The Jellicoe Committee believed that this body's lack of knowledge of the prison and its personalities would lead to an emphasis on the safeguards of due process. (JUSTICE, 1975, pp. 70-2)

The mixed nature of present proceedings means that making complaints is compounded by the risk of a discipline charge of making 'any false and malicious allegation' against an officer. The system, in JUSTICE's view, seems to be biased against the prisoner/complainant, and the existence of this offence in particular is incompatible with a just and effective complaints sytem. (JUSTICE, 1983, p. 46) JUSTICE recommended that the discipline function should be separated and given over to a panel of local justices. The view taken by the May Committee was that as the courts now allowed judicial review of board hearings, this would protect the interests of accused prisoners. The final and conclusive argument against making the hearings more like a court in the May Committee's view was that of cost. (Committee of Inquiry into the UK Prison Service, 1979, p. 109)

A number of commentators have stressed the importance of the boards of visitors not merely being independent, but also appearing to be so. There is a good, instructive example of what may happen if a member of a board of visitors actually tries to act in an independent way: the case of Mr Rod Morgan. Morgan, a Senior Lecturer in Criminology at the University of Bath, was until 1984 a member of the board of visitors of Pucklechurch Remand Centre. Morgan wrote to The Times in May 1983 arguing that improvements in prison conditions could only be forced on the government from below (i.e. by prisoners), or from outside the prison system. His suggestion that unconvicted prisoners were justified in demonstrating to gain improvements in their conditions was quickly attacked by the national chairman of the POA, who argued that Morgan should be dismissed from the board as he would not be able to conduct his official duties properly. (The Times, 25 May 1983) In April 1984,

Morgan resigned from the board of visitors as the local branch of the POA had resolved not to escort him around the Remand Centre or to co-operate with him. (Morgan, 1984) Clearly the Home Office was not prepared to support Morgan in his attempt to assert the board member's legal rights of access to the prison.

In spite of all of the criticisms that have been made, especially in the 1970s, the continued existence of the dual functions of the boards of visitors seems to be assured. It is open to argument whether change could have been accomplished by either the Weiler working party or the May Committee. On the one hand, the Weiler working party had the advantage of being composed of civil servants who had considerable knowledge of the prison service. It might well be thought that such a group of informed insiders would be in a good position to bring about change. Unfortunately, the working party's terms of reference were limited to procedures within the existing system. The May Committee, chaired by a High Court judge, might be seen to have been equally well placed to overhaul the system. The Committee's terms of reference could have been used to link changes in this area with changes in the general working conditions of staff, but the May Committee suffered from the double disadvantages of having to report as quickly as possible and of being more concerned with managerial issues than with fundamental problems of justice in the prisons.

In May 1984 the Home Secretary responded to the growing number of prison discipline cases before the courts and the European Court of Human Rights' decision in Campbell and Fell v. United Kingdom (see chapter 4) by appointing a Committee to inquire into the Prison Disciplinary System under the chairmanship of Peter Prior. The Committee reported in October 1985 and recommended a new national tribunal to handle all serious offences against discipline. The tribunal was to be independent, its members having no other connection with prison management. Each panel of the tribunal would consist of a legally qualified chairman and two lay members. The Committee recommended changes in the discipline code, creating new criminal offences to deal with the more serous offences against discipline. (Home Office, 1985, chapter 6) The white paper, The Prison Disciplinary System in England and Wales, published in 1986 has been set aside and the Home Office subsequently decided not to change the system by means of new legislation.

The other body in this category of semi-independent protections and safeguards is the prison inspectorate. The origins of inspection of prisons have been traced back to the late eighteenth century, when justices of the peace were empowered to examine the local prisons and report back to the quarter sessions. (Stockdale, 1983, pp. 210-1) When the local prisons were nationalised in 1877, an inspectorate was established. The number of posts was fixed at six and they set off about their task with some vigour. Their effectiveness was diminished as they necesarily came into conflict with Sir Edward du Cane, the forceful head of the Prison Commission. A period of decline began and inspection slowly reverted to a system of self-inspection by inspectors who were part of the administration of the prisons. (Stockdale, 1983, pp. 216-22)

The title of inspector was revived again by Earl Mountbatten in his report on prison escapes and security. Mountbatten recommended the appointment of an Inspector General. This new appointment was intended to be a professional head of the prison service rather than an administrator as the former Prison Commission Chairman had been. Rather surprisingly an outsider was appointed in 1967, but in 1971, the Inspector General's post was redefined and downgraded in an internal management review and the title was changed to Chief Inspector of the Prison Service. The next Chief Inspector was a former prison governor. (Stockdale, 1983, pp. 223-4)

In the 1970s, the Expenditure Committee of the House of Commons made new demands for an independent inspectorate. (Expenditure Committee, 1977, para 176) The Home Office took the view that the existing programme of regular inspection of prisons had as its primary task the assessment of the 'life style' efficiency and administration of establishments. The existing Inspectorate was integrated into the management structure and the inspection teams were augmented by specialist staff from the regional offices (i.e. educational and medical). (Home Office, 1979, p. 237)

For the Home Office, independence had two possible meanings, an inspectorate could be independent of the government, or it could be independent of the service being inspected. Each of these meanings had consequences for the appointment of inspectors and their relationship with the administration of the prison service. The Home Office argued that the two existing functions of the inspectorate, efficiency and propriety, both required the inspectorate to be a part of the management structure. Efficiency auditing was necessary to ensure continuity throughout a geographically diffuse service. Propriety auditing was an adjunct and reinforcement of the activities of boards of visitors, concentrated on the maintenance of standards. These functions were concerned with management and this kind of quality control had of necessity to be part of the management in order to remedy any defects.

The Home Office argued that a completely independent inspectorate would create a constitutional innovation. If a new inspectorate was outside the Home Office the provision of criticisms of the prison system would be difficult to reconcile with the tradition of ministerial responsibility and accountability to Parliament. On the other hand, an inspectorate without executive powers to remedy defects would suffer from a lack of credibility.

The May Committee recommended that there should be within the Home Office an independent department called the Prisons Inspectorate headed either by someone entirely independent of the civil service or by a senior ex-governor with the post of Her Majesty's Chief Inspector of Prisons. The department would include staff from both the Prison Service and the Home Office. This new inspectorate would be available to make ad hoc inspections of incidents and should make unannounced inspections of particular establishments. The inspectorates's reports should be published except where security considerations applied.

In 1980 the Home Secretary accepted these recommendations on the new style inspectorate and appointed Mr William Pearce, a former Chief Probation Officer. Mr Pearce died in January 1982 and was succeeded by Sir James Hennessy, a former colonial administrator. The third Chief Inspector, Stephen Tumim, a circuit judge, was appointed in 1988.

When Mr Pearce gave evidence to the JUSTICE Committee on prisoners' rights, he described how the inspectorate went about its work. One week was allotted to the actual visit to each establishment and a second week was spent writing up the results. Before each prison was visited a written report from the chairman of the board of visitors was requested and a meeting between the inspector, the chairman and the governor was then arranged. The inspector also examined the records of complaints in each wing so that any pattern of grievances could be discovered and as a result lead to recognition of an administrative defect. This was the alternative to looking into individual grievances, which are outside the inspectorate's terms of reference. (JUSTICE, 1983, pp. 37-9)

The effectiveness of the Inspectorate is difficult to evaluate. It has produced annual reports, reports on inspections of individual institutions and a number of 'thematic reviews'. One of the thematic reviews was on prisoners' complaints and the authors recommended among other things that there should eventually be a statutory code of prisoners' rights. (Home Office, 1987) It is dificult to detect any sense of improvement from the general tone of the annual reports but they have the virtue of routinely collecting and publishing information on an otherwise closed world. Some of the reports present details of living conditions, hygiene standards and staff attitudes that come as shock after years of bland reports on the work of the prison service.

Since the Criminal Justice Act 1982, the Inspectorate has had a statutory basis and this has reduced the scope for Home Office intervention in its work. There is no mention of requiring the Home Secretary's consent or approval to carry out the Inspectorate's official duties. (Zellick, 1983) The statutory basis of inspection does not of course necessarily mean that members of the Inspectorate will be more independently minded.

Morgan has suggested that the Chief Inspector has exercised independence of judgement and that the annual reports contain detailed, if coded, criticisms of successive and systematic managerial failure to provide better prison conditions. On the other hand, the reports of individual inspections say little about the regime, costs, staffing ratios etc. These reports do not provide the basis for long-term comparisons. The Inspectorate has also failed to produce a coherent set of standards by which their job can be done. Morgan argues that the production of standards would be the 'most important contribution to the creation of a more accountable system'. (Morgan, 1985, pp. 122-3)

Official independent grievance mechanisms

The third category of grievance mechanisms for prisoners comprises applications to Members of Parliament and the Parliamentary Commissioner for Administration (P.C.A.). As a result of section 3 of the Representation of the People Act 1983, convicted persons are legally incapable of voting at any parliamentary or local government election during the time when they are detained in a penal institution. Prisoners do however continue to be seen as constituents by the MP in the constituency where they lived on conviction, and prisoners may correspond with their MP. The regulations concerning the contents of such letters are located in the Standing Orders. Until 1981 the regulations in force were particularly restrictive and to make matters worse they were also confidential.

In 1981, the Home Office published a revised Standing Order concerning prisoners' correspondence as a result of the judgment of the European Court of Human Rights in the Silver case (see chapter 4). One of the categories referred to is that addressed to MPs. The only explicit prohibition on correspondence of this kind relates to 'complaints about prison treatment which the inmate has not yet raised through the prescribed procedures' i.e. via the governor, the board of visitors and the Home Secretary. There is also a general provision that contents of correspondence must not endanger the security and good order of the establishment. (Birkinshaw, 1982, pp. 82-3)

Unfortunately there is no real information available on the effectiveness of MPs on behalf of their prisoner constituents. Until the 1981 change, the complaint had to have been raised and investigated fully within the prison before it could be raised with the MP. This may well have had the effect of putting off the MP who received a personal letter from the Home Secretary stating that the complaint had already been investigated and rejected as groundless. The MP would then be able to write to his constituent regretting the lack of success. The general impression among prisoners is that the chances of an MP achieving anything for a prisoner are slight, but there may be a psychological benefit to the prisoner who is able to wave a letter on House of Commons stationery at his fellows and at the prison staff.

The second, and related, means by which prisoners' complaints can be investigated is that of the P.C.A.. Under the Parliamentary Commissioner Act 1967 he is empowered to investigate any action taken by or on behalf of a governmental department or certain other authorities provided that there is no court or tribunal in which such action may be challenged. (Yardley, 1981, pp. 209-14) The Commissioner begins his investigation only on receipt of a complaint that there has been maladministration. The complaint is sent initially to the complainant's MP and the MP is then free to decide whether it should be submitted.

The Commissioner conducts his inquiries in private, and the choice of procedure to be followed is entirely within his discretion. Section 8 of the Act gives the Commissioner the right to compel any Minister or officer or member of a department or authority to produce documents or to provide information relevant to the investigation. The Commissioner has similar powers to those of a court in that witnesses must attend and reply to questioning. Ministers and civil servants are not entitled to claim Crown Privilege to avoid replying. At the end of an inquiry, the Commissioner must send a report to the MP who instigated the investigation. The report either gives the results of the investigation, or the Commissioner's reasons for deciding not to conduct an inquiry. Similar reports are sent to the original complainant and to the principal officer of the department or authority concerned.

The initial legislation did not attempt to define or describe the nature of maladministration although the late Richard Crossman's catalogue of 'bias, neglect, inattention, delay, incompetence, ineptitude, perversity, turpitude, arbitrariness and so on' gives a good indication. (House of Commons Debate, 18 October 1966, col 51) This absence of a statutory definition was intentional as it left the way open for any holder of the post to discover new examples of maladministration. The Parliamentary Select Committee which oversees the Commissioner's work recommended a more adventurous approach to the early holders of the post, all of whom had formerly been civil servants. The Commissioner began with a staff of 60 of whom none were lawyers, and the total number of staff has risen subsequently to 110. These staff are usually on secondment from various government departments. Set a thief to catch a thief, perhaps.

The impact of the P.C.A. on the lives of prisoners has been mixed. According to the Geoffrey Wener writing for the Prison Reform Trust, the P.C.A. had dealt with 65 prison cases up to 1981. (Wener, 1982) This number represents an average of five cases per annum since the inauguration of the scheme; the number of petitions to the Prison Department is about 720 per month. The P.C.A. 'success' rate in relation to prisoners' complaints is rather poor. None of the individual cases dealt with has been upheld in its entirely although there have been partial successes (cp. 38% successes in the case of other complaints).   The P.C.A. has had some success in changing Home Office administrative practice, e.g. the Home Office was calculating parole eligibility dates wrongly in the opinion of prisoners. (Wener, 1982, p. 6) The P.C.A. has also come up against Home Office intransigence: in the <u>Knechtl</u> case (see chapter 4) the P.C.A. suggested that the Home Office should review the rules governing the granting of permission to prisoners wishing to seek legal adivce in order to sue Home Office staff.   The Home Office did review its policy, but decided that no modification was necessary.   The Select Committee took issue with this reply and a change in policy was eventually forthcoming. (Wener, 1982, pp. 6-7)

Unfortunately it is generally recognised by all those who have looked at the P.C.A.'s work in prisons that there are probably more disadvantages than advantages.   The criticisms that have been made fall into seven main areas

1. Prisoners' complaints only reach the P.C.A. at the end of a fairly lengthy chain of events.

2. The number of complaints reaching the P.C.A. from prisoners is low. John Prescott (MP for Hull East) reported in 1976 that only 7% of a sample of his colleagues knew of this right. (Prescott, 1976, para 5.20)

3. The P.C.A can only deal effectively with certain issues as the work of the P.C.A. tends to be paper oriented.

4. The P.C.A. tends to concentrate on procedures rather than the content of decisions.   (Wener, 1982, p. 8)   The P.C.A. is not in a position to question the Prison Rules or the Standing Orders.

5. On those occasions when the P.C.A. has found the Prison Rules to have been broken, he has concluded that no injustice has been done. (JUSTICE, 1983, p. 29)

6. Because the P.C.A. investigations are of single events it may not be possible to detect an underlying defect in the system.

7. The activities of the boards of visitors are outside the scope of review by the P.C.A. as they are not governmental bodies.

Recommendations to reform the P.C.A. system to help prisoners in particular have come from the large-scale study of the early history of the P.C.A. by Gregory and Hutchesson, and from the JUSTICE report <u>Our Fettered Ombudsman.</u> (Gregory and Hutchesson, 1977, p. 158; JUSTICE, 1977, chapter vi)   Both reports stress the special needs of prisoners as a highly vulnerable group in need of protection.   The history of the P.C.A. led the JUSTICE Committee to say that the P.C.A. has failed to live up to expectations in this area of work.   The Committee argued that the P.C.A. should have been used to investigate the prison riots rather than this being done by Home Office staff.   The Committee recommended free access by prisoners either to an MP or to the P.C.A. 'and for the latter to make full use of his powers'. (JUSTICE, 1977, pp. 51-2)

It is not entirely clear who originated the idea of a separate prison ombudsman, but both John Prescott MP and Dr Graham Zellick proposed it after the Hull prison riot.   John Prescott proposed the establishment of a separate prison ombudsman in the report of his indepenent inquiry into the riot and its aftermath.   Zellick made a similar proposal in an article in <u>The Times</u> shortly after the announcement of the Fowler inquiry into the Hull riot.   Zellick argued that the existing P.C.A. scheme was a cumbersome procedure and was ill-suited to dealing quickly and effectively with the problems of a prison system with 42,000 inmates.   An important point which Zellick also raised was that complaints made by prisoners might be ignored as being too trivial to warrant consideration when seen in the context of the work of the P.C.A., a prisons' ombudsman, on the other hand, would be aware of the different proportions assumed by problems for those in custody. (Zellick, 1976)

The idea of a prison ombudsman was discussed in the Home Office evidence to the May Committee. The Home Office's argument is framed in terms of constitutional problems of reconciling the power to override decisions made by the Prison Service with the notion of ministerial responsibility. Unless the ombudsman had this power, it would be difficult to distinguish the new post from the existing P.C.A. scheme. The Home Office concluded that it would not wish to exclude the possibility of establishing a new prison ombudsman, but could not take the view that a sufficient case for one had yet been made. (Home Office, 1979, p. 241) The report of the May Committee simply re-states the constitutional issue before passing on to other matters. (Committee of Inquiry into the UK Prison Service, 1979, pp. 93-4) What both manage to overlook is the more basic question of the effectiveness of the existing scheme.

The suggestion was repeated in the JUSTICE report Justice in Prison and in Geoffrey Wener's report A Legitimate Grievance for the Prison Reform Trust. (JUSTICE, 1983, pp. 39-42; Wener, 1982, pp. 18-9) The JUSTICE report argues that the new ombudsman should have the objective of ensuring that the treatment of prisoners is fair, reasonable and just. The ombudsman's power should not go beyond that of making recommendations. These recommendations would have the authority of Parliament in that annual reports to Parliament would list those recommendations which have not been complied with. An important difference from the present arrangements would be the recommendation that complaints or communications would not be subject to disciplinary measures under the Prison Rules. (JUSTICE, 1983, pp. 40-2)

Wener reports on the experience of prison ombudsmen in Sweden, Denmark, New Zealand and Canada. In each country ombudsmen exist either to deal specifically with prisons, as in Canada, or more generally for all government activity, as in Sweden, Denmark and New Zealand. The common conclusion is that ombudsmen can play an important and effective role in dealing with prisoners' grievances and in acting as a check on the quality of prison administration. (Wener, 1982, pp. 18-9) Wener argues that 'with a unique combination of independence, impartiality, accessibility and investigative power, an ombudsman could constitute a significant "fail-safe" component in prison grievance procedures'. (Wener, 1982, p. 18) He does not, however, say how this ombudsman would fit into the administration of the prisons, or on the extent of the ombudsman's power to investigate and remedy grievances.

Unofficial independent grievance mechanisms

Pressure groups also assist prisoners and safeguard their rights. Of particular importance in this context are the Howard League for Penal Reform, JUSTICE, the National Council for Civil Liberties (NCCL) and the PROP. The first three of these organisations are of a different type from PROP in that they are more or less approved by the Home Office and prisoners may write to them about their complaints. PROP on the other hand set out to be a prisoners' union. Prisoners are allowed to write to the Howard League, JUSTICE and NCCL about their case leading up to conviction or about prison conditions. This was an important exception to the former rule which until 1981 prohibited complaints about prison conditions. (Zellick, 1971, p. 340)

The Howard League is the oldest penal reform group and its origins can be traced back to 1866. (Rose, 1961; Ryan, 1978) The Howard League includes in its statement of aims campaigning for the individual prisoner 'if the case in question reflects a principle which, in the League's view, needs to be clarified or altered'. (Howard League, 1982, p. 7) The League also publishes a pamphlet, Prisoners' Problems, on how to make requests and complaints within the prison system.

JUSTICE is predominantly composed of lawyers, and its general aims are to uphold and strengthen the principles of the rule of law, and to assist in the maintenance of the highest standards of administration of justice and in the preservation of the fundamental liberties of the individual. As far as prisoners are concerned JUSTICE tends to be a last resort.   This is because of JUSTICE's criteria for dealing with individual cases, there has to have been an element of injustice, the complaint has to be one to which lawyers can contribute, and finally there has to be the probability of affecting change within a decade. (Darbyshire, 1980, p. 6)   The Annual Reports of JUSTICE usually list details of the cases in which the organisation is currently taking an interest.

JUSTICE has also been important because it has organised a number of committees to investigate administration and to recommend reforms. JUSTICE committees were influential in the establishment of the P.C.A. and have subsequently produced detailed criticisms of its activities. In the area of prisoners' rights JUSTICE members (with members of NACRO and the Howard League) formed part of the Jellicoe Committee which produced a report, Boards of Visitors of Penal Establishments, in 1975.   In 1983 a committee under the chairmanship of Sir Brian MacKenna, a retired High Court judge, produced the report entitled Justice in Prison.

The NCCL was founded in 1934 to provide an independent watchdog organisation to oversee the activities of the police in relation to hunger marchers. (Cox, 1975, p. 23)   Since the 1930s, the NCCL has acted as a non-party political pressure grop seeking to protect civil and political rights.   An additional activity has been concerned with justiciable rights, i.e. those which may be established in a court of law.   In a recently published collection of essays to celebrate NCCL'S fiftieth anniversary, it is stated that its most valuable work in recent years has been on behalf of those without an effective voice of their own. (Wallington, 1984, p. 2) Ironically while there are essays on a wide range of 'client' groups, there is no essay on prisoners.

In reality, NCCL has been involved in providing assistance to prisoners who have been trying to have their cases reviewed in some way. The lack of a large legally qualified staff (two solicitors were employed full-time in 1976) has not prevented the Council from being involved in some of the more important prisoners' rights cases of recent years.   Laurie Taylor recounts the history of the NCCL's involvement with Peter Rajah, who had tried to have the board of visitors' adjudication reviewed by the courts, finally to become one of the plaintiffs in St Germain. (Taylor, 1980, pp. 37-8)

The NCCL was also involved in Williams v. Home Office.   Harriet Harman, then legal officer of the NCCL, worked as the instructing solicitor in what turned out to be a long and complicated series of litigation. (Leigh, 1980) In order to bring the case it was necessary to get access to internal Home Office policy papers.   The means of gaining this access is called 'discovery', a process by which parties can obtain information of the existence and contents of all documents relevant to the matters in dispute between them.   The object of discovery is to eliminate surprise at the trial and 'to promote fair disposal of the case'. (Walker, 1980, p. 363) The Home Office fought very determinedly to prevent the disclosure of many of the relevant documents on the grounds that it was against the public interest to disclose the documents, as these included advice given by civil servants to ministers. The Treasury Solicitor mentioned the possible conflict of interest for Ms Harman as a solicitor for Williams and legal officer for NCCL, and said that he did not wish to see the documents used for NCCL's purposes.

Some of the disclosed documents were referred to during the trial as exhibits and hence were made public. Some were also quoted at greater length in a Guardian article published shortly after the trial. The article entitled 'How ministry hardliners had their way over prison units', explained the policy and personalities involved in some detail. (Guardian, 8 April 1980) The official reaction was almost instantaneous. The Treasury Solicitor complained immediately to the NCCL about the article rather than the newspaper.

An action alleging civil contempt of court was brought against Ms Harman. The contempt consisting in a breach of the implied undertaking given to the court that documents would not be disclosed for any other purpose. Ms Harman was held to have committed a contempt of court and although she was not punished she did have to pay the Home Office substantial costs. An appeal to the Court of Appeal was dismissed and eventually an appeal in the House of Lords was also dismissed. Lord Diplock said, when giving judgment, that the case was not about the freedom of the press or openness of government, but rather it related to an aspect of the law of discovery and documents in actions before the High Court. The contempt of court lay in the 'collateral or ulterior motive of her own or NCCL'. (Home Office v. Harman, p. 338) The work of the courts was not to satisfy public curiosity but to hear the actions brought before them, so any argument about the public interest could not be sustained.

PROP is distinctive because of its insistence on being an organisation run by ex-prisoners for prisoners and ex-prisoners. Other people may apply for membership but, if granted, this is limited to associate membership only. PROP began its public existence in May 1972 and was announced as a prisoners' union. (Fitzgerald, 1977, chapter 5) In the first part of 1972 there had been a series of peaceful protests about prison conditions and PROP was organised to represent prisoners. PROP adopted a 'Statement of Intent' which included a 'Charter of Rights'.

The demands were sent to the media and to the then Home Secretary (Reginald Maudling). A covering letter to the Home Secretary included a request to begin negotiations to bring about the implementation of the prisoners' rights listed in the Charter. The letter was never answered. PROP tried to accomplish its aims by general publicity and through organisation within the prisons themselves.

Throughout the summer of 1972 there was a wave of demonstrations and strikes in the prisons which PROP attempted to orchestrate. One of the organisational problems faced by PROP was to gain legitimacy among prisoners themselves, as a starting point from which to take on the Home Office. The POA objected to any official contact with PROP and received assurances from the Home Secretary that he had no intention of negotiating with PROP. (The Times, 4 September 1972)

The decline of PROP began in August 1972 with the riot in Albany prison. The popular press reported the riot in considerable detail, and commented on the problems caused by disruptive prisoners. PROP was split by an internal crisis when one of its founding members resigned in a blaze of damaging publicity and promptly began bankruptcy proceedings against PROP. Fitzgerald reports that prison staff and boards of visitors began to re-assert their control through restrictions on prisoners' activities and by giving severe punishments to anyone engaging in demonstrations. PROP's decline continued in part because of its inability to validate its claim to speak for the majority of prisoners; access to its claimed membership was always problematic, and this led to frustration and recriminations.

Since 1972 PROP has divided into two groups, one in Hull and the other in London. The Hull section has been concerned with running a hostel for ex-prisoners, and with providing speakers for educational establishments. The London group has had the general aim of changing public attitudes to crime and punishment. This has entailed working through local councils and trade unions to widen the knowledge of different groups on prison conditions in paticular. London PROP is also working as a clearing house in the sense that it steers prisoners and their families to other specialist organisations which can provide help or advice.

PROP is still actively involved in campaigning on behalf of prisoners; the book Frightened for My Life brings together case studies of the deaths of seven prisoners. (Coggan and Walker, 1982) The authors argue that these cases demonstrate the urgent need for prisoners to have access to independent medical advice, of their own choice, and for the integration of the prison medical service into the NHS.

PROP's concern with prisoners' rights is quite unlike that of any of the other pressure groups. Its approach is confrontational and has produced a considerable amount of conflict. PROP's attempt to establish a list of prisoners' rights in its Charter is important as it represents the first real attempt by prisoners themselves to draw up a list of rights, in contrast to rules draw up by prison administrators. The failure of PROP both as an organisation and in its initial aims is of importance, demonstrating as it does the view of what the Home Office considers legitimate political activity by prisoners and the difficulty of organising a radical self-help group among prisoners who do not see themselves as having a common cause.

Conclusions

The picture which emerges from this review of the administrative remedies for prisoners' complaints and grievances is one of complexity and considerable overlap. Two issues which emerge from this review seem to be of major importance - independence and effectiveness. The question of independence is complicated by the probability that an organisation which might appear to outsiders to be independent of either the Home Office or the Prison Department may not be seen in the same way by prisoners who experience the routine decision-making process. The location of bodies such as the boards of visitors will mean that their integrity is always open to attack. The more autonomous members of boards of visitors try to become, the more likely they are to run into trouble from prison staff and management as demonstrated by Dr Rod Morgan's experiences.

Effectiveness is equally difficult to evaluate. The simple fact of a prisoner's complaint being heard by an independent person or organisation could on occasions be all that the comlainant wanted. Other claims against the prison system may be in the power of the governor, and a simple change in policy might bring about changes which are significant to prisoners but which appear trivial to outsiders. The point is that effectiveness and independence are not invariably related; but there does appear to be negative relationship in the sense that the greater the independence of the body, the less immediately effective it will be. Independence brings problems of caseloads and skill or ability to come to grips with the peculiarities of prison administration.

The boards of visitors and the Prison Inspectorate appear at first sight to have great advantages over the other organisations that have been described. Both comprise people who are knowledgeable about the prison world, and who are in a position to take a sustained interest in prisons. The effectiveness of both the boards and the Inspectorate as organisations which provide quality control is diminished by each body having more than one area of responsibility. The boards of visitors are disciplinary boards as well as hearers of complaints. The Prison Inspectorate is in practice a form of management consultancy concerned with the smooth running of the prison system. The history of various prison inspectorates that have been established since the 1830s has been characterised by repeated instances of incorporation into the management structure.

No single organisation or person is able (or appropriate) to deal with prisoners' grievances. Some are less suitable than others. Complaints can range from matters of daily routine to policy considerations, so a number of mechanisms will always be necessary. Not all complaints should be the subject of some sort of review. What is a source of worry is that in the complexity of the present patchwork some important legitimate grievances may not be ventilated at all.

3 Prisoners' rights in English law

The English courts have traditionally taken little interest in the lives of prisoners after sentence. The rights of the accused have always had priority, a belief stemming from the days when the penalties were extremely harsh. Accused persons were to be protected from wrongful conviction by adherence to rigid procedural rules. This did not mean that the nineteenth-century judge did not have a significant effect on the conditions experienced by a prisoner. (Advisory Council on the Penal System, 1978, chapter 3) The conditions of custody depended on the nature of the offence; offences were divided into felonies and misdemeanours. In English common law a felony was a serious crime which involved forfeiture of the felon's land to the crown, and offences such as murder, wounding, arson, rape and robbery were felonies. Forfeiture was abolished in 1870 but the distinction continued until 1967 and new felonies were created by statute up to that date. Misdemeanours were defined as offences other than treason and felony. Not all of the misdemeanours were less serious offences, for example conspiracy, riot and assault were misdemeanours, but most were minor offences.

In the middle of the nineteenth century a series of Acts, such as the Penal Servitude Act 1853, was passed which substituted sentences of penal servitude for sentences of transportation. Imprisonment was a lesser penalty and could be used as a sanction for either felonies or misdemeanours, to a maximum of two years. The distinction between imprisonment and penal servitude was important. Imprisonment involved isolation, silence, separation from other prisoners, a sentence so severe that two years was thought to be the maximum that could be safely inflicted. Penal servitude was served in the central government convict prisons. The Prison Act of 1877, which brought all prisons under central government control, allowed for modifications in the 'hard labour, hard fare and a hard bed' system imposed in the 1865 Act. A system of progressive stages was introduced which allowed a little improvement in the prisoner's conditions.

When the Forfeiture Act was enacted in 1870 other penalties were substituted, e.g. felons were deprived of the right to hold office under the Crown, to receive any public pension, or to vote. More importantly, those sentenced to penal servitude for felony were not able to sue, dispose of or mortgage property or make a contract. The right to sue was restored in the Criminal Justice Act 1948 and included the possibility of suing the prison authorities.

Individual prisoners have brought cases against their gaolers before the courts, but the success of these cases has depended largely on the kinds of issues raised. The prisoners' rights cases have been divided into five major groups, defined by the main themes of the cases. These thematic groups are as follows
- access to the courts;
- the classification of prisoners and prison conditions;
- the duty of care;
- natural justice in prisons;
- enforced medical treatment.

Access to the courts

One of the curiosities of the history of prisoners' rights litigation is that prisoners had been bringing cases before the courts for many years before the right of access to the courts was finally and authoritatively established. Since the emergence of the prisoner's right to sue, the prison authorities have exercised a high degree of control over prisoners' litigation. [1] The Prison Rules 1964 include rule 34(8) which requires the leave of the Home Secretary before a prisoner may engage in any legal business. This rule does not apply if the prisoner is already a party to legal proceedings, e.g. criminal trial or subsequent appeal. The requirement in rule 34(8) included for many years legal proceedings in relation to divorce, although prisoners serving 12 months or more have been allowed for some years to institute such proceedings without permission. In other cases it has been necessary to seek special permission which has not been granted automatically. (Zellick, 1977, p. 65)

The Home Office has used the Prison Rules to control access to legal advice. Letters to legal advisers have been censored or stopped by the prison authorities. The rules were used to prevent prisoners from writing to people they did not know before the sentence and to control the contents of the letters, which meant that complaints could only be made to organisations such as NCCL. If a prisoner asked his family or friends to instruct a solicitor, the Home Office could refuse the solicitor access to his potential client. The Home Office insisted until 1975 on seeing a prisoner's evidence and assessing his case when deciding to give permission, even in cases when the Home Office was itself the potential defendant.

Since 1976 the prisoner's path to the courts has still not been an easy one. Unless the prisoner has the money to pay for legal advice, he will be limited to whatever advice may be given under the legal aid 'Green Form' scheme. This scheme allows people on low incomes, including prisoners, to receive legal advice and assistance up to the current financial limit. Even with this aid, the prisoner's difficulties may not be over, as his next problem is making contact with a solicitor.

Many prisons are located in the countryside and solicitors may be reluctant to spend the time.

After the Golder case (see chapter 4), the Home Office amended the Prison Rules relating to contacts with solicitors. Prisoners were allowed contact with a solicitor with a view to instituting civil proceedings subject to the directions of the Home Secretary. (Zellick, 1976, p. 139) The main regulation was that of the 'prior ventilation' rule, i.e. the Home Secretary would not allow suits concerning the administration of prison establishments until internal investigations of complaints had been completed. This rule has subsequently been replaced by the 'simultaneous ventilation' rule which means that a complaint has to been made to the prison authorities at the same time as litigiation is brought before the courts. Even this rule has been declared unlawful by the courts (in ex parte Anderson), and prisoners may now bring their complaints directly to the court. The barriers to speedy access to the courts have been removed without the courts being deluged by the threatened flood of litigation.

The act of a prison governor in stopping a prisoner's application to the High Court for leave to issue proceedings was the subject of litigation, and finally established prisoners' rights of access to the courts. In Raymond v. Honey (1981) it was held that interference with a prisoner's access to the courts was a contempt of court. In the Divisional Court, it was held that breaching the confidentiality of correspondence was a contempt, either if it was calculated to prejudice the right to unhindered access to the courts, or if it interfered with the due course of justice or with lawful process, provided the applicant was a person whose common law rights had not already been restricted. A person held in prison retained all of his civil rights except those which had been taken from him either expressly or by implication. The prison governor was held to be acting within the Prison Rules by opening and stopping the first letter, but stopping the application to commit the governor for contempt amounted to conduct which prejudiced a citizen's unhindered access to the courts. As the delay had only been temporary, the court did not make any order other than costs.

The Home Office appealed to the House of Lords – the first time a prisoner's rights case had been to the House of Lords. Lord Wilberforce, giving judgment, dismissed the Home Office appeal, basing his decision on two principles. First, it was an established principle in English law that conduct calculated to prejudice a party's access to the courts, or to obstruct or to interfere with the due course of justice or the lawful process of the courts, was a contempt of court, and that access to the courts was a right guaranteed by the European Convention on Human Rights. Second, it was an established principle that a convicted prisoner, in spite of his imprisonment, retains all of his civil rights that are not taken away by his conviction or by other legislation. Lord Wilberforce accepted the argument that the Prison Rules would be ultra vires if they were to be interpreted to deny the right of access. The Standing Orders could not be interpreted to have greater legislative power than the Rules from which they were derived.

Three other Law Lords concurred, while Lord Bridge of Harwich dissented on the gounds that he wished to add a third principle to those stated by Lord Wilberforce

> that a citizen's right to unimpeded access to the courts can only be taken away by express enactment.

The importance of the Wilberforce judgment is liable to exaggeration.

The rights which a prisoner has not lost either as a result of legislation or through imprisonment still remain to be delineated. The right of access to the courts does not, of course, have any significance in how the courts will deal with substantive issues.

In the summer of 1983, the Prison Department amended its policy in relation to private prosecutions by prisoners. These had previously been prohibited by the same rules as those which governed civil actions. The Prison Department took the view that Raymond v. Honey applied equally to criminal prosecutions. However, the Home Office added that the government would consider sympathetically and carefully any request for the Treasury Solicitor to advise on an accused officer's defence. (The Times, 1 June 1983)

It is appropriate to mention here the question of access to the institutions of the ECHR. Although the Convention will be dealt with in more detail in chapter 4, it has been the subject of a case. In Guilfoyle v. Home Office (1981) it was held that the prison authorities could open and stop correspondence dealing with an application to the European Commission of Human Rights.

Lord Denning said that while the European Court was a court of judicature (i.e. exercising a judicial function), the European Commission was more like a tribunal which could make enforceable orders. Lord Denning also said that there was the matter of deciding when someone actually becomes a 'party' to 'legal proceedings', even if the European Commission could be described as legal proceedings. In his view, this only happened when an application had been accepted as admissible, in much the same way as applying to the High Court did not make one a party to legal action, which only happened when leave to appeal was granted and proceedings began.

Lord Denning concluded that Guilfoyle was not 'a party to any legal proceedings' under rule 37(1). The letters to and from his solicitor could be read by the prison governor. On the other hand, if the correspondence was connected with a petition which had reached the European Court of Human Rights, it could be read but not stopped. This had been stated by the Home Secretary as a matter of policy in answer to a Parliamentary Question. The appeal was dismissed as in Lord Denning's opinion the Home Office, the prison governor and all concerned had acted properly.

Until December 1983, the Rules required that complaints had to be lodged with the prison authorities before the prisoner could seek legal advice. In R v. Governor of Wormwood Scrubs Prison, ex parte Anderson Lord Justice Goff said that while it was proper for the Home Office to regulate the access of prisoners to solicitors, it was clear from Raymond v. Honey that a prisoner's right of access to a solicitor to initiate proceedings should be unimpeded. The applicant's request to see a solicitor was an inseparable part of his right of access to the courts themselves. The requirement that an inmate made a complaint as a prerequisite of access to a solicitor went beyond the control of the circumstances of access and constituted an impediment to his right of access to the civil court, the Standing Order was therefore ultra vires.

The right of access to the English courts seems to have been firmly established, but there are still important barriers to effective access. The restriction on legal advice has been particularly important in this respect. The government has accepted the need for duty solicitor schemes in prisons, but so far progress has been very slow, only two prisons (Camp Hill on the Isle of Wight and Manchester) had such schemes by March 1984. (Lord Chancellor's Deptartment, 1983; NACRO, 1984, p. 21)

The classification of prisoners and prison conditions

Historically the largest single category of prisoners' rights litigation
concerns the related issues of the classification of prisoners and the
conditions of imprisonment. The first of these topics stems directly
from the comment at the beginning of this chapter, that the offence
determined the conditions of custody. The second topic relates to the
conditions of imprisonment, and attempts by prisoners to obtain some
form of external review or supervision of the actions of their gaoler.

In the nineteenth century the courts were asked to intervene on seven
occasions which were recorded in the law reports. In these cases the
courts were prepared to intervene when there was a breach of the system
of classification. For example, in Osborne v. Angle (1835) the Court of
Common Pleas accepted that it had a duty to protect a debtor from a
greater degree of severity and coercion than his circumstances
warranted. The Court rejected the claim in this case recognising the
proper exercise of the warden's discretion in the prevention of escapes.
A similar view was taken in Yorke v. Chapman (1839). In Cobbett v. Grey
(1850) the court decided that moving a prisoner to a part of the prison
in which, by law, he should not have been kept was a trespass. Both the
Home Secretary and the gaoler were liable for wrongly classifying the
prisoner.

In 1869, the courts concluded in Moone v. Rose that the gaoler was an
officer with a duty to obey the law and if he was responsible for
holding a prisoner illegally beyond the expiry dte of a warrant then the
prisoner could sue. The issue was re-stated in Osborne v. Milman in
1886 when the courts accepted the principle that treating a misdemeanant
as a felon was a matter for the courts. The Court of Appeal eventually
decided that Osborne had actually been dealt with in the appropriate way
but the principle had been accepted.

Other cases brought in the nineteenth century where prisoners were
asking for the courts to intervene in prison administration were firmly
rejected. In The King v. Carlile (1822), the prisoner asked for the
same opportunity to take exercise as permitted to felons. Chief Justice
Abbott said the courts were willing to do what by law they had the power
to do. The management and control of the prisons were in the hands of
the county magistrates subject to the approval of the justices of
assize. Other means of regulation were therefore available although this
did not mean that gaolers could ill treat prisoners. In 1843, the
Queen's Bench Division judges decided that they could not interfere with
the regulations of Stafford gaol when asked to do do in R v. Cooper.

Nothing further seems to have emerged from this line of development in
the nineteenth century cases. The landmark case on the nature of prison
rules is Arbon v. Anderson (1943). The principle raised in two linked
cases dealt with by the King's Bench was whether the instructions issued
by the Home Secretary for the detention of enemy aliens, and the Prison
Rules 1933, conferred rights on detained persons which could be the
basis of actions before the courts.

Lord Justice Goddard gave the judgment which established the basis of
prisoners' litigation up to the present day. He said that the Home
Secretary's instructions for the detention of enemy aliens were nothing
more than departmental administrative instructions which could be
altered by him at any time. There had been no breaches of the Prison
Rules and even if there had been, these rules did not confer rights upon
prisoners which could be enforced by legal action. The rules were made
under the Prison Act 1898, for the 'government' of prisoners. There was

nothing in the Act or its Rules to show a legislative intention to confer rights which could be enforced at law. The nineteenth century cases which had been discussed because they appeared to make breaches actionable could be distinguished from the present case: Cobbett v. Grey was concerned with imprisonment in the wrong place, and Osborne v. Milman was concerned with the nature of the offence. Arguments based on claims that prisoners had suffered some inconvenience or detriment could not be the basis of action.

Lord Justice Goddard continued, saying that the proper avenue for complaints by prisoners was that provided by the governor, the visiting committee and the Secretary of State. There is a strong element of policy contained in the remark that

> It would be fatal to all discipline in prison if governors and warders had to perform their duty always with the fear of an action before their eyes if they in any way deviated from the rules.

His Lordship added that even if there were proof of a breach of the rules, there would have been no cause for legal action.

The Prison Act 1952 did not change the legal position of prisoners. In Silverman v. Prison Commissioners (1954) a declaration was sought to show that because Silverman was being held in a prison which did not provide the special treatment involved in Preventive Detention sentences which he believed was required by the Criminal Justice Act 1948 this action was ultra vires. Silverman argued that the Prison Commission had exceeded its legal powers in keeping him in a local prison and not providing special treatment.

The Queen's Bench Divisional court rejected Silverman's calim saying that no cause for action lay against the Prison Commissioners, as they did not make the Prison Rules. The judge did, however, consider the merits of the case. The conditions covering the different stages of a sentence of preventive detention, and the matter of how much remission of sentence was given, all contributed to the special treatment. Those were aspects of preventive detention which differentiated it from an ordinary sentence of imprisonment.

The judge also referred back to Arbon v. Anderson to point out that the Prison Rules did not confer positive rights on prisoners. Authority was also cited for the proposition that the court had no jurisdiction to grant a declaration except when an enforceable legal right had been infringed.

Silverman appealed to the Court of Appeal and the lower court's judgment was upheld. On this occasion, the Court of Appeal looked at the facts of the case, and took the view that the rule was within the scope of the Criminal Justice Act. This approach removed any need to consider the rules or their effect on prisoners' legal rights.

The next case in which there was a statement of the legal status of prisoners occurred as a part of Alfred Hinds' long-running battle with the Home Office, the courts and the police over his conviction for the part he was alleged to have played in a storebreaking. Hinds was sentenced to 12 years' preventive detention, although he continually protested his innocence and claimed that police officers had committed perjury to obtain the conviction.

Hinds escaped from prison and was eventually re-arrested in Northern Ireland in 1961 on a warrant alleging the common law misdemeanour of escaping from lawful custody. Hinds applied to the Divisional Court to argue that he could not have escaped from lawful custody if his initial imprisonment was unlawful. This application had initially been dismissed on the grounds that it was frivolous and vexatious.

Hinds appealed to the Court of Appeal, and in dismissing the application Lord Justice Sellers commented on the nature of the Prison Rules and the legal status of prisoners. Hinds appeared to think that he could carry on litigation as if he was a private individual (presumably meaning a free citizen). Lord Justice Sellers then went on to say

> The privileges afforded to prisoners were dealt with under certain rules which had been made and retained under the Criminal Justice Act 1948. A person in custody had not the same rights as ordinary individuals. In order to safeguard the rights of prisoners in custody the rules provided that with the consent of the prison authorities prisoners were able at their discretion to seek legal advice and bring actions in some cases. These rules were administrative only and if there was any breach of them then the way in which they could be put right was to complain to the visiting Justices.

This judgment re-asserts the limited nature of the rules and quite unequivocally states the need to protect the prison authorities from litigious prisoners. Prisoners had no legitimate interest in litigation concerning prison conditions, which were the preserve of visiting justices.

The next landmark case was Becker v. Home Office (1972), when only the Court of Appeal hearing was reported. Mrs Becker was imprisoned in 1965 for a bankruptcy offence. During the course of that sentence, she asked the Home Office for permission to continue a legal action as a trustee of her children which she had begun before the sentence of imprisonment. The Home Office granted the permission provided that Mrs Becker would pay her own costs i.e. the expense of escorts to and from the courts and the costs of travel. These costs had to be paid in advance to the Home Office. Mrs Becker agreed to this condition. Mrs Becker eventually won her case, but the costs of escorts were not included in the judgment. The prison governor then recovered these costs (£8.17) from Mrs Becker's property held by the prison. Mrs Becker then brought an action against the Home Office to recover this money and to claim damages against the Home Office for the wrongful detention of a cheque for £30 which had been sent to the prison. This cheque seems to have been held by the prison authorities for a while, but then it disappeared and was never subsequently found. The issue did not involve the loss of the cheque itself but rather damages for its unlawful detention.

In the first trial, the judge held that Mrs Becker was entitled to recover the £8.17 from the Home Office but dismissed the claim for damages in respect of the lost cheque. The Home Office appealed against the award of the expenses while Mrs Becker cross-appealed in respect of the lost cheque.

In the Court of Appeal, Lord Denning, the Master of the Rolls, in giving the leading judgment reviewed the historical precedents for the production of prisoners in the courts. Under the Prison Act 1952, the Home Secretary had discretionary power to release prisoners to appear in court. The Act also allowed the Home Secretary a discretion in how to administer the prisons and in deciding who should pay any expenses incurred. The Prison Act contained regulatory directions only, and did not give any prisoner a hint of a right to have anything provided to him free of charge. If the Home Secretary wanted to extend privileges to any prisoner on the condition that the prisoner paid for it himself, then he was entitled to do so.

Lord Denning rejected the claim in respect of the £30 cheque on the grounds that a convicted person cannot have delivered property which comes into the prison addressed to him. The prisoner is not allowed personal possessions, or contraband. In a similar way, cheques can be withheld and it is within the discretion of the prison authorities to decide how they are to be dealt with.

Lord Denning in giving judgment then went on to say that if the courts were to hear cases from disgruntled prisoners, the governor's life would be made intolerable. The discipline of the prison would be undermined. He re-affirmed Lord Justice Goddard's view of the rules: 'The Prison Rules are regulatory directions only. Even if they are not observed, they do not give rise to a cause of action'.

The most important recent case to challenge the Prison Rules is Williams v. Home Office which was decided in 1981. The Williams case was mentioned earlier as it involved Ms Harriet Harman, the legal officer of NCCL.

The case is important as it concerned the status of the Prison Rules, the ways in which the Prison Department could attempt to deal with difficult prisoners, and the argument that the regime of the unit in which Williams was detained was contrary to the aims of the Prison Act 1952. The main object of complaint was the nature of the regime in the control unit at Wakefield prison in which Williams was held. The control unit was developed by the Home Office in 1974 as a way of coping with prisoners regarded by the prison authorities as being subversive troublemakers who disrupted the normal discipline of maximum security prisons. The plan was that prisoners in the control unit were held in solitary confinement for the first 90 days. If the prisoner was of good behaviour during that time, he was allowed to associate with any other prisoners in the unit in the same stage. If at any time, a prisoner failed to conform he would have to begin the whole process again, regardless of any discretion the governor might feel like exercising. The history of the policy on control units has been the subject of heated argument, and the Home Office has been accused of having tried to launch the new policy without public announcements, although J.E. Thomas has argued that when the control unit policy was announced in Parliament, no one there or outside made any response: the outrage was supplied three months later by the Sunday Times. (Thomas, 1975, p. 99)

Williams, who had been in the control unit from 23 August 1974 to 10 February 1975, when he was transferred to another prison, contended that his imprisonment in the control unit had been unlawful for the following reasons

1. because the nature of his imprisonment was different from and worse than in the remainder of the prison system, and breached of the Prison Rules 1964;
2. the Home Office could not rely on section 12(1) of the Prison Act 1952 to justify his detention in the control unit since the Home Secretary was merely empowered to confine him to prison, and was not concerned with the nature of that imprisonment;
3. the Home Secretary had no power to place him in the unit, as a prison governor was the only person authorised to order the segregation of a prisoner;
4. even if the Home Secretary did have the power to act under rule 43 (by which a prisoner can be placed in solitary confinement for administrative purposes), his detention was unlawful after his first month since there was no review in accordance with rule 43(2) (i.e. monthly thereafter);
5. the regime was punitive and contrary not only to the policy and

object of the 1952 Act and the 1964 Rules but also to the Bill of Rights 1689 which prohibited the infliction of 'cruell and unusuall punishments'; and,

6. contrary to the rules of natural justice, the plaintiff had not been specifically told why he was being transferred to the unit nor was he given any opportunity to make representations why he should not be detained there.

This case probably represents the most detailed review of any aspect of prison policy by a judge in England. In his review of Williams' claim, Mr Justice Tudor Evans said that the claim being made was that the form of detention was unlawful and amounted to false imprisonment. Also a claim was made that compensation should be paid to Williams for the effect on his personality of time there. It was claimed that the experience had frightened, depressed and disoriented him, although no psychiatric evidence could be produced to substantiate this claim. There was an additional claim for exemplary damages because of 'oppressive, arbitrary and unconstitutional action by servants of the government'. It was submitted that the control unit and its regime had been introduced secretly and without any advance publicity. When Home Office ministers had admitted the existence of the control unit in reply to a Parliamentary Question, they had omitted any reference to the deprivation of human company.

The judge said that he was ultimately concerned with three questions of law

1. the proper construction of section 12(1) of the 1952 Act; did the section lawfully justify the detention of a prisoner in any prison?
2. what, if at all, was the relevance of the conditions of imprisonment to the lawfulness of the detention?
3. what, if at all, was the relevance of a breach or non-compliance with the Prison Rules with respect to the issue of lawful detention?

Mr Justice Tudor Evans answered these questions saying that Williams had been lawfully convicted and sentenced in 1971. While in prison he had shown himself to be a persistent troublemaker who disrupted the life of the prison. The Home Secretary had the power to act in such cases under rule 43 of the Prison Rules. The governor could remove any prisoner from association with others either generally or for particular purposes when it appeared desirable for the maintenance of good order or discipline. The control unit committee could equally lawfully exercise this power. There had, however, been no further request for authority to hold Williams in segregation after the first month in the unit. The control unit committee did not review each man's progress every month as required by rule 43; the rules were internal regulations and were not mandatory.

The second question concerned the nature of the control unit. There was evidence to show that the regime was disagreeable. The judge did not believe that the regime was designed to punish; punishment was not within the ambit of rule 43 which was designed to be a preventative measure by isolating the individual.

As to the third issue, Mr Justice Tudor Evans did not think that the lawfulness of detention could be affected by the conditions of custody,. The question of the conditions of imprisonment was a matter for the Home Secretary. The safeguards against abuse were ample. Other cases, R v. Hull   Prison Board of Visitors, ex parte St Germain and Others (see below) and Payne v. Home Office (see below), were quoted to demonstrate the administrative nature of the prison conditions. The actions of prison administrators had considerable consequences for the lives of prisoners but they could not be reviewed by the courts.

Mr Justice Tudor Evans quoted Lord Goddard in Arbon v. Anderson both to justify the statement that the Prison Rules did not confer rights, and for the protection of prison governors from judicial interference. Lord Denning's views on disgruntled prisoners in Becker v. Home Office were also cited.

One argument was of particular importance in terms of principle. Mr Justice Tudor Evans rejected the appeal made to the Bill of Rights. The argument concentrated on the meaning of the words 'cruel and unusual' and whether the regime as a matter of fact was either or both, dependent on the construction adopted. The clause in the sentence, "That excessive bail ought not to be required nor excessive fines imposed nor cruel and unusual punishment inflicted' might have two meanings: first, it might be read conjunctively to imply that it is only a punishment which is both cruel and unusual which must not be inflicted; or second, that the clause might be read disjunctively to imply that the Act prohibits the infliction of cruel punishment and, separately, prohibits the infliction of unusual punishments. On this second interpretation the unit would be in breach of the Act if it was either cruel or unusual. On the first interpretation, it would be lawful in modern England to inflict a cruel punishment provided it was not unusual, i.e. that it was commonly inflicted. Counsel for Williams had argued that the phrase had been read disjunctively by the Canadian courts to have the effect of limiting the cruelty of a usual punishment (the Supreme Court of Canada has subsequently decided that the words should be read conjunctively and rejected the American usage), but Mr Justice Tudor Evans proposed that it be read conjunctively. (R v. Miller and Cockrriell)

The judge thought that the control unit was not unusual when compared with other regimes in the English system, for example, the segregation units proposed in the Radzinowicz report, consequently there was no breach of the Bill of Rights. In fact he was mistaken as to the similarity of these regimes. The Advisory Council on the Penal System had suggested that disruptive prisoners should be held in a segregation unit within a larger prison 'so that there can be some continuity of treatment, some possibility of ready transfer between the unit and the main prison, and above all so that the prisoner, however difficult he may be, is not treated as having been abandoned by the prison system as a whole'. (Advisory Council on the Penal System, 1968, para 42) The details of life in such a segregation unit would have been far removed from those in the actual control unit, e.g. some association or group activity was possible if the governor thought this advisable. Any one allocated to a segregation unit would only have to remain there for as long as a local committee deemed necessary and a quick return to the main prison was to be the main objective. (Advisory Council on the Penal System, 1968, paras 165-6)

On the question of cruelty the court had heard lengthy arguments about prison standards as recommended in the United Nations Standard Minimum Rules, those inherent in the Universal Declaration of Human Rights and the European Convention on Human Rights. Counsel had quoted two cases, Waddington v. Miah and R v. Secretary of State for Home Affairs, ex parte Bhajan Singh, as to how these international conventions should be approached in the courts. The judge then quoted Lord Denning in Bhajan Singh

The courts can and should take the Convention into account whenever interpreting a statute which affects the rights and liberties of the individual.

Mr Justice Tudor Evans said that he had taken the provisions of the conventions into account when considering whether the control unit regime was cruel. The courts, it was argued, should reflect public standards of morality to prevent standards of custody from falling. Some standards might slip when there was an urgent need to cope with troublemakers and subversives in the prisons. He had, however, looked at the regime, and had no doubt that it did not fall below the irreducible minimum standard. The court had been presented with comparative material on North American prison regimes which had been held to have violated the constitutional prohibition on cruel and unusual punishment, and by those criteria the control unit was not cruel.

The judge accepted that the Home Office had infringed some of the rules relating to the continuation of detention in the control unit but rejected the claim of false imprisonment. Counsel for Williams apparently thought it pointless to base the case directly on the breach of the rules, as the court was bound by precedent that damages could not be recovered when the rules had been broken. When the case went to appeal in 1982 the Court of Appeal was similarly bound by authority. The Court of Appeal was asked to grant leave to appeal to the House of Lords where the question of the justiciability of the Prison Rules could be examined. The appeal was dismissed as was leave to appeal to the House of Lords on the grounds that the appellant would be altering the basis of the case and the lower courts would not have had any opportunity to decide the issues.

The Prison Rules and the laws relating to the classification of prisoners provide the longest single strand of litigation in the area of prisoners' rights. The judiciary have been reluctant to intervene in the central areas of everyday life in prison. The authority which has been followed stemmed from Arbon v. Anderson which was an unusual piece of litigation based on an action brought by enemy aliens held under emergency legislation. To make matters worse, the claim brought in the case probably looked frivolous at the time, the middle of World War II when the general population was suffering considerable hardship. Precedent was created from this case where the merits of the actual claims seem to have been rather poor, certainly the applicants were regarded as undeserving. The possibility that better claims might be examined has been precluded by the authority of this judgment.

Hostile and unflattering attitudes shine through a number of these cases; the Becker case provides the best example. Lord Denning took great exception to the activities of Mrs Becker whom he described as 'a vexatious litigant' and he seems to have been anxious to avoid any examination of prison practices and procedures. First, the courts have treated the Prison Rules differentially; those rules which have to do with problems and issues peculiar to prison life have been treated as 'administrative directions'. Even the word direction has been watered down on occasions, for example, Mr Justice Tudor Evans stated that a failure by the Home Office to obey these rules would not lead to civil liability. In Becker, it seemed that a prisoner's property could be mislaid without any consequences for the staff. Why then were these rules brought into existence? From the behaviour of the judges which has been quoted here it would seem that the Home Office had saddled itself with a series of unnecessary and unnecessarily benevolent rules.

The second, related theme is that the judiciary have refused to become involved in the supervision of prisons. There has never been any attempt to assess the effectiveness of these other supervisors, e.g. the governor, boards of visitors and the Home Secretary. There might be fewer grounds for concern if the courts had refused after a detailed examination of internal grievance mechanisms. The judges have frequently given the impression that their decisions were based on detailed knowledge of penal policy and prison practice, this impression disappears quickly on detailed inquiry. The belief expressed by Mr Justice Tudor Evans in the similarity of the regimes of control units and the proposed segregation unit is a good example. The judiciary considers generally that it is self-evident that prison administrators should be allowed to get on with their work unhindered by outsiders.

The duty of care

Prisoners are protected by the common law duty of care owed to them by the prison authorities. This common law duty stems from the origins of prisons as places of safety until the judge arrived to hold trials. There have been several attempts to discover the boundaries of this common-law duty. These cases are important because they raise issues about a prisoner's right to personal security.

In the first, Ellis v. Home Office, which reached the Court of Appeal in 1953, Ellis claimed damages from the Home Office for injuries he had suffered when attacked by another prisoner. Ellis claimed damages on two grounds: first, because the staff had been negligent; or, because of the breach of the duty owed him by the prison authorities under the Prison Rules. The Home Office claimed Crown Privilege in relation to the police and medical reports on the assailant. Mr Justice Devlin expressed grave concern at Ellis's inability to test the evidence about his attacker (a possible mental defective); if the prison authorities knew or suspected that the man was likely to be violent, they should have protected other prisoners. The case was dismissed in the High Court because of the absence of official documents.

The Court of Appeal rejected the claim for damages but stressed the duty of care. The Court stated that those responsible for running prisons had a duty to take reasonable care for the safety of those detained against their will. This duty was not as high as that expected of those dealing with the insane but the duty of care was placed on prison authorities even though they could not be expected to provide constant supervision. (The government no longer claims Crown Privilege, and the notion has been superseded by what is called 'public interest immunity'.)

A very similar case occurred three years later in D'Arcy v. Prison Commissioners. D'Arcy alleged that he had been attacked by three fellow prisoners and then brought an action against the Prison Commissioners claiming damages for negligence. In his direction to the jury, Mr Justice Barry said that the law did not presume that the Commissioners ensured the safety of each prisoner, and the mere fact that one prisoner attacked another did not itself indicate any negligence by the authorities. D'Arcy was, however, entitled to as much damages as any law-abiding citizen if he proved his case. The jury found in D'Arcy's favour and assessed the damages at £200 but found that as D'Arcy was 5 per cent to blame the judgment should be for £190 plus costs.

The safety of a prisoner was raised again in 1978 in Egerton v. Home Office. Egerton claimed damages for negligence from the Home Office on the ground that prison staff had failed to supervise properly the prisoners who had attacked him. Egerton, who was serving a 12 year sentence for sexual offences, had been segregated from other prisoners for his own protection under rule 43. He had subsequently asked to rejoin the main prison population, and this permission had been granted. The attack had taken place in the lavatory of the workshop where he was working. There were 60 prisoners in the shop, supervised by five prison officers, none of whom knew that Egerton was just off rule 43 or the nature of his offences. As a result of the assault, Egerton's right arm was rendered virtually useless.

Egerton's claim was dismissed by Mr Justice May. The Home Office had to exercise reasonable care in all the circumstances relating to a particular prisoner. Greater care should have been taken in this case, the level of supervision was not adequate and the workshop staff should have been told about Egerton's offences. But the Home Office and its staff could not have reasonably anticipated a spontaneous attack such as this, and for that reason the claim failed.

The suggestion made by Mr Justice May that the Home Office and its staff could not have anticipated an attack on Egerton is impossible to accept. No one with even the slightest knowledge of prison life could accept this claim. Prisoners who have been convicted of sexual offences are frequently assaulted by their fellow prisoners and for this reason are allowed to opt out of the general life of the prison, to go on 'rule 43' as it is often phrased. The presence of a man serving 12 years for sexual offences would be common knowledge in the prison and for this reason it is not possible to accept that the workshop staff would not have know about him. Even the fact that such a man had come off rule 43 and had rejoined the general prison population would itself have been a subject of great interest and general comment within the prison.

In 1988, the Queen's Bench Division rejected a claim for negligence against the Home Office in Porterfield v. Home Office. Mr Justice Roach said that the assistant governor involved had acted reasonably in the light of facts known at the time and could not be judged by the facts known later. The prison staff were not to be faulted for failing to tell the prisoner about the likelihood of an assault as he would already have known of it.

Work is an important aspect of prison life but the position of prisons in relation to the Health and Safety at Work Act is complicated. The major provisions of the 1974 Act 1974 bind the Crown but the Home Secretary has a power to exempt the Crown either generally or in part in the interest of the safe custody of those in lawful detention. (Halsbury, 1982, para 1153) A further reason for the non-applicability of some of this legislation is that prisoners are not employees. In Pullen v. Prison Commissioners (1957) an action was brought against the Prison Commissioners for a breach of the statutory duty to protect Pullen from dust and fumes as required by the Factories Act 1937. Lord Goddard dismissed the claim on the ground that a prison workshop was not a factory within the definition of 'factory' in the 1937 Factories Act, there being no relationship of master and servant or employment for wages in the case of a prisoner.

Responsibility for the safety of prisoners when working has been the basis of action more recently in Ferguson v. Home Office (1977). The claim for damages was based on the argument that Ferguson had not been instructed adequately in the use of the machine by the prison authorities. Mr Justice Caulfield was principally concerned with whether or not the Home Office owed a duty of care to the plaintiff when the accident occurred. This question was answered positively as the wood being sawed was the property of the prison authorities. There was a duty on the prison authorities to instruct prisoners in the use of machinery. Ferguson was awarded £1,500 in special damages, £7,000 for future loss of earnings and £7,000 for general damages.

The outcomes of these cases are not very satisfactory for two reasons. The protection of prisoners from assault by their fellows is an important principle to be upheld. One of the aims of any penal system is that known as 'Montero's aim' after the Spanish jurist who emphasised it. He argued that offenders and suspected offenders should be protected from unofficial retaliation. (Walker, 1972, p. 17) The general standards of British prisons have been the subject of considerable official criticism, and prisoners do live in a greater degree of squalor than people outside but there is no real need for them to live in high risk environments. Prisons do not need a fire certificate and the inspectorate established under the Fire Precautions Act 1971 does not have jurisdiction over prisons and there is no right of entry under that Act. If prisoners be injured at work, they are not covered by the industrial injuries scheme although other benefits may be available.

Natural justice in prisons

The most rapidly developing aspect of prisoners' rights litigation has been that requiring that various aspects of prison decision-making such as discipline boards, security classification and allocation, and parole selection and revocation be subject to the rules of natural justice. While the rules of natural justice can be traced back to mediaeval ideas about natural law, the concept has been reactivated as a fundamental part of administrative law in England since 1963. (Jackson, 1979, chapter 1) The House of Lords' decision in Ridge v. Baldwin has led to the gradual introduction of the doctrine that any power which affects people's rights must be exercised judicially i.e. fairly. In administrative law, natural justice involves two rules of fair procedure: first, that a man may not be a judge in his own case, and second, that a man's defence must be fairly heard. The first rule has not been as important in the context of prisoners' litigation as the second. The intention of judicial activity in this area is to make a fair hearing as much a part of good administrative practice as it is thought to be of good legal practice. (Wade, 1961, p. 442) There are links between this rule of natural justice and the due process of law requirements of the Fifth and Fourteenth Amendments to the US Constitution (see chapter 6), and Article 6 of the European Convention on Human Rights (see chapter 4). The developing requirements of natural justice in two areas will be discussed
- prison disciplinary hearings; and,
- security categorisation and allocation;

Prison disciplinary hearings

The cases brought before the courts seeking judicial of prison discipline have covered five distinct areas: first, the initial question of whether prison discipline is liable to judicial review; second, the nature of offences and the process of bringing charges; third, the procedures to be followed in hearings; fourth, the issue of legal representation; and fifth, governors' disciplinary decisions.

a) Judicial review of prison discipline In R v. Hull Prison Board of Visitors, ex parte St Germain and Others heard in 1977, the applicants applied to the Divisional Court of the Queen's Bench to grant certiorari against the Hull Prison Board of Visitors for their failure to observe the rules of natural justice. [1] The applicants had all been charged with offences arising from the Hull Prison riot and the Board of Visitors had imposed punishment involving loss of privileges, especially the loss of remission.

Lord Widgery had to decide on the nature of a board of visitors before he could answer whether certiorari could be applied to their activities. Certiorari would go against the boards if they were sitting as a panel of magistrates, or if they were acting judicially. But he then referred to a distinction that had been made authoritatively elsewhere that certiorari was limited to bodies which were both under a duty to act judicially and were performing a public duty; private and/or domestic tribunals were outside of the scope of certiorari. At first, Lord Widgery had thought that this would apply only to the prison governor's disciplinary powers, but the board of visitors had to be included because they also sit as part of the disciplinary machinery of the prison. The court could not allow only one part to be liable to judicial review as the board of visitors is intimately related to the organisation of the prison.

In 1979 St Germain and the other prisoners involved appealed on a single issue of law. This was whether boards of visitors were subject to judicial review when acting as a discipline body. The first issue for the Court of Appeal was to decide whether the deliberations of boards of visitors were 'any criminal matter or cause' in which case appeal was to the House of Lords directly. The telling point was that prison discipline offences were 'offences against discipline' as opposed to 'offences against the public law', i.e. they applied only to prisoners and could not be tried before the criminal courts.

On the second issue Lord Justice Megaw took the view that the boards were not part of the administration of the prison when acting as an adjudicatory body. The boards' activities were materially different from those of a governor when dealing with discipline offences. The courts were the ultimate custodians of the rights and liberties of the subject whatever his status, and however attenuated those rights and liberties were as a result of some punitive process, unless Parliament decreed by statute that it should be otherwise. Under the Prison Act a prisoner retained residuary rights regarding the nature and conduct of his imprisonment despite the deprivation of his general liberty. The appeals were allowed and the issues were remitted back to the Divisional Court of the Queen's Bench for hearing and determination.

The main substantive issues were heard by the Divisional Court later in 1979. St Germain and the other applicants asked again for certiorari to quash the decisions of the board of visitors on the grounds that they had not been given a proper opportunity of presenting their cases in accordance with rule 49(2) of the Prison Rules and that the board had failed to observe the rules of natural justice by refusing to allow them to call witnesses in support of their cases. It had also admitted and then acted on statements made during the hearing by the governor which were based on reports by prison officers who had not given oral evidence.

Lord Justice Lane granted the application for six reasons. First, the chairmen of boards had to exercise their discretion to ask questions on behalf of the prisoner in a reasonable way, in good faith and on proper grounds, as prisoners could not be given the same liberty to conduct their own defences as in an ordinary criminal trial. There was evidence that the chairman had refused to call witnesses as he thought that there was ample evidence against the accused. Second, there was the matter of whether administrative convenience was an acceptable reason for refusing to call witnesses. This reason was not enough as 'convenience and justice are often not on speaking terms'. Third, a fair chance of exculpation cannot be said to have been given without hearing an accused's witnesses. Fourth, the right to be heard included, in appropriate cases, the right to call evidence. The Prison Rules would be a mockery (including phrases like 'proper opportunity' or 'full opportunity') if there was no opportunity of calling evidence likely to establish the facts at issue. Fifth, boards of visitors were not masters of their own procedures; natural justice requires that the procedure before any tribunal acting judicially shall be fair in all circumstances. Finally, the admission of hearsay evidence was also subject to the overriding obligation to provide a fair hearing; a prisoner had been convicted without the opportunity of commenting on what the governor had said; he was not aware of the charge against him.

Lord Justice Lane added that the conclusion that some of the findings should be quashed had been arrived at with some reluctance. The Court felt that the board had reached the right decisions in spite of the irregularities. The accused were prisoners, some were dangerous and all were difficult, and all were to some extent untrustworthy; but they were entitled to a fuller hearing than they had in fact received. The findings had been quashed for lack of procedural fairness so that the charges could be brought again before a differently constituted board of visitors. There is no information as to whether or not these charges were ever brought again.

In 1985, it was held that a board of visitors, just as a bench of magistrates, could be held liable for torts as a result of acting in excess of their jurisdiction. But while upholding this principle the court held that a variation in the conditions of confinement, e.g. cellular confinement as a punishment for a breach of discipline, could not constitute the common law tort of false imprisonment. (R v. Board of Visitors Gartree Prison ex parte Sears)

Mention was previously made to Marin's extremely detailed comparison of prison discipline in Britain and the US. Marin's response to the Court of Appeal's decision in St Germain was positively enthusiastic, describing it as the most significant decision in the history of British prison law. Marin was concerned that this one case did not necessarily establish a whole field of law. He was worried by the American experience, where cases have been interpreted narrowly to re-assert limitations on prisoners' rights. (Marin, 1983, p. 271)

b) The nature of prison offences and charges In February 1982 the Divisional Court clarified the process of formulating charges in R v. Board of Visitors of Dartmoor Prison, ex parte Seray-Wurie. Seray-Wurie was charged with assaulting a fellow prisoner but when the matter came before the governor he referred it to the board of visitors under rule 51(2) of the Prison Rules which states that 'where a prisoner is charged with any serious or repeated offences against prison discipline for which the governor's powers of punishment seems insufficient, the governor may..refer the charge to the..board of visitors'. Seray-Wurie contended that the governor's action had been ultra vires as the offence with which he was charged was neither serious nor repeated in that he had never previously been convicted of an assault.

Mr Justice Forbes rejected the application on the ground that the point of the rule was the sufficiency or otherwise of the governor's power to punish. The governor could not be said to have acted unfairly in taking the view that someone with 249 days' loss of remission was a case where his powers of punishment were insufficient.

Mr Justice Forbes seems to have misunderstood the rule on serious and/or repeated offences. The judge seems to have accepted that a total of 249 days' loss of remission was itself clear evidence of serious and/or repeated offending against the Prison Rules. It would have been safer to inquire how this total had been reached, whether Seray-Wurie had committed many minor offences or a smaller number of major ones, only then would it be possible to conclude that the governor's powers were sufficient or not.

In September 1982 the nature of prison discipline offences was considered in R v. Board of Visitors of Highpoint Prison, ex parte McConkey. Prison discipline offences generally are open to the criticism of vagueness in wording and none more so than rule 47(20) which states that a prisoner shall be guilty of an offence against discipline if he 'in any way offends against good order and discipline'. McConkey was charged with this offence for remaining in a room knowing that other prisoners were smoking cannabis, and on being found guilty, lost 90 days' remission. In an affidavit, the chairman of the board of visitors' panel said that they were satisfied that McConkey had known of the cannabis smoking and remaining in the room constituted an offence under rule 47(20).

Mr Justice McCullough took the view that the special problems of prisons justified the existence of rules that would be intolerable in the outside world, but such problems did not provide any reason for adopting an interpretation harshly at odds with the generally accepted notions of criminal responsibility. The implication of the board's decision was that his presence had been a deliberate encouragement to the others. Because this had never been explained fully to McConkey, he could not have mounted an adequate defence and had suffered as a consequence. The board's decision was quashed - and the remission restored.

In 1985, the Court of Appeal held that boards of visitors had no jurisdiction under the Prison Rules to substitute and convict a prisoner on a lesser charge once they had concluded that the more serious offence had not been made out. (R v. Dartmoor Prison Board of Visitors ex parte Smith) Later in 1985, the Queen's Bench Division stated that it would be better if the particulars of an offence were given in addition to the formal wording of the rule alleged to have been broken. It did not accept that failure to do this would be sufficient to overturn the outcome of a disciplinary hearing. (R v. Board of Visitors of Swansea Prison ex parte Scales) In the same year the Divisional Court held that a board of visitors panel had a discretion whether or not to try different charges against the same prisoner together or to try one charge knowing of the existence of another. The board of visitors had to decide how to avoid circumstances would constitute a situation of apparent bias. (R v. Board of Visitors of Walton Prison ex parte Weldon)

Kate Akester, a solicitor specialising in prison law, has reported that quite a large proportion of applications for judicial review never come to court. Prisoners have had remission restored but the point of law has been lost. She has noted one case in which this had happened where a prison officer stated that an act deemed to be a discipline offence in one prison might not be in another institution. (Akester, 1988, p. 8)

c) The procedure of boards of visitors' hearings In the wake of the St Germain decision a steady stream of applications for judicial review of boards of visitors has gradually established the detailed requirements of natural justice in this area. The first was R v. Board of Visitors,

Nottingham Prison, ex parte Moseley heard in January 1981. Moseley had been charged with assaulting a prison officer. Moseley sought an order of certiorari on the ground that the chairman had refused to allow him to call witnesses to support his plea of self-defence. The affidavit provided by Moseley giving his account of the board meeting differed from that of the chairman. A question of law for the judge was whether the Divisional Court could intervene in a case where there was a conflict of evidence as to a point on which the dispute turned. Lord Justice Lane had said in the St Germain case that if such a conflict occurred it was proper for the court to lean in favour of the chairman's account. Mr Justice Glidewell said he was satisfied that on the balance of probabilities the evidence was that Moseley had not been refused the right to call certain witnesses and there was nothing to suggest that the board had acted with deliberate unfairness. Not every error or informality was a ground for quashing the board's decision.

The Divisional Court took a slightly different position in the next case heard in November 1981. In R v. Board of Visitors of Gartree Prison, ex parte Mealy. Mr Justice Hodgson took the opportunity to set out general principles to be applied when considering the fairness of adjudication hearings:

1. The Chairman should follow as strictly as possible the procedure set out in the document Explanation of Procedure which the prisoner had to prepare his defence. The chairman should explain what he was doing and why.
2. Allowance should be made for prisoners' lack of knowledge especially the difference between a defence and a plea of mitigation.
3. It was important to distinguish between matters of procedure and principles of fairness in making decisions such as allowing prisoners the notes taken at the investigatory stage of the process.
4. Prisoners should be informed of the reasons for changing the order in which charges were to be heard - generally to be avoided as it might surprise the prisoner.
5. As the prisoner cannot examine witnesses directly and all questions have to be put by the chairman it is important for the chairman to try to discover what the prisoner hopes to adduce from each witness.
6. The Explanation of Procedure document should be followed and prisoners should be given the opportunity to provide further information at the end.

The judge said that this case had fallen below a standard of fairness and a substantial injustice had been caused. The board's decision was quashed and the 60 days' loss of remission was restored.

Later in 1982 the issue of witnesses was again the subject of litigation. In R v. Blundeston Prison Board of Visitors, ex parte Fox-Taylor, the prisoner had been charged with an offence against discipline after fighting another prisoner. Fox-Taylor sought an order of certiorari, contending that because he had been denied the opportunity of having a witness who could have given evidence in his defence there had been a breach of natural justice.

The judge granted certiorari and held that the prison authorities were under a duty to take reasonable steps to see that the names of potential witnesses were known to boards of visitors so that a full and fair investigation could be made. In this case there was no reason why the witness was not made known, and that inaction had substantially prejudiced the applicant's defence, causing him to lose 90 days' remission. This official inaction had vitiated the proceedings of the board.

In February 1985 there was a slight back tracking on the importance of procedures when the Queen's Bench Division dismissed an application for judicial review holding that it was not part of its duties to lay down the precise procedure which a board of visitors ought to adopt. However, there might be cases where it would be a breach of the rules of natural justice and unfair not to allow the prisoner to sit down, or to allow him materials to make notes. (R v. Board of Visitors of Pentonville Prison ex parte Rutherford)

Later in 1985 the Queen's Bench Division held that it was desirable in the interests of natural justice being seen to be done that, at a disciplinary hearing before a board of visitors, a prisoner should be shown a welfare report on him even though he had not specifically requested to see it. In this case the breach of the rules of natural justice was marginal and the application was dismissed. (R v. Board of Visitors of Wandsworth Prison, ex parte Raymond)

In 1986, the Queen's Bench Division dismissed an application for judicial review stating that it would be inevitable that members of boards of visitors would know a great deal about prisoners as they perform administrative as well as adjudicatory functions within the prison. Members of panels could disqualify themselves from hearings if they wished but prior knowledge of a prisoner in another context did not disqualify anyone. ((R v. Board of Visitors of Frankland Prison, ex parte Lewis)

d) Legal representation The first case asking for the application of the rules of natural justice to prison disciplinary hearings was Fraser v. Mudge (1975). Fraser was accused of assaulting a prison officer, and initially asked the High Court for a declaration that (i) he was entitled to legal representation at a disciplinary hearing before the board of visitors; and (ii) he be granted an injunction restraining the board of visitors from enquiring into the charges until he had been given legal representation. Both of these applications were rejected and Fraser then appealed.

Lord Denning said that prison discipline was like the system of military discipline, where a man was brought before his commanding officer, in which legal representation had never been the practice. Legal representation would lead to delay. Prison discipline must be fair - the man must be told the charge against him and be given a proper opportunity of presenting his case - but this could be done without legal representation. Lord Denning added 'We ought not to create a precedent such as to suggest that an individual is entitled to legal representation'.

The Divisional Court was asked in late 1983 to hear two sets of issues brought by prisoners facing serious charges against prison discipline. For simplicity's sake the case is referred to as R v. Secretary of State for the Home Department, ex parte Tarrant. When the various applicants had appeared before adjudication panels the boards of visitors had refused requests for legal representation on the ground that they had no power to grant representation in any case. The applicants were charged with offences categorised in the Prison Rules as either 'grave' or 'especially grave'.

The judge's view was that the court was bound by the decision in Fraser v. Mudge that there is no right to legal representation before boards of visitors. But the question which then arose was whether the boards had a discretion to allow legal representation. According to Raymond v. Honey a convicted prisoner retained all civil rights which have not been taken away expressly or by necessary implication. A board of visitors was master of its own procedure, and there was no common law rule or decision which could deprive it of its discretion to permit legal representation. Every board had a discretion to grant legal representation at any hearing before it.

Mr Justice Webster said that a board should take six points into account before deciding to allow represenation

1. the seriousness of the charge and the potential penalty;
2. whether any points of law were likely to arise - such questions would arise rarely save in the case of mutiny charges;
3. the capacity of a prisoner to present his own case;
4. procedural difficulties, bearing in mind that a prisoner would normally be kept apart from other prisoners inhibiting him in the preparation of his case;
5. the need for reasonable speed in making an adjudication; and
6. the need for fairness between prisoners and between prisoners and prison officers. That was not a comprehensive list.

The issue of whether the board had exercised its discretion properly is totally unexpected in the context in which the boards of visitors were then working. The whole of the discussion on the adjudication functions of boards of visitors in the previous seven or eight years had taken place against the background provided by the Weiler report on procedures. The official Home Office view throughout that time had been antithetical to legal representation. The Working Party had been against allowing any outsiders to represent prisoners on the grounds that they would not be sufficiently familiar with prison life to be effective. It was also argued that the employment of an insider would create other difficulties. The Working Party concluded that the prisoner should be responsible for his own defence. The gap between this guidance and a discretion to allow legal representation is enormous.

Once the possibility of allowing legal advice had been established there was an attempt to apply it retrospectively. The Court of Appeal rejected an application made in 1984 in respect of adjudications held in 1981. The amount of time elapsed would have been detrimental to 'good administration' within the Supreme Court Act 1981. (R v. Board of Visitors of Swansea Prison ex parte McGrath)

In 1988, the House of Lords finally decided that prisoners have no legal right to representation in disciplinary proceedings. In R v. Board of Visitors of the Maze Prison, ex parte Hone, the House of Lords held that two prisoers in the Maze Prison, Northern Ireland, were not entitled to legal representation when facing charges of assaulting prison officers. Lord Goff rejected the argument that because a charge before a disciplinary tribunal related to facts that in law constituted a crime, the rules of natural justice required the tribunal to grant legal representation. Everything depended on the circumstances as the list provided in Tarrant made perfectly clear.

e) Governors' disciplinary decisions The Court of Appeal seemed to have excluded any possibility of judicial review of a governor's disciplinary decisions in St Germain. The arguments in R v. Deputy Governor of Camp Hill Prison, ex parte King stemmed from charges relating to the discovery of of a hypodermic needle which had been found in the cell shared by King and three other prisoners. The deputy governor found the charge proved and ordered that each should lose 14 days' remission. The Court of Appeal had to decide two issues: (i) whether an application for judicial review could lie against an adjudication and punishment determined by a prison governor; and (ii) whether the punishment should be overturned because the deputy governor had misunderstood the Prison Rules relating to the possession of unauthorised articles. The court dealt with these issues in the logical order and considered first the interpretation of the rule relating to unauthorised possession. Lord Justice Lawton held that the deputy governor had misconstrued the rule and the punishment given to Smith and his cell-mates was ultra vires the governor's statutory powers.

The issue which then arose was whether judicial review was available to correct the error which had led to King spending an extra 14 days in custody. Was the deputy governor exercising a managerial function or a judicial one? The discipline offences made under the Prison Rules were held to be rules for management. The deputy governor was a manager appointed by and responsible to the Home Secretary. The discipline powers were necessary for the proper and efficient discharge of their duties as managers. To grant prisoners access to the High Court whenever they thought that the governor had abused his powers, or had failed to give them a fair hearing or had misconstrued the rules would undermine the governor's authority and make management very difficult. If a prisoner had a well-founded complaint that a governor had misconstrued the rules and the Home Secretary had rejected his petition requesting a review, the prisoner might be entitled to judicial review of the Home Secretary's decision.

In 1988 the House of Lords resolved this inconsistency in Leech v. Parkhurst Prison Governor by deciding that decisions of prison governors made in the exercise of their disciplinary powers were susceptible to judicial review. This came about because at the the time that the Court of Appeal was deciding the King case, the Northern Ireland Court of Appeal was taking the opposite view in relation to corresponding Prison Rules in Northern Ireland. The Law Lords held that a governor adjudicating on a charge against prison discipline bore all the hallmarks of an authority subject to judicial review. The existence of the right to petition the Home Secretary did not preclude the possibility of judical review. If judicial review of the Home Secretary's decision was applied for as suggested in King then the court would not be able to consider the evidence on which the Home Secretary had made his decision. If the social consequences of the greater availability of judicial review were as detrimental to the functioning of the prison system as predicted in King, then it was open to Parliament to exclude it.

There has been a remarkable change in a very few years as to the procedural protections granted to prisoners facing discipline charges of a serious nature. The likely consequences are difficult to predict as the more significant changes are so recent. No doubt prison staff will have more work to do, and will have to be careful that they are aware of the ramifications of these decisions. The decision by the Lord Chancellor in 1984 to extend the provision of legal aid funds to pay for legal representation where this has been permitted by the board of visitors will probably mean that legal representation will become a more prominent feature of adjudication hearings in more serious cases although the future of legal aid is currently under review. One of the more noteworthy points to come out of this review of recent cases and the discussion of boards of visitors in chapter 2 is that these changes requiring greater attention to procedural rules have come at a time when the proportion of magistrates on the boards has been declining. At a time when selection policy has encouraged boards to behave less like benches of magistrates, the courts are requiring them to behave more judicially when sitting as adjudication panels.

Three additional points should be made about these cases. First, the courts have concentrated exclusively on the second rule of natural justice and have not been asked to consider the first rule which prohibits a man from being a judge in his own case. Second, in order to distinguish between summary discipline and adjudications by boards of visitors the courts frequently used what can be called the military analogy. The courts suggested that the activities of the governor when dealing with discipline are similar to those of a commanding officer in the armed services in the sense that they are executive and managerial rather than judicial. Decisions of this kind require speed and informality to be effective. It would be absurd to suggest that a commanding officer should be supervised judicially, and exactly the same argument was held to apply to prison governors. The courts have never followed through the logic of this argument. If they had done so then some form of representation before boards of visitors would have been established some time ago and it would be universal. When the War Office Committee on courts-martial inquired into the procedures followed in courts-martial the recommendation was made that while legal representation was impracticable, it was the duty of any company or commanding officer to ensure that advice and assistance was given to any man charged with an offence which might be tried at court martial. The adviser was to be competent to inform the accused of his rights and to advise the accused as to the conduct of his defence. (War Office, 1949)

Third, this whole area has been bedevilled by the courts taking inconsistent or even contradictory views of issues which appear to be the same or very similar. In Fraser, Lord Denning rejected his own precedent so as to deny a prisoner the right of legal representation. In St Germain and in Tarrant, the courts have taken opposite views on the issue of whether boards of visitors were to be considered 'masters of their own procedures'. In St Germain, the answer was no, while the court in Tarrant answered the question positively. The outcomes might be considered just, but the Court of Appeal could hardly be accused of being consistent.

Security categorisation and allocation

The courts have been willing to intervene in the discipline system which affects the lives of some prisoners, and there have been attempts to get them to intervene in the system of classifying prisoners which affects all prisoners. The prison allocation system is designed primarily for the prevention of escapes and internal control over prisons. The higher the security category a man has, the more control there will be over his daily life. Category 'A' men have to be escorted within the prison by two prison officers and are signed for at each hand over. The system of deciding the prisoner's category is an internal administrative activity within the Prison Department and the precise criteria used are not made public nor are the reasons for particular decisions.

The security category system has been challenged in the courts on one occasion, although not a great deal is known of the arguments as the case was reported as a news item rather than as a Law Report. In 1977, Roger John Payne asked the High Court to hold that the rules of natural justice should apply to categorisation decisions and that he should have been told why he had been kept in category 'A' for more than six years. (The Times, 3 May 1977) The argument was dismissed by Mr Justice Cantley, who said that in his view Parliament in the Prison Act 1952 had never intended that prisoners should be given that information by the Home Office or be allowed to present a case as to how they should be classified. The judge was also quoted as saying 'In my view the full panoply of the rules of natural justice is wholly inappropriate to the classification of prisoners'.

An attempt was also made in the Williams case to apply these rules of natural justice to the decision of the control unit committee which sent Williams to the control unit in the first instance.

Mr Justice Tudor Evans said that the fact that the control unit committee had failed to follow all of the procedural steps did not show that they acted unfairly or that they should have given the prisoner the right to make representations. The judge did not think that the principles of natural justice required that the prisoner should have been given notice of the intention to transfer him or to make representations to prevent the transfer. The committee had not failed to comply with the rules of natural justice.

Both security categorisation and allocation are areas of prison life which affect all prisoners because all have a security classification and have been left firmly outside the scope of judicial review provided that Prison Department staff act fairly when making their decisions. The whole topic is regarded as one for the administrators, who should be given the opportunity of getting on with their job. The difficulty lies in the issue of fairness; unless the prisoner knows how a decision has been made and on what information it has been based, he cannot challenge it. The administrator's fear is that once reasons have to be given for decisions, the decision can be challenged and the whole process is quickly seen as as an invitation to debate decisions.

Enforced medical treatment

Medical treatment provided to prisoners has been the subject of considerable debate and criticism. The prison authorities are required to provide a medical officer for each prison. A convicted prisoner has no right to consult an outside doctor unless he is a party to legal proceedings, although he is allowed to write to his own doctor. (Halsbury, 1982, para 1154) The quality of hygiene in prisons has been criticised publicly by a member of the Prison Medical Service who was later censured for having done so. (The Times, 7 November 1983) There has also been considerable controversy over the prison medical service's use of drugs, and Fitzgerald and Sim, who commented on the subject in their book British Prisons, were sued for libel by the medical staff at one prison and lost, having to apologise and pay undisclosed damages. (The Times, 1 August 1980) A similar case was reported in 1983 when the Daily Mirror had to apologise and to pay undisclosed damages to the medical staff of Brixton prison. The paper admitted that a report it had published on the use of tranquillisers as an aid to discipline was unfounded. (British Medical Journal, 1983, p. 153)

The use of drugs in prisons led to a claim for damages in Freeman v. Home Office (1984). Freeman alleged that drugs which had been prescribed for him had been administered to him without his consent between September and October 1972. Freeman also alleged that he had actively resisted the administration of these drugs but had been forcibly overcome by the medical officer and prison officers. Freeman also claimed that he was incapable of consenting to this treatment because he wasa prisoner in the Home Office's custody. The High Court rejected these arguments and Freeman appealed to the Court of Appeal. The Court of Appeal also rejected the claim for damages for the claims of assault, battery and trespass against the person. The Court of Appeal had decided elsewhere that the American concept of informed consent had no place in English law. Real consent provides a complete defence to a claim based upon the tort of trespass. Consent could not however be real if it had been procured by fraud or misrepresentation; consent in fact amounts to consent in law.

One of the issues raised in the Freeman case was that prison medical officers had a dual responsibility as both medical men and a members of the prison staff. The potential for conflict which is inherent in this situation has been the subject of discussion by Brazier who suggests that the prison medical officers' mandate to give a prisoner drugs depends on the level of deterioration of the prisoner and the possibility that the prisoner will damage himself or other people. Prison medical officers are caught in a double-bind situation, they are criticised for both under use and the over use of drugs. (Brazier, 1982, pp. 283-4) The Home Office is at pains to stress that prison medical officers are like general practitioners although they are clearly not in the same confidential relationship with their patients.

Conclusions

The history of litigation brought by prisoners has seen an important series of changes over the last 170 years. The most surprising change has been the gradual extension of the rules of natural justice to the prison disciplinary system. Gradually the requirements of natural justice have been applied to other sectors of administration outside the prison. The doors to legal representation before boards of visitors seemed until very recently to be closed for ever and the Home Office for its part was equally reluctant to allow outsiders into the disciplinary system.

It is too easy to overestimate the extent of the changes in judicial attitudes towards prisoners. The application of the rules of natural justice represents only the tip of the iceberg. The remainder demonstrates a remarkably high degree of continuity. The judges have always taken a poor view of prisoners appearing before the courts to challenge prison administrators. On some occasions the judges' comments have taken the form of disparaging remarks about the particular litigant. The more usual kind of comment has been one more closely related to the matter of policy - whether the courts should allow prisoners to make life difficult for prison governors by allowing cases to be brought. Certainly the courts cannot be accused of encouraging litigation as a consequence of generous decisions. The everyday conditions experienced by the vast majority of prisoners remain firmly outside the scope of review by the courts.

The Prison Rules, the Standing Orders and the Instructions which provide the framework for administrative decision-making have been held not to provide the basis for legal action. There have been one or two exceptions, as in the case of disciplinary hearings, but these are peripheral. The unwillingness of the courts to tackle some issues has been particularly disturbing. The lax ways in which a prisoner's property may be dealt with seem especially unacceptable, adding a degree of arbitrariness to prison life. The system's failure to ensure the safety of prisoners in its care is equally deserving of criticism although the courts have been quite naive in their view of the responsibility of the prison authorities. Indeed one writer on prisoners' rights litigation has concluded from examples such as these that the zealous use by the courts of dangerously far-reaching principles to defeat the unmeritorious and perhaps vexatious litigant may in future defeat the meritorious claimant. (Tettenborn, 1980, pp. 88-9) In a series of cases decided in the last seven years, the courts have established the principle that prisoners' complaints may only be dealt with by judicial review, and have rejected other means such as declarations sought through the Chancery Division. The general attempts made by the judiciary to reduce procedural complexity have failed in this area; new procedural distinctions have been introduced. (Emery and Smythe, 1986) In O'Reilly v. Mackman (1982), the House of Lords rejected any attempt to bring prison decisions which might have the effect of reducing the protections afforded to the prison authorities before the courts.

The courts' unwillingness to become involved in the more mundane processes of prison life is understandable as there are literally thousands decisions which might overwhelm the courts themselves. What seems regrettable is the courts' apparent unwillingness to provide any structure for the wide discretion available to the prison authorities.

Notes

[1] The term 'prison authorities' has been used as the prisons were controlled by the Prison Commission until 1963 when the prisons became the direct responsibility of the Home Office.

[2] 'Certiorari is an order which may be used to quash a decision if the person or body deciding failed to observe the rules of natural justice, or acted without, or in excess of jurisdiction'. (Walker, 1980, p. 198)

4 Prisoners' rights under the European Convention on Human Rights

Prisoners held in English prisons have the European Convention on Human Rights and its Institutions as a way of establishing their rights and redressing some of their grievances. Only a relatively small number of cases have been brought before the European Convention's institutions, but the effects of the Convention are far-reaching.

The European Convention on Human Rights owes its existence to the movement in post-war Europe to prevent a recurrence of the large-scale deprivation of civil and political rights to which the Jews and others had been subjected in Nazi Germany. The belief existed that the horrors of the extermination and concentration camps came about through the systematic deprivation of civil rights. The Convention was drawn up to prevent this from happening again. The drafting of the Convention was carried out by a Committee of Experts in 1948 and 1949; the Committee took the United Nations Universal Declaration of Human Rights as their pattern. The resulting Convention was signed in Rome on 4 November 1950, and came into general force in September 1953. The drafting of the Convention presented considerable problems, as the notion of what was a general right was open to dispute. (Beddard, 1980, p. 24) There was also the problem of the conflict of two distinctive legal philosophies and their legal systems, the common law tradition of the British and the civil law tradition of the Western Europe.

The drafting of the rights guaranteed by the Convention was heavily influenced by the British participants, who argued for as precise definitions of rights as could be achieved. The effects of this approach on the limitation of the development of rights will be discussed below.

Britain accepted and signed the European Convention as it would any other foreign treaty. The Convention was signed on 4 November 1950 in Rome, and the United Kingdom ratification was deposited on 8 March 1951.

It was presented to Parliament in October 1953. (Foreign Office, 1953) Between 1953 and 1966, the British government was liable only to actions brought against it by other signatory states, the High Contracting Parties as they are called in the Convention. Part of the novelty, and the importance, of the Convention is that it envisaged the possibility of a citizen taking his or her state to task before an international organisation for an alleged violation of rights. The right of individual petition is guaranteed by Article 25

> 1. The Commission may accept petitions addressed to the Secretary-General of the Council of Europe from any person, non-governmental organisation or group of individuals claiming to be the victim of a violation by one of the High Contracting Parties of the rights set forth in this Convention, provided that the High Contracting Party against which the complaint has been lodged has declared that it recognises the competence of the Commission to receive such petitions. Those of the High Contracting Parties who have made such a declaration undertake not to hinder in any way the effective exercise of this right.

Signatory states could decide not to allow this right of individual petition while accepting the rest of the Convention; Britain accepted Article 25 in 1966, and has renewed this acceptance on a five-yearly basis ever since.

Since the acceptance of both the right of individual petition and the compulsory jurisdiction of the European Court of Human Rights, prisoners, amongst other British citizens, acquired a new means of holding the government to account. Prisoners are allowed to petition the European Commission of Human Rights without the leave of any prison official. Their correspondence with the Commission can legitimately be opened and read by the prison authorities, but in no case will it be stopped, and it must be posted immediately by the authorities.

The material to be discussed in this chapter and in chapter 5 can be seen as complementary to the two important essays on the European Convention on Human Rights and the British prison system by Zellick, and Douglas and Jones which deal with many of the early cases.

There are important differences between the discussion here and the essays. Zellick is concerned primarily with a wider discussion of Human Rights Conventions in relation to penal policy and the law on penal practice in England. He uses the United Nations Declaration of Human Rights, the European Convention on Human Rights and the European Standard Minimum Rules for the Treatment of Prisoners as bench marks against which the English penal system can be evaluated. Douglas and Jones take a more specific approach, dealing with the findings of the Commission and Court of Human Rights in cases brought by prisoners and offenders in the UK.

Rights guaranteed by the European Convention on Human Rights

The European Convention on Human Rights is a multi-purpose document. It is a treaty which places a number of obligations on its signatories, and it specifies the mechanisms which give force to those obligations. The ratification of a treaty by the British Parliament does not mean that the Convention becomes a part of British law, it exists and operates at a supra-national level. It is also important to note at this point that the government and its agencies alone can be the object of petition. The

British government has to defend or justify the violation of a complainant's rights as guaranteed by the Convention, assuming it wishes to do so.

The original text of the Convention includes sixty-six Articles and four Protocols. Those which have provided the most frequent basis for petitions by British prisoners are quoted in full below. It is not intended to imply that these have been the only grounds used: those less frequently employed will be referred to as they occur, on a case by case basis.

Article 3 states 'No one shall be subjected to torture, to inhuman or degrading treatment or punishment'. This is the only Article in the Convention which is not subject to some form of qualification or restriction of the right that is guaranteed. It is not possible to claim any derogation from its terms even in time of war or public emergency.

Article 6 states

1. In the determination of his civil rights and obligations or of any criminal charge against him, everyone is entitled to a fair and public hearing within a reasonable time by an independent and impartial tribunal established by law. Judgment shall be pronounced publicly but the press and public may be excluded from all or part of the trial in the interests of morals, public order or national security in a democratic society, where the interest of juveniles or the protection of the private life of the parties so require, or to the extent strictly necessary in the opinion of the court in special circumstances, where publicity would prejudice the interest of justice.
2. Everyone charged with a criminal offence shall be presumed innocent until proved guilty according to law.
3. Everyone charged with a criminal offence has the following minimum rights:
(a) to be informed promptly, in a language which he understands and in detail, of the nature and cause of the accusation against him;
(b) to have adequate time and facilities for the preparation of his defence;
(c) to defend himself in person or through legal assistance of his own choosing or, if he has not sufficient means to pay for legal assistance, to be given it free when the interests of justice so require;
(d) to examine or have examined witnesses against him and to obtain the attendance and examination of witnesses on his behalf under the same conditions as witnesses against him;
(e) to have free assistance of an interpreter if he cannot understand or speak the language used in court.

This Article appears to be concerned exclusively with the procedural requirements necessary to achieve a lawful conviction for an offence. Two phrases in Article 6(1) have been important in cases brought by British prisoners. The phrase 'the determination of his civil rights and obligations' was important in the Golder case where the phrase was used to give a right of access to the courts, there being no other place in the Convention where this right is specified. The procedural safeguards that are listed in the Convention would be of little use unless citizens could actually go to court. The phrase 'criminal charges' has been important as it was used in Campbell and Fell to bring prison disciplinary hearings within the scope of the Convention. This interpretation is based on the argument that some matters which are

treated as being disciplinary are in reality criminal offences and should consequently attract the protection of the Article.
Article 8 states

1. Everyone has the right to respect for his private and family life, his home and his correspondence.
2. There shall be no interference by a public authority with the exercise of this right except as is in accordance with the law and is necessary in a democratic society in the interest of national security, public safety or the economic well-being of the country, for the prevention of disorder or crime, for the protection of health or morals, or for the protection of the rights and freedom of others.

This Article has been central to the petitions brought by British prisoners since the right of individual petition was accepted. The control of correspondence by the prison authorities has resulted in cases which the British government has always defended fiercely.
Article 10 states

1. Everyone has the right to freedom of expression. This right shall include freedom to hold opinions and to receive and impart information and ideas without interference by public authority and regardless of frontiers....
2. The exercise of these freedoms, since it carries with it duties and responsibilities, may be subject to such formalities, conditions, restrictions or penalties as are prescribed by law and are necessary in a democratic society, in the interests of national security, territorial integrity or public safety, for the prevention of disorder or crime, for the protection of health or morals, for the protection of the reputation or rights of others, for preventing the disclosure of information received in confidence, or for maintaining the authority and impartiality of the judiciary.

The rights guaranteed here have been used to challenge the censorship of prisoners' letters on the grounds that their contents offend in some way.
Two points need to be made at this stage in the description. First, the rights guaranteed by the Convention are limited to those considered important by drafters working in the period 1948 to 1950. Items now considered essential, e.g. the right to privacy, may be inferred through judicial interpretation. But judicial interpretation is a haphazard business. Second, in order to secure unanimity among the High Contracting Parties, a number of permissible restrictions to these guarantees have been inserted. Some restrictions were written into the Articles themselves, as permissible exceptions. States can also make reservations about particular Articles or the Protocols, e.g. articles may not apply to dependent colonies. Also, states are permitted what is called the 'margin of appreciation' in their actions, e.g. the state may ask to be given the benefit of any doubt.

The procedures and institutions of the Convention

The Convention provides for two institutions to accomplish its objectives. The Commission acts as the secretariat and the investigating body. For those States which accept its compulsory jurisdiction, there

66

is also the European Court of Human Rights. If a case on which the Commission has submitted a report has not, within three months, been referred to the Court, the final decision is taken by the Committee of Ministers. The Committee of Ministers consists of the Ministers of Foreign Affairs of the member states of the Council of Europe. The Committee has two duties, first, to decide the question of violation of the Convention in cases not referred to the Court; and second, to supervise the execution of its decisions and the judgments of the Court. The Commission consists of a number of members equal to the number of High Contracting Parties and it has been the case traditionally that there is a national of each High Contracting Party on the Commission. (Beddard, 1980, pp. 36-7) Members of the Commission do not act as representatives of their country, they are there in an individual capacity.

Complaints against a High Contracting Party may be made under two Articles of the Convention, namely Articles 24 or 25. The first refers to what are called inter-State cases where the complainant is another State. An example of this was the Irish government case against the British government over the alleged use of torture in Northern Ireland. The second is the right of individual petition when a citizen accuses his government of violating, or permitting the violation of, rights guaranteed by the Convention. Individual applications must be in writing, signed by the applicant or a representative. Applications have to include the name and address of the applicant or a representative, the name of the High Contracting Party against whom the claim is being made, and whenever possible the object of the claim and the provisions of the Convention alleged to have been violated. (Beddard, 1980, p. 38)

When an individual petition is received by the Commission, one member is nominated to act as a rapporteur who examines the application and reports to the Commission on its admissibility. The rapporteur may ask either party for further information. On receipt of the report, the full Commission may declare the application inadmissible.

The criteria of admissibility are complicated, with the result that the majority of complaints are rejected as inadmissible. Estimates vary, but it has been suggested that only about two per cent of applications are accepted. (Beddard, 1980, p. 138) There are seven main grounds for rejecting applications and several are confusing and less than consistent, either with each other or the apparent aims of the Convention.

1. 'All domestic remedies have been exhausted, according to the generally recognised rules of international law'. This requirement is designed not only to prevent vexatious applications but also to give the States opportunity to rectify administrative mistakes before these are brought to the attention of other States.
2. After the exhaustion of local remedies, the application to the Commission must be within six months of the final decision.
3. Article 27(1)(a) states that the Commission shall not deal with applications if there is no way of identifying the applicant.
4. Unless new evidence or information has become available, the Commission will not reconsider any case that has already been examined, nor will it consider applications which depend on the presentation of new legal arguments.
5. An application cannot be accepted if it is incompatible with the provisions of the Convention, for example, if it claims violation of a right not guaranteed by the Convention, or it claims the right to engage in activities which would destroy the other rights conferred in the Convention.

6. It will reject applications which are 'manifestly ill-founded', a phrase introduced to protect the High Contracting Parties from frivolous complaints.
7. The Commission will not consider cases where there has been persistent and negligent disregard for the rules laid down by the Secretariat for the preparation of a petition; or when there is no prima facie evidence of a violation; or where abuse has been the cause of inadmissibility.

If a petition survives this stage in the process, the Commission then examines the merits of the application. The facts are established by written pleadings and further oral argument. The Commission may call witnesses, carry out visits, or take whatever actions it considers to be necessary. The Commission's task is always to bring about a friendly settlement between the parties, consequently the proceedings take place in camera and avoid a court-like appearance. If no settlement is achieved, the Commission is then required to draw up a report of the facts and providing an examination of the legal issues involved. The final report is sent to the Committee of Ministers and has to include proposals for action. The Committee of Ministers is the executive body of the Council of Europe and it provides a political input into the Convention. No State may be taken before the Court of Human Rights without its consent, and unless the State accepts the compulsory jurisdiction of the Court, it is for the Committee of Ministers to decide the merits of an application. Some States have preferred to accept the jurisdiction of the Committee as its decisions require a two-thirds majority for action to be taken whereas the Court can act on a simple majority decision.

The Court can only deal with a case which has been examined by the Commission which has not resulted in a friendly settlement, and which has been referred to the Court by the Commission or a State.

The Convention provides that the Court should consist of a Chamber of seven judges. The Court's procedure is inquisitorial rather than adversarial. The Rules provide that the Chamber decides whether to hear witnesses or experts; if it wishes, it may depute one or more of its members to conduct an enquiry either through site visits or whatever means thought appropriate. The judgment of the Court is final. It is read by the President at a public hearing and is then taken to the Committee of Ministers which has the duty of carrying out the decision. There is a limited power to award compensation. There may be complications when a finding of the Court requires an amendment to the national law or administrative practice.

The outcome of cases brought by British prisoners

It is not possible to give any figures for the number of applications made by prisoners to the European Commission of Human Rights since 1966. A few have been declared admissible in whole or in part, and have then gone on to the Court as no 'friendly settlement' had been achieved and the Commission or Government has referred it. The system of reporting the cases decided by both the Commission and the Court has been rudimentary even by comparison with that found in the English courts. For this reason it is difficult to produce a synthesis of the jurisprudence which has been developing. [1] The cases will be referred to by the designations used in the European Human Rights Reports or the Yearbook of the European Convention on Human Rights. Often the Yearbook refers simply to an application number and states that it is a case of X against the UK. No further identification is available.

Complaints under Article 3

Article 3 is one of the briefest and most succinct prohibiting torture, inhuman or degrading treatment or punishment. Prisoners in British penal establishments are reported to have claimed violations of this prohibition in six cases; only one (Reed) of these claims has survived scrutiny by the Commission of Human Rights.

The first, known by the number 3868/68, was decided in May 1970. The applicant alleged that his treatment while in prison constituted inhuman and degrading treatment and hence violated his rights as guaranteed by Article 3. The applicant complained that he had been held in one prison while awaiting transfer to a training prison but no vacancy was available. During this time he was deprived of various privileges such as home leave, association with other prisoners, the use of a personal radio and a hobby set in his cell.

The initial assessment of the Commission was that the application was inadmissible but the parties were invited to comment. The British government submitted that the matters complained of, by reason of their very nature, were not capable of constituting inhuman or degrading treatment The applicant argued on the other hand that there was a considerable contrast between the conditions experienced by prisoners in different kinds of prison. The Commission declared this application as inadmissible on the ground that it was manifestly ill-founded.

In Kiss v. United Kingdom decided in December 1976, the applicant claimed that an assault by a prison officer on him constituted ill-treatment in violation of Article 3. The Commission found that the incident complained of was relatively trivial as it was only a push. There was no evidence of injury. This did not amount to a breach of the Article.

The Commission was asked in 1978 to consider allegations that Article 3 in the case of Hilton v. United Kingdom. Hilton complained that he had been ill-treated by prison staff and produced a list of some 50 occasions or incidents which made up the claim. The ill-treatment varied from assaults and threats of violence by prison staff, officially incited threats made by fellow prisoners, solitary confinement, threats to transfer him to a special hospital, and the lack of medical care when ill. Hilton also alleged that these incidents were further aggravated by racial prejudice against him because he was black. When he took up these matters with the prison governor, he was charged with prison disciplinary offences which were false and had been brought maliciously. The UK did not accept any of these allegations and contested all the claims.

The Commission had to decide whether the treatment in particular instances, and/or whether the treatment in general, amounted to inhuman or degrading treatment or punishment contrary to Article 3 of the Convention. On the first issue, the Commission used the definition given by the Court in 1969 in the Greek case, the systematic use of torture and mistreatment of political opponents of the Colonels' regime in Greece.

> The notion of inhuman treatment covers at least such treatment as deliberately causing severe suffering, mental or physical, which, in the particular situation is unjustifiable.
>
> Treatment or punishment of an individual may be said to be degrading if it grossly humiliates him before others or drives him to act

against his own will or conscience.

The standard applying in an inter-State case might not necessarily be relevant to an individual application; ill-treatment in individual cases may be relative.

The Commission found there was no objective evidence to support these allegations, and investigations tended to reduce their credibility even further. The Commission concluded that there appeared to be no breach of Article 3 of the Convention in respect of specific incidents of ill-treatment. This conclusion still left the question of whether the applicant's general treatment, by act or omission, in its cumulative effect, amounted to a violation. The Commission decided that there was no evidence that Hilton had been treated in a degrading manner. The Commission came to this conclusion after reviewing Hilton's progress, or rather his decline, through the prison system.

The Commission rejected the argument that they should consider the cumulative effect as a violation of Article 3 by a majority of ten votes to four. The dissenting members said that in their opinion the cumulative impact of the conditions did constitute degrading treatment contrary to Article 3. They agreed that Hilton had been an uncooperative, difficult prisoner but argued that it was unacceptable that a prison system should reduce a prisoner to an 'animal-like state'; a phrase that was frequently used in this case. More important was the extremely repressive application of disciplinary measures. These had a destructive effect on the applicant which amounted to a violation - to degrading treatment contrary to Article 3 in their view.

The details of Hilton's decline through the prison system are important in any discussion of the effectiveness of the Convention. Hilton was apparently one of those individuals who comes into conflict with the prison system, for whatever reason, and it is quite clear that the system could only respond by hitting back. The almost inevitable outcome is the destruction of the prisoner. The prison system has more people, more energy, more power and ultimately more force with which the official view of events can be imposed.

Reed v. United Kingdom, decided in December 1979, raised issues concerned with the admissibility of prisoners' applications. Reed alleged that he had been assaulted at Hull prison on 4 September 1976, i.e. in the aftermath of the riot. He complained that these assaults constituted a violation of Article 3 in that they were inhuman or degrading treatment. The government did not contest Reed's version of events but submitted that the application was inadmissible as he had failed to exhaust all the available domestic remedies. He had not brought civil actions for damages against the prison officers allegedly responsible for the assaults.

The Commission decided to consider the application in order to see if there were any special circumstances e.g. the fact that Reed had been denied access to professional legal advice. Reed was also required to exhaust the prison system's internal complaints procedure before going elsewhere. The Commission concluded Reed was in a situation where his access to an effective and adequate remedy was made dependent on the completion of a separate preliminary internal procedure and on the outcome of criminal prosecutions. Neither of these constituted 'domestic remedies' in the Commission's opinion.

This complaint was found admissible because the Commission considered it to be of fundamental importance that a remedy for an alleged violation of the Convention should in principle be immediately available to every one wishing to complain of alleged mistreatment. For these reasons, the application was declared admissible and was considered on its merits.

Following the decision on the admissibility of Reed's application and its deliberation on the merits, the Commission placed itself at the disposal of the parties in the hope of achieving a friendly settlement. Agreement was finally reached in November 1981 and consisted of a £2,000 ex gratia payment, the replacement of the 'prior ventilation rule' with the 'simultaneous ventilation rule', and payment of 6247.30 French Francs in respect of Reed's fees and costs.

An issue highlighted here is the time taken for a complaint to be dealt with. One defence available to any bureaucratic organisation is delay. The longer the time taken to deal with a complaint, then the less likely people are to complain. The usual bureaucratic rationale, that the organisation should be given the opportunity to correct its own errors, is plausible at first sight, even laudable. But the disadvantage is that complaints may never become public. The Commission took the view that it was of great importance that complaints should be heard quickly in the civil courts, rather than waiting upon the outcome of internal administrative reviews which lack the force of law.

The Commission also decided in December 1979 on the admissibility of an application by Ian Brady (convicted in 1965 for his part in the 'Moors Murders') who claimed that the cumulative effect of imprisonment as a category 'A' prisoner breached Article 3. Brady claimed that despite the publicity given to his case, he had gradually been allowed to participate in prison life. Participation included cooking daily meals, doing braille work and association with other prisoners. In 1971 these privileges were terminated. With the introduction of greater general security, he was transferred to other prisons where he was kept almost continuously in solitary confinement without any opportunity for exercise outside his cell. Unofficial local arrangements had been made to allow him greater freedom of movement, but these conflicted with his official status and could be removed at any time.

The Commission rejected Brady's application on the grounds that a prisoner's security classification was not a matter which fell within the scope of the Convention. The cumulative effect of these conditions might in time have been in breach of Article 3 but his circumstances had improved since 1975. The application was rejected as being manifestly ill-founded.

Prison conditions generally seem to be outside the scope of Article 3 which seems to be interpreted exclusively in terms of the way prisoners are dealt with by prison staff. Most applications relate to allegations of abuses by individual members of staff - the type of allegation that by its very nature is difficult to prove. There have been attempts to argue that official policy, especially high security imprisonment, constitutes a breach because of the long-term effect of restrictive conditions, but these claims have been rejected as prisoners have only been exposed to these conditions, two or three years.

Complaints under Article 4

Only one complaint seems to have been made by a British prisoner under Article 4 which prohibits slavery or servitude and forced or compulsory labour, subject to exceptions. Ian Brady alleged breaches of Article 4 to support his principal claim that his rights under Article 3 had been violated. The report of the Commission's deliberations on admissibility does not specify precisely the substance of the Article 4 claim. The Commission declared this application inadmissible because the improvement in circumstances made it manifestly ill-founded.

Complaints under Article 6

Two phrases in Article 6(1) have been important in cases brought by British prisoners. The phrase 'the determination of his civil rights and obligations' was used to secure a right of access to the courts. The phrase 'criminal charges' brought prison disciplinary hearings within the scope of the Convention. This Article can be thought of as the 'natural justice' or 'due process' Article, linking with the English and American legal systems respectively. Article 6 also concerns access to legal advice.

The Knechtl (1970) case is important in the development of the British cases heard by the Commission, as it was held to be admissible and it raised for the first time the question of prisoners' access to the courts. Knechtl alleged that he had lost a leg through the negligence of the prison medical staff and the main complaint in his application was that he had been refused access to a solicitor when he wished to consider bringing legal proceedings against the prison authorities. He alleged violations of his rights under Article 6(1).

The Commission decided that as Article 6(1) had not been interpreted before, this application should also be judged on its merits. The Commission rejected the argument that prisoners did not have equal protection under the Convention compared with free citizens. It was discovered that if Knechtl was prevented from beginning litigation until his date of release, he would not have been able to bring an action against the surgeon, as the statutory time limit on beginning an action would have expired, and if the Home Office defended the action they would also escape litigation. In the light of these considerations, the Commission declared the application admissible and Knechtl accepted an ex gratia payment. Subsequently the British government changed the prison Standing Orders when prisoners wish to seek legal advice in cases involving negligence by medical staff.

The Golder case (1975) is of great importance as it was the first British prisoners' rights case to reach the European Court of Human Rights. Specifically, the Court was asked to consider whether the Home Secretary had violated Golder's rights by denying him access to the courts in refusing his applications for permission to contact a solicitor with a view to bringing a libel action against a prison officer.

In 1969, when Golder was in Parkhurst prison there was a serious disturbance. Golder was interviewed by the police following an allegation that he had assaulted a prison officer, and was told that a prosecution was being considered. Later, the prison officer who had identified Golder changed his evidence absolving Golder of any involvement. The plans to bring either criminal or prison discipline charges were dropped. In the following year Golder petitioned the Home Secretary requesting a transfer to another prison. Golder also stated that he believed material relating to the assault allegations was still on his file. In the petition, Golder asked for permission to consult a solicitor with a view to bringing a civil action for libel in relation to the assault allegation or as an alternative, that there should be an independent review of his file. At this stage Golder petitioned the Commission of Human Rights and the application was declared admissible in part in March 1971. The Commission accepted the complaints relating to the denial of access to legal advice.

The Commission gave the opinion that Golder's rights had been violated in so far as Article 6(1) guarantees a right of access to the courts, and that there was no inherent limitation on the right of prisoners to initiate legal proceedings. The British government did not accept this opinion and a friendly settlement could not be achieved. The case was referred to the Court of Human Rights by the UK government.

The European Court held that the right of access to a lawyer was an essential and inherent part of the right to a fair trial. The Court took the view that the fair, public and expeditious qualities of judicial proceedings are of no value if judicial proceedings cannot take place. Article 6(1) was not restricted in its application solely to criminal charges, despite the fact that civil litigation is not specifically mentioned. The phrase 'the determination of his civil rights and obligations', which is used in the first line of the Article was interpreted to include civil proceedings which would be necessary to decide the individual's 'obligations'. Sir Gerald Fitzmaurice, the judge of British nationality, said that the method of interpretation used to find against the British government was creating a right that was not actually listed in the Convention; the Court's decision would only serve to bring the Convention into disrepute among signatory states.

The Times noted an ironic twist to the case in that Golder himself had not been in touch with his solicitor for more than two years. A short time after instituting proceedings Golder had ceased to take an interest in them. The solicitor said that he last saw Golder shortly after his release from prison on parole in 1972; and that he had no idea of Golder's current whereabouts. Two weeks after the decision, the then Home Secretary announced that the Prison Rules were to be amended in the light of the judgment.

The Kiss claim in respect of Article 6 (1976) was dealt with by the Commission after the Golder judgment had been given, but it related to earlier events. The Commission's decisions are in one sense a reiteration of the Golder judgment as well as a slight elaboration. The importance of the case lies in its concern with the conditions of imprisonment.

Kiss complained to the Commission on four grounds: i) ill-treatment by a prison officer; ii) insufficient medical treatment; iii) the allegedly false charge brought against him as a consequence of the ill-treatment, and the subsequent unfair disciplinary proceedings; and iv) the refusal of the Home Secretary to allow him to institute legal proceedings. The third and fourth complaints relate to Article 6.

The Commission had to decide whether Article 6 applied to hearings before boards of visitors. In a previous case (Engel), the Court had decided that Article 6 did apply to disciplinary hearings in the Dutch Armed Forces although the Court had said that this decision should not be followed blindly as military discipline was different from the general system of law. The Commission decided that Article 6 should not apply to prison disciplinary hearings, as these hearings were unlike those concerning criminal offences. The Commission also held that the penalty of loss of remission does not constitute a deprivation of liberty. Any remission of the sentence for good behaviour 'is a mere privilege and loss of that privilege does not alter the original basis for detention'. Consequently this part of the application was rejected as being manifestly ill-founded.

The final part of Kiss's complaint was that the Home Secretary's refusal to allow him to institute legal proceedings violated his right of access to the courts, as interpreted by the European Court in the Golder case. The Commission stressed the importance of the principle of access to the courts. Kiss had been refused permission to institute legal proceedings. The European Court had upheld prisoners' rights of access to institute civil proceedings only, so Kiss could only be allowed access to those courts and part of his complaint could not be upheld. The application was declared admissible and the Commission then considered the merits of the case.

It is not clear what happened after this decision. There is no further reference to the Kiss case in any of the more recent Yearbooks. It may be assumed that the parties reached a friendly settlement because neither the UK government nor the Commission took the case any further.

Although most of the Hilton application related to alleged breaches of Article 3 there was a complaint under Article 6(1). Hilton complained that the prison authorities had violated his rights by refusing to allow him to instruct a solicitor concerning an injury to a finger. The first application in June 1971 was refused before the Knechtl and Golder cases, and the policy changes made by the Home Office consequent upon these decisions. The second application in July 1972 was refused - and the government accepted that this was a regrettable oversight as the application was obscured by many other petitions made by Hilton. The Commission voted unanimously that the Home Secretary's action concerning the denial of access to the courts was a violation of Article 6(1). During the examination of the case by the Committee of Ministers, the British government announced that it accepted the Commission's conclusion in respect of this article. Reparation had been offered to Hilton and this had been rejected. The Committee of Ministers decided that no further action by the British government was called for.

Ian Brady alleged that his rights under Article 6(1) had been violated in that both the membership of the committee which decided prisoners' security classifications and its deliberations were surrounded by secrecy. The Commission held that the complaint was not covered by any of the provisions of the Convention; Article 6(1) was concerned with criminal charges brought before the courts. Classification of prisoners was an administrative procedure. The complaint was declared inadmissible as the rights claimed were not part of the Convention.

In Campbell and Fell v. United Kingdom which was decided by the Commission in May 1982, the Commission was asked to consider again the applicability of Article 6 to the proceedings before boards of visitors.

Campbell complained that Article 6(1) had been violated in proceedings against him before a board of visitors, in which he was convicted of mutiny and personal violence to a prison officer. The punishments given for these offences were the loss of 570 days' remission, 91 days' loss of privileges, exclusion from associated work, cellular confinement and stoppage of earnings. Both Campbell and Fell complained that Article 6 had been violated when they had both been refused permission to consult a lawyer without first exhausting the internal complaints procedure. Fell also alleged that Article 6(1) was violated when he was refused permission to consult his lawyer out of the hearing of a prison officer.

The first task was for the Commission to decide whether Article 6 applied to hearings of boards of visitors. The Court of Human Rights had established criteria to distinguish between disciplinary and criminal law. The distinction was important, as the Court had held that Article 6 does not apply to a purely disciplinary offence unless it amounts to a criminal matter. The factors which the Court took into account were
1. whether the provisions defining the offence charged belong according

74

to the legal system of the respondent State, to criminal law,
disciplinary law or both concurrently;
2. the nature of the offence; and,
3. the degree of severity of the penalty which the person concerned
risks incurring.
The Commission applied these criteria to the facts of Campbell's
complaint. First, the offences of 'mutiny' and 'gross personal violence
to an officer' are covered by disciplinary law in the Prison Rules. The
Commission believed that the charges here were plainly offences against
prison order. Second, the Commission rejected the argument by Campbell
that the loss of remission was equivalent to a further long period of
imprisonment, and hence fell into the criminal sphere. The Commission
could not regard loss of remission as equivalent to a sentence. Third,
the severity of the penalty in this case was however different from
anything the Commission had considered previously. The offences charged
were described as 'especially grave' in the Prison Rules and there was
no limit on the penalties which could be inflicted. In the Commission's
view, the range of possible punishments went beyond 'what could be
properly regarded as a purely "disciplinary" penalty and fell within the
criminal sphere'. The Commission considered that the charges brought
against Campbell were criminal for the purposes of Article 6 of the
Convention, and the provisions of this article were applicable to some
hearings before boards of visitors.
The Commission then considered whether the adjudication hearing had
complied with the requirements of Article 6. The Commission considered
first the issue of the 'independent and impartial' nature of boards of
visitors. The case law of the Commission and the Court required that for
a tribunal to be 'independent' within the meaning of Article 6(1) it had
to be independent of the executive and both parties to a dispute. A
board of visitors' duty to act impartially and independently did not
meet the caselaw standard; they were not sufficiently institutionally
independent, as their members were appointed by the Home Secretary, and
their other functions brought them into daily contact with prison
officials. Hearings did not meet other requirements of Article 6, in
that neither hearings nor judgments were announced publicly.
Additionally, the applicant was not allowed either legal advice to
prepare his defence or legal representation at the hearing. The
Commission concluded that the proceedings before the board of visitors
had violated Campbell's rights under Article 6.
The Commission next considered the claims made by both Campbell and
Fell that their rights to a fair and public hearing under Article 6(1)
had been violated by the delay in contacting a legal adviser imposed on
them by the prison authorities. The delay was imposed by the
requirement in the Prison Rules that all internal grievance mechanisms
had to be exhausted first. The Commission concluded unanimously that the
delay in allowing both applicants access to legal advice involved a
breach of Article 6(1). In the Commission's view, a substantial delay
in access to the courts might itself breach Article 6(1). There was no
justification for giving unlimited priority to internal investigations.
Fell also complained that when he was allowed to consult a lawyer, he
was not initially permitted to consult him out of the hearing of a
prison officer. In the Commission's view, where access to the courts is
allowed only under conditions in which the potential litigant is denied
the benefit of privilege as normally afforded under domestic law (i.e.
the law of the Contracting State), this amounts in principle to an
interference with the right of access guaranteed in Article 6(1).
In September 1983, the British government invited the Court to decide

the case as it did not accept the Commission's view on the applicability
of Article 6 to boards of visitors; to declare that Campbell had failed
to exhaust all domestic remedies available to him; and to note the
changes in law and practice in the UK relating to communications between
prisoners and their legal advisers since the judgment in the Golder
case.

The Court rejected the government's plea that Campbell had failed to
exhaust domestic remedies. The Court held by a majority of four votes to
three that Article 6 of the Convention applied to boards of visitors'
proceedings. The main issue then was whether the board of visitors'
hearing complied with the guarantees in Article 6 which apply to those
facing criminal charges. The Court said that it was not opposed to
states distinguishing between 'criminal' and 'disciplinary' law but this
distinction was not binding for the purposes of the Convention. If the
Contracting States had the discretion to decide the classification of an
offence and hence to remove it from the operation of Articles 6 and 7,
the application of these provisions would be subordinated to their
sovereign will and would lead to results incompatible with the object
and purpose of the Convention.

The guarantee of a fair hearing is one of the fundamental principles
of a democratic society. The Golder judgment had shown that justice
cannot stop at the prison gate and there is no warrant for depriving
inmates of the safeguards of Article 6 in appropriate cases.

The Court then applied the three criteria from the Engel case to test
the 'criminal' nature of these disciplinary hearings. The Court rejected
the claim that boards of visitors' proceedings violated the requirement
that criminal charges should be heard in public. There were sufficient
reasons of public order and security to exclude the press and public.
However, a majority of the Court decided that Article 6(1) had been
violated because the board of visitors had not announced its decision
publicly. Public order and security considerations did not apply to this
issue. In the context of prison discipline, a public announcement was
designed to ensure scrutiny by the public of the judiciary with a view
to safeguarding the right to a fair trial.

Several of the issues relating to prisoners' access to the courts were
decided by the Court of Human Rights in Silver v. United Kingdom.
Judgment was given in March 1983. Access to the courts comprised a
small part of this case only as it was principally concerned with the
censorship. Silver's complaint stemmed from his petition to the Home
Secretary for permission to seek legal advice concerning allegedly
negligent treatment in prison. He petitioned in November 1972 and was
refused in April 1973. In July 1973, Silver petitioned again, and
requested leave to seek legal advice about his dental treatment. This
second petition was apparently granted in October 1973, but Silver
claimed that he was never informed of this. The Prison Rules did not
then allow prisoners to seek legal advice about civil proceedings
without the Home Secretary's permission i.e. before the change in the
Rules stemming from Golder. The Commission had received the first
petition from Silver in 1972 and for that reason it was declared
admissible and proceeded to the Court, eleven years later.

The Court held unanimously that there had been violations of the
applicants' rights of access to legal advice in connection with claims
for personal injuries. The Court held that a subsequent change in the
rules did not restore rights denied at any earlier date. The Court
expressed its belief that for evidentiary and other reasons, speedy
access to legal advice was essential in personal injury cases.

Applications claiming breaches of Article 6 have effectively challenged prison administration. The prison Standing Orders and Circular Instructions which were changed after the decisions in <u>Golder</u> have helped to allow prisoners greater access to legal advice when considering legal action against prison staff. The <u>Golder</u> decision was significant in recognising that Prison Rules imposed blanket prohibitions which did not distinguish between cases. The decision was also important in that it stated a right of access to the courts and legal advice seven or so years before the domestic courts considered the question. The decisions in <u>Campbell and Fell</u> constitute another element of the attack on the disciplinary functions of boards of visitors.

Complaints under Article 8

Article 8 guarantees the right of respect for private and family life, home and, most importantly, correspondence. Section two of Article 8 lists a number of exceptions such as national security, public safety, and the prevention of disorder or crime. The Prison Rules in Britain include powers to stop and censor prisoners' letters. Prisoners have to have the Home Secretary's permission to correspond with any one outside the prison. The Prison Rules are formulated in general terms, and more detailed instructions are contained in the Standing Orders.

A significant part of Golder's case was that his rights guaranteed under Article 8 had been violated. The claim concerned the refusal by the prison authorities to allow him to write to a solicitor and various other correspondents. The Home Secretary's actions could not be justified by any of the exceptions in Article 8(2). Only the complaint in relation to a legal adviser was declared admissible by the Commission.

The Court had to decide two issues in relation to Article 8
1. can a convicted prisoner who wishes to write to his lawyer in order to institute proceedings rely on the protection given by Article 8 of the Convention to respect for correspondence?
2. if answered positively, did the facts disclose the existence of a violation of Article 8?

The Court took the view that the Home Secretary's refusal of Golder's petition had the direct and immediate effect of preventing Golder from contacting a solicitor by any means whatever. Impeding someone from even initiating correspondence constituted the most far-reaching form of 'interference' with the exercise of the 'right to respect for correspondence'. If Golder had attempted to write to a solicitor without the Home Secretary's consent, any letter would have been stopped and Golder could then have invoked Article 8. That would lead to the paradoxical result that by complying with the Prison Rules on correspondence, the prisoner loses the benefit of Article 8 of the Convention.

The Court stated that Article 8(2) exhaustively defines the limitations which may be applied and rejected the argument that a sentence of imprisonment inevitably affects the operation of other Articles in the Convention. The British government argued that interference with correspondence was justified to prevent disorder or crime. This was rejected by the Court because the facts showed that Golder was trying to contact a legal adviser. The Court took issue with the claim that some interference was justifiable 'in a democratic society'. This argument had to be rejected, as Golder was trying to exercise a right guaranteed under the Convention. The Court concluded this demolition of the government's argument by saying that there had been a violation of Article 8. In this conclusion, the Court was unanimous. The Prison Rules were amended in the light of this judgment.

It is appropriate to continue the theme of censorship of prisoners' correspondence by referring to Silver v. United Kingdom which was decided by the Court of Human Rights in March 1983. This case is frequently referred to as the Prisoners' Correspondence case, concentrating as it does on the issue of censorship. Complaints were made by six people serving sentences of imprisonment and one other person who was corresponding with a prisoner friend that their letters were stopped by the prison authorities. The Commission had selected these seven applications to provide a test case to examine the validity of the censorship of prisoners' mail in Britain.

Censorship of mail was delegated by the prison governor to a subordinate, who could stop any letter thought to offend against the provisions of Home Office Instructions and Standing Orders. The prisoner was given the opportunity of re-writing the letter but omitting the offending material. Any prisoner might complain about a censor's decision to the governor, and if this proved unsatisfactory, the prisoner could then complain to the board of visitors. The last resort would be a petition to the Home Secretary.

At the time of the events complained of, and until 30 November 1981, the Standing Orders and Instructions contained rules and guidance of a general nature concerning prison administration as well as more specific directives on the control of prisoners' correspondence. The Orders and Instructions were made available to Members of both Houses of Parliament for reference, but were not available to either the public or prisoners; prisoners are given information about aspects of the control of correspondence on a card placed in each cell. Under Prison Rule 34(8) prisoners had to seek the Home Secretary's leave to correspond with any person other than a close relative; normally the prisoners were allowed to correspond, without such permission, with other relatives or existing friends. The governor retained a discretion to forbid any correspondence he felt potentially disruptive of good order or to prevent crime. Governors also had a discretion to allow correpondence with other people not known to the prisoner before he came into custody, but a prisoner could not usually write to other prisoners, ex-prisoners, marriage bureaux, or specified categories of pen friends.

Prisoners were also given leave to write to legal advisers, MPs, consular and commonwealth officials, organisations such as NCCL, JUSTICE, and the Howard League for Penal Reform, and the European Commission of Human Rights. The Standing Orders specifically prohibited a convicted prisoner from making representations on matters concerning his trial, conviction or sentence to any judge, public authority, or representatives of Commonwealth or foreign governments. Such representations could, however, be made to the Home Secretary. Prisoners were not allowed to send letters requesting other people to communicate what they were not permitted to do directly. Additionally, prisoners were prohibited from including in their letters complaints about the courts, the police and the prison authorities; threats of an incitement to violence; objectionable references to persons in public life; discussion of crime and criminal methods or of the offences of others; material intended for publication or for use on wireless or television; and, allegations against prison officers. This listing is not exhaustive but contains the main categories then included in the Standing Orders.

The case arose from the stopping of 62 letters written by the applicants. The reasons given by the prison authorities for stopping the letters are presented in Table 4:1.

Table 4:1
Reasons for stopping applicants' letters

Offical Reason Given		Number
Complaints about prison treatment		
addressed to MPs	16)	
addressed to legal representatives	4)	36
addressed to other people	16)	
Prohibition on correspondence other than with relatives or friends		11
Prohibition on letters dealing with legal matters without permission		1
Prohibition on business transactions		1
Prohibition on letters containing material intended for publication		4
Prohibition on letters using improper language		4
Prohibition on letters holding prison authorities up to contempt		1
Prohibition on letters complaining about trial, conviction, or sentence		1
Miscellaneous		3
Total		62

Three themes recurred throughout the Commission's decision. First, the prohibitions were over-broad, or blanket, ones. Correspondence should be dealt with on individual merits. Second, many of the prohibitions contained in the Standing Orders were not 'in accordance with the law', because they could not be foreseen in the Prison Rules. Finally, the Commission could not discern any legitimate interest threatened by allowing particular kinds of correspondence, i.e. they rejected the justification that censorship prevented disorder.

On the other hand, the Commission found that there had been no violation of Article 8 when letters had been stopped because they contained threats of violence. The instances of letters being stopped because of the prohibition on discussion of crime in general, or the crimes of others, were not violations of Article 8, as the prisoners could re-write any letters stopped for these reasons.

The British government did not accept the Commission's conclusions, and the case was referred to the Court of Human Rights by the Commission in 1982. The principal task for the Court was to decide whether these interferences were covered by the exceptions listed in paragraph 2 of Article 8. The Court found a violation of Article 8 because the censoring of some letters was not 'in accordance with the law' and the censor's behaviour was not foreseeable from the text of the Rules. The question, 'Did the interferences have legitimate aims under Article 8(2)?' was not discussed before the Court. The Court concluded that a total of 57 letters had been stopped when it was not 'necessary in a democratic society' in violation of Article 8 of the Convention.

A prisoner's right to correspond was an additional issue decided in Campbell and Fell v. United Kingdom by the Court in June 1984. Father Fell claimed that he had been refused permission to correspond with a Sister Monica Power because although she had been known to him before he came into custody, their relationship was not considered to be 'a close personal friendship'. The Commission had concluded that this refusal constituted a violation of Article 8. The British government stated that they did not wish to contest this opinion in the light of changes made after Silver. The Court held that there had been a violation of the Convention as there were no reasons to depart from the Silver decision even though Father Fell was a category 'A' prisoner at the time of the refusal.

The issue of censorship has great survival qualities and was the reason for a further judgment against the British government as recently as March 1988. In Boyle and Rice v. United Kingdom (1988) the complaint referred to the stopping in 1981 of a letter intended for a 'media personality' by Boyle who was then a prisoner in Scotland. The British government conceded that the stopping of the letter was a breach of Article 8 since the letter was a purely personal one.

A few attempts have been made to use the other provisions of Article 8. In March 1982, the Commission considered the admissibility of an application, X v. United Kingdom, (1982) claiming that the requirements that prisoners wear prison clothes constituted a violation of the guarantee in Article 8(1) of respect for private life. The Commission took the view that the wearing of prison clothes was lawful and necessary in a democratic society, and rejected as manifestly ill-founded.

In October 1982, the Commission considered the limitation of visits to prisoners as a violation of the respect for private life clause in Article 8(1). In another case cited as X v. United Kingdom (1982) the claim was that an attempt to send out a visiting order to the Chairman of the Citizens' Commission on Human Rights (a body sponsored by the Scientologists) was stopped by the prison authorities on the grounds that the prisoner did not know this individual before the sentence.

The Commission considered that family and private life is limited by the nature of lawful detention. It would not be feasible for there to be unlimited visiting facilities. In this case the reason for the visit was not part of the applicant's private life, but was to further the public campaign of the Citizens' Committee on Human Rights. The application was inadmissible as it was manifestly ill-founded.

Complaints under Article 10

Article 10 of the Convention protects freedom of expression, including the right to receive and impart information and ideas without interference. The second paragraph allows exceptions which have to be justified if invoked by the state. The control of books and letters by the prison authorities in Britain as a matter of course has made it more or less inevitable that prisoners would claim violations under this Article, although the first case was in fact an attempt to use Article 10 as a substitute for a Freedom of Information Act.

In 1979 the Commission was asked to consider a claim by Ian Brady that the Home Office's refusal to provide him, and those interested in his case, with the names of the members of the board responsible for the allocation of maximum security prisoner's classification was a breach of Article 10. The Commission rejected this claim on the ground that while the public had a right to receive information and ideas in areas of public interest the concept of information was not so extensive as to oblige the divulgence of the names of members of an administrative committee. The application was rejected as being manifestly ill-founded.

In the first case referred to as X v. United Kingdom, the Commission was asked to consider what can be seen as a more predictable claim under this Article. The applicant claimed violations of Article 10 on the grounds that his use of writing material was restricted while in prison, and any notes written there would be scrutinised on his release. He also complained that he had no access to a library or newspapers for part of the sentence, this was a punishment given by the board of visitors on one occasion. Other periodicals and papers sent to him were put away with his property. The Commission considered that the matter of writing paper and the uses to which it could be put, and the scrutiny to which it was subjected, raised issues of a general character under Article 10 the merits of which deserved full examination. The application was declared admissible and the result of the hearing of the merits of this application is still awaited.

It seems slightly paradoxical that a prisoner's rights to express his own ideas in writing may be liable to greater protection than the same prisoner's right to receive ideas and information. While this may be laudable, it is not likely to be a very widely used right.

Complaints under Article 12

Article 12 of the Convention states that 'Men and women of marriageable age have the right to marry and to found a family, according to the law governing the exercise of this right'. In the past, prisoners in England who wished to marry had to ask permission of the Home Secretary and this was only rarely granted, as it involved the temporary release of the prisoner from custody.

In Hamer v. United Kingdom decided in December 1979, the Commission considered the merits of Hamer's complaint that the refusal of permission by the Home Secretary to allow him to marry was a violation of his rights under Article 10.

The right to marry was regarded by the Commission as a right to form a legal relationship, to acquire a status. The exercise of this right by prisoners did not involve a general threat to prison security or good order. The marriage ceremony itself could take place under the supervision of the prison authorities. In the Commission's opinion, national laws on marriage could not be used to deprive a person, or category of persons, of full legal capacity of the right to marry. Nor could it interfere with their exercise of that right.

The government submitted that Hamer was merely in a position where, as a result of his own actions, he was unable to exercise that right for a time, as he was unable to go to a place authorised under the domestic law of marriage. In the Commission's view this was not a situation that could be described as an act of choice; Hamer had not chosen to be celibate in the same way as a priest. Nor could it be said that Hamer's inability to marry was an inevitable result of his imprisonment.

On these grounds, the Commission concluded that Hamer's right to marry as guaranteed by Article 12 had been violated, and reported this to the Committee of Ministers. The Committee was then informed that the British government accepted the Commission's report, and had changed its practices in relation to prisoners who wished to marry. Furthermore, a decision had been made to amend British law to allow persons to be married in prison. The Marriage Act 1983 permits prisoners to marry in prison.

Complaints under Article 13

Article 13 provides that: 'Everyone whose rights and freedoms as set forth in this Convention are violated shall have an effective remedy before a national authority, notwithstanding that the violation has been committed by persons acting in an official capacity'. Jacobs has argued that it is clear that Article 13 is one of the rights guaranteed by the Convention, although it is anomalous that the right to a remedy should itself be classed among the guaranteed rights. (Jacobs, 1975, p. 215) The British government has had to defend a number of complaints brought under Article 13, as it has been argued that there is nothing in the British system of justice which is capable of dealing with the sorts of issues raised by the Convention.

The landmark case was Silver v. United Kingdom where, in addition to the other issues, the Court considered an alleged violation of this Article. The Commission of Human Rights had decided by a majority of fourteen to one that the absence of effective domestic remedies for the claimed censorship of correspondence in violation of Article 8 constituted a violation of Article 13. The government had replied by denying a violation and argued that the revised Standing Orders did not violate Article 8.

The Court examined the four channels of complaint available to prisoners: application to the board of visitors, the P.C.A., petition to the Home Secretary, and proceedings before the English courts. All of these avenues suffered from one or more defects - they were not sufficiently independent, or had no binding powers to grant redress, or had limited jurisdiction. In the Court's view there could be no effective remedy as required by Article 13 and consequently there had been a violation. The Court then went on to reserve the decision as to the action to be taken.

The issue of effective domestic remedies was briefly discussed in Campbell and Fell. In June 1984, the Court of Human Rights discussed two claims made in respect of Article 13, one in conjunction with Article 6(1) and the other in conjunction with Article 8. The Court decided that Fell's complaints under Article 6(1) concerning access to legal advice and the refusal to allow confidential consultation with his lawyer raised no special issue under Article 13. The reasons for this decision were first that the requirements of Article 13 were less strict than those in Article 6(1) itself, and second that these complaints were both absorbed by those made under Article 6(1). Complaints made in conjunction with Article 8 were dealt with separately as these related to personal correspondence. The Court held that there had been a violation of the Convention as no effective remedy existed within the English system in respect of restrictions on correspondence and access to legal advice.

Conclusions

Since the right of individual petition became available in 1966, British prisoners have had an alternative set of institutions through which they can bring complaints about their treatment while in prison. The significance of this alternative is that the Convention provides a formal, written set of rights which the signatory States are expected to respect. Any deviation or departure from the Convention by a High Contracting Party has to be justified. Several ringing phrases have been used to describe this change of relationship. James Avery Joyce's notion of 'the State in the Dock' and Hurwitz's 'The State as Defendant'. (Joyce, 1978, p. 79; Hurwitz, 1981) It is a new departure for sovereign governments to be held to account for what they do as everyday administrative procedures. The change is particularly important in countries like Britain which has not had elaborate systems of control over governmental activity. Citizens are able to challenge the actions of their government before a tribunal which can compare administrative practice across Europe. Powers which are regarded as essential to the maintenance of government and administration by British governments may not exist elsewhere, and reasons given by British governments for their continued use may well fall on deaf ears at Strasbourg.

Changes in prison policy and practice have come both from these cases and from others which were the subject of friendly settlements after opinions had been given by the Commission of Human Rights.

The European Court of Human Rights held in Golder that the Home Secretary had violated rights concerning access to the courts when permission to contact a solicitor in respect of a libel action was refused. Also it held that the refusal of permission to allow the applicant to write to a solicitor was an interference with his right to respect for correspondence.

In Silver, the European Court of Human Rights held that the interference with prisoners' mail by the prison authorities violated the Article guaranteeing respect for correspondence. This action was held not to be in accordance with the law because the individual could not foresee the consequences of his actions. The Court also held that the Convention had been violated in that any one complaining about censorship did not have access to an effective remedy before a national tribunal. The avenues by which a prisoner could complain were either not sufficiently independent, or if independent, did not have the jurisdiction to deal with such complaints.

The Court held in Campbell and Fell that Article 6 applies to the disciplinary hearings of boards of visitors when charges involving 'especially grave offences' were being dealt with. This decision meant that both the boards and their procedures have to meet some of the safeguards and standards of the courts. But it was held that the only way that the hearing violated the Convention was that its decisions were not announced publicly as required by Article 6(1). The Court also decided that the Convention had been violated in that the applicants had no right to legal representation when facing these disciplinary charges. Additionally the Convention had been violated in that consultations with a solicitor had to take place within the hearing of a prison officer.

The Commission of Human Rights has been important because its opinions have led to friendly settlements which have had important consequences for prisoners. Alternatively the British government has accepted the Commission's opinions because similar issues to those raised in a Court decision had been involved. The Commission also admitted the complaint in Reed that the requirement of having to exhaust internal grievance procedures before being allowed access to the courts was a violation of rights guaranteed by the Convention. The Home Office subsequently replaced the 'prior ventilation rule' with the 'simultaneous ventilation rule'. In Hamer the complaint was that refusing to allow prisoners to marry was a violation of the Convention and the law was later amended to allow marriages to take place in prisons.

Convicted prisoners are not treated as a highly stigmatised group in international law. It is recognised that prisoners are vulnerable as a group, and have to be protected. In Silver the Court held that blanket prohibitions on correspondence violated prisoners' rights under the Convention. In doing this it recognised prisoners as people with a legitimate right to correspond with others. The Convention protects prisoners and staff equally. British penal administration and practice have been opened up to review. The European institutions have refused to accept many of the justifications based on simple claims of lawful authority. There has been an air of unreality on recent occasions when the British government has had to argue that rules have changed and that similar complaints would not arise now. The Court has held quite rightly that something should be done about rights which have been abrogated and cannot now be restored.

The picture is not, however, one of complete success. The British experience is a good example of the problems inherent in the enforcement of international law. The procedures are both lengthy and complicated, and many applications fail at the admissibility stage, often for the lack of competent advice. Both the Commission and the Court sit infrequently so that progress is slow, and there are multiple opportunities for commenting on each party's responses. The end result of a Court decision may not be very dramatic. The British government changed the law on marriage after Hamer, and the Home Office altered the rules governing access to legal advice after Knechtl and Golder. On the other hand, the Silver case was the third case to raise somewhat similar issues. The reluctance of the Home Office to allow prisoners access to lawyers has not been removed by these decisions. What ground has been given has been yielded only after the full procedure of a Court of Human Rights.

Note

[1] In this context jurisprudence is a translation of the French legal term 'la jurisprudence' meaning 'the course of decisions, the body of case-law on a topic' rather than 'the study and knowledge of law', see D.M. Walker, 1980, p. 678.

5 Issues and trends in Britain and Europe

The discussion of prisoners' rights cases in the English courts cannot
not take place in isolation from the cases brought before the
institutions of the European Convention on Human Rights. There is
overlap, interaction and possible conflict between the two. It is
essential to look at the issues which transcend the individual cases.
Also it is important to see how the principles have changed over time.
Seven topics which highlight the issues are discussed in this chapter:
(i) the status of the Prison Rules; (ii) the medical care of prisoners;
(iii) the procedures of the European Convention on Human Rights; (iv)
changes in the interpretation of the Convention; (v) the relationship
between British domestic law and the European Convention on Human
Rights; (vi) the problems of enforcing court decisions made against the
prison authorities, and their long-term effects; and, (vii) the matter
of how the courts see the legal status of prisoners.

The status of the Prison Rules

Much of the prisoners' litigation is based on interpretation of the
Prison Act 1952 and its Rules. This is true whether cases are heard in
the domestic courts or in the European institutions. Since 1898, it has
been left to the Home Secretary to make rules which provide the basis of
prison life. The Prison Commission and subsequently the Prison
Department have both enjoyed a high degree of freedom from external
scrutiny. The Prison Commission was greatly relieved to be given the
authority in 1898 to control its daily affairs without detailed
Parliamentary intervention. Parliamentary control over rule making has
been limited, on the grounds that the Home Secretary should be left to

decide what is appropriate. It has been possible to change the administration without going through the complete legislative process. This has meant that prison standards have been set by the executive itself. The stated rationale also conflicts with the view of one writer on the subject, Peter English, has suggested that the movement away from Parliamentary control has its basis in a belief in the increasing professionalism of prison service personnel. (English, 1973, p. 207)

The prisons are governed by the Prison Act 1952 and the Prison Rules 1964 as amended to give effect to the decisions of the European Court of Human Rights, as well as changes in English statute law. The Prison Act and Rules are publicly available, but only a summary which lists the offences against prison discipline is generally provided for prisoners themselves. Copies of the Prison Rules are held in prison libraries and prisoners may apply to the governor in order to buy a personal copy. (House of Commons Debate 13 November 1980, col 355 WA) The Prison Rules are not the only guidance given to the prison administrators. There are also the Standing Orders. Though the Standing Orders are technically not confidential documents, the only external scrutiny to which they were liable was that of members of the two Houses of Parliament, as copies of the Standing Orders were placed in the Libraries of the Palace of Westminster. For many years ministers resisted making the Standing Orders more widely available on the grounds that they were 'management instructions issued for official purposes'. (House of Lords Debate, 27 June 1977, cols 993–4 WA) This has changed since the Golder judgment and the subsequent publication of the revised Standing Order 5 on correspondence. Now the Standing Orders are being made more widely available as they are reprinted.

Zellick has suggested that the Rules can be seen as falling into five categories.
1. Rules of general policy objectives which describe the objectives of penal policy and the treatment of prisoners. For example rule 1 – 'The purpose of the training and treatment of convicted prisoners shall be to encourage and assist them to lead a good and useful life'.
2. Rules of a discretionary nature which specify the areas over which the staff have discretionary powers, e.g. the grant of remission.
3. Rules of general protection which relate to minimum standards of health and welfare. They are not framed so as to be the basis of litigation, but they cover important areas of prison life, e.g. the duty of care towards prisoners.
4. Rules as to institutional structure and administrative functions which are concrete, specific rules which are liable to strict supervision.
5. Rules of specific individual protection which are concrete and precise in nature, and relate to discipline and the maintenance of order. Parliament has specified the maximum penalties which may be imposed when the rules are broken. (Zellick, 1981, pp. 612–6)

The importance of this categorisation lies in the question of whether these Rules provide the basis for the prison administration's legal responsibility towards prisoners. The language is frequently vague, and the courts have traditionally been reluctant to become involved in litigation over vaguely worded Acts of Parliament, or contracts. Rule 1 is an example of an abstract rule, but it can be seen as providing an ethos for the prison system. That view of the rule does not lend itself to judicial review in the sense that the prison administration are in some way in breach of contract if they fail to provide either the means or the desired outcome: the latter may not be in their power. It is important to note that Lord Kilbrandon has suggested that a failure by the Prison Department to provide proper conditions in prisons lies in the hands of the judges

> The Judges might say, 'We are authorised by law to impose the punishment of deprivation of liberty, but we are not authorised by law to impose the punishment of mental, physical and moral degradation. Unless there are places where we can order persons to be confined, deprivation of liberty being the only penalty imposed, we shall cease to send people to prison, because when we do so we are doing something which is beyond the powers which have been given to us. (British Institute of Human Rights, 1975, p. xiii)

The implication is that the judges could link the general statements of the Prison Rules to a test of the totality of prison conditions. The totality of the conditions would in turn form a test of the constitutionality of prison conditions. At present, no other way is available to look at the sum of prison life. Normally the legality of imprisonment depends on the conviction by the courts and the Prison Act itself. But the legality of a sentence, and the constitutionality of the conditions of the sentence are not the same thing.

The Prison Rules are delegated legislation, promulgated by statutory instrument, and subject to the negative resolution procedure of Parliament. This procedure normally allows Parliament to avoid wasting time with the minutiae of administration. But it should be noted that not all delegated legislation is of equal status. Importantly the Prison Rules fall into a weak category. This seems to be the outcome of both Parliamentary intention and judicial interpretation. As seen above, the courts have frequently held that Prison Rules are merely administrative directions, so that non-compliance does not affect the validity of what has been done. It is more usual with other delegated legislation for non-compliance of some mandatory requirement to lead to the overturning of that action by the courts.

It is useful at this stage to draw some conclusions from the courts' decisions and this will be done by looking at decisions under three headings - prison classification, prison conditions and natural justice.

One of the few principles to be established in the litigation against the prison authorities is that prisoners should be properly classified. In the past, up to 1948, the matter of classification was extremely important. There are relatively few classes of prisoner at the present time, but the importance of classification has not diminished. Although it did not reach the courts, there is the complaint to the P.C.A. in 1968 by a man held for eight days as a convicted prisoner when he had been remanded for medical reports. The Home Ofice paid out £100 as an ex-gratia settlement. (P.C.A., 1968, p. 46)

Once the prisoner has been sentenced, the courts have been reluctant to intervene. The modern authority for this policy derives from Lord Justice Goddard's dictum in Arbon v. Anderson, and was re-asserted in Silverman, and Becker v. Home Office. The statement by Lord Justice Goddard that no civil action was possible for a 'breach of statutory duty' towards prisoners has persisted into an era when the judges have taken a greater interest in both administration and the discretionary powers of ministers and civil servants. The Prison Rules relating to the conditions of everyday life continue to be seen as 'merely directory'. More recently, Lord Denning's views of litigation by prisoners, as expressed in Becker, have re-inforced the separateness of prison life. In Becker the court was asked to review the prison authorities' behaviour in relation to an explicitly-worded prison rule, and the implication was left that as long as prisoners' property was not actually stolen, the prison authorities could not be held accountable for negligence.

Decisions seem to have been affected in three ways by the courts' view of litigants. First, as a matter of policy prisoners should accept their lot once the sentence has been passed, and he appeal procedure has been exhausted. Second, prisoners have a great deal of time and strong motives to concoct frivolous and vexatious cases against those in lawful authority over them. Third, because prisoners are disaffected and antagonistic people by definition, and the prison administration needs to be able to exercise a flexible response to those in its charge. The effect of these views is that the courts have been less concerned with the merits of the cases before them and have concentrated on the character of the litigants. This assumed conflict of good and evil has led one writer, Tettenborn, to conclude that the courts have often used procedural issues to defeat the substance of prisoners' complaints. (Tettenborn, 1980, pp. 88-9)

The Prison Rules need to be treated differentially when seen in the context of natural justice. The paradox is that the Rules are not enforceable in terms of statute law requirements on prison administrators in respect of prison conditions, but they are enforceable in respect of judicial notions of natural justice. This trend can be traced through the series of cases involving boards of visitors (ex parte St Germain, ex parte Fox-Talbot, and ex parte Mealy). A somewhat similar, though not identical trend, can be seen in Raymond v. Honey. The rather grand phrase 'natural justice' really means fairness in this context. The courts have gradually come to the view that boards of visitors need to act fairly when reaching their decisions. In the case of ex parte Fox-Talbot, the board's decision was overturned even though the board was not responsible for the failure to call witnesses.

Prisoners suffered from the general reluctance of the courts to consider the issue of fairness, and were also subject to the distinction made by the courts between bodies which exercised judicial as opposed to disciplinary powers. The latter were concerned with privileges rather than rights, and decisions of internal disciplinary bodies about privileges were held not to imply a right to a hearing. (Jackson, 1979, p. 18) The application of the requirements of natural justice to the adjudications of boards of visitors lagged nearly twenty years behind the re-introduction of the general principle in other contexts.

The application of this right to a fair hearing for men involved in the Hull Prison Riot seems all the more remarkable considering the argument that the judges have used procedural faults to reject claims made by prisoners. In this instance it appears that the characteristics of the rioters (all were serving long sentences, it was alleged that an estimated £2 million worth of damage had been caused to the prison and many members of the staff had been injured) may have led the judges to reject the prisoners' claims to fair disciplinary proceedings.

The developments which have occurred since the Court of Appeal's decision in the St Germain case in 1979 seem quite remarkable. A series of cases has challenged the procedures of the boards of visitors sitting as disciplinary boards. The right to legally qualified representation at disciplinary board hearings which was rejected in 1975 (Fraser v. Mudge) has been permitted, at the discretion of the Board, in late 1983 (ex parte Anderson) although the House of Lords ruled in 1988 that it is not a right. The courts refused to allow direct judicial review of the summary discipline of prison governors until the House of Lords decision in 1988. Suggestions that some similar requirement applied to decisions about allocation to the Control Unit (in the <u>Williams</u> case) or to prison security classification (<u>Payne v. Home Ofice</u>) have so far been firmly excluded.

The courts have accepted the importance of access to the courts by prisoners. The case of <u>Raymond v. Honey</u> is remarkable for several reasons. The decision that prisoners have the full right of access to the courts has been given by the House of Lords - the first time a prisoners' rights case has been decided there. The paradox is, however, that while this right of access is now ensured, there are relatively few areas which can be litigated; while the courts hold to the view that the Prison Rules are 'merely directory' the bulk of prison life will remain beyond judicial review.

Medical care of prisoners

One of the innovations of the 1830s was the detailed planning of a healthy environment for the prisoner. The ancient curse of 'gaol fever' was to be eliminated by providing a better environment and the appointment of a medical officer to each prison. The cell was originally designed with much thought given to the space necessary to allow the circulation of air and the dilution of carbonic acid gas exhaled by the single prisoner who occupied the cell. Many of the same cells are now inhabited by three prisoners. There is surprisingly little modern research evidence as to the effects on prisoners' physical health of current prison conditions. (Walker, 1983, pp. 61-3)

The Prison Rules state that prisoners may request to see the prison medical officer, and these requests have to be passed on quickly to the medical officer. Medical officers may, at their discretion, call another medical practitioner into consultation and are expected to do so before performing any serious operations.

At this official and formal level there is no real problem. The two areas which cause concern in practice relate to the problems of the adequacy of medical care, and the alleged misuse of drugs. The second of these concerns has already been mentioned in the discussion of inspection and of enforced medical treatment. The standard of medical care has been the subject of comment by the medical profession as well as by critics of the prison system. These criticisms begin with understaffing and badly trained staff, the cursory nature of examinations, through to callousness and deliberate neglect; it is argued that the prison medical officers share a working assumption that all or most prisoners who complain of ill-health are malingering. (Cohen and Taylor, 1978, pp. 62-6)

The prison medical services have also been subjected to criticism because of the number of prisoners who have died in custody from unnatural causes or suicide. (Coggan and Walker, 1982) The prison suicide rate, six times higher than for the general population, is one cause for criticism, but Coggan and Walker have also produced a series of case studies of deaths in custody allegedly caused by neglect, professional incompetence, and in one case, assaults by staff.

In 1987, a prisoner applied for judicial review claiming that he had been refused adequate medical treatment by the prison authorities for injuries received at the time of his arrest. He used this approach on the grounds that the Home Secretary had failed to fulfil his responsibility for the maintenance of the applicant under the Prison

Rules, and the governor and medical officer were in breach of their duties. Mr Justice McNeill struck out the aplication on the grounds that judicial review could only be granted where a breach of some public duty was propounded. The complaints were being made in respect of questions of prison management which are not subject to judicial review. At best a claim of common law negligence could be made. (R v. Home Secretary and Others, ex parte Dew)

Many of the criticisms and complaints about medical care in prisons begin and end with the prison medical officer. The prison medical officer has complete discretion over the assessment of medical matters; if he decides that there is no medical problem there is nothing the prisoner can do to challenge this opinion. This total absence of challenge or appeal is unique in the prison system.

Several remedies have been suggested. First, a change in the Prison Rules which would allow the prisoner to consult with another medical practitioner. (House of Commons Debates, 11 November 1981, cols 904-6) Second, the more radical suggestion that the Prison Medical Service should be integrated into the National Health Service. (JUSTICE, 1983, pp. 20-1)

The abolition of the Prison Medical Service is seen by some as the necessary first step towards the improvement of prison medical services e.g. Cohen and Taylor, Coggan and Walker. It is not self-evident why this would lead to an improvement, except that prisoners would then be able to choose a general practitioner, and prison medical officers would no longer be Home Office employees.

It is apparent that the prison medical service is sensitive to criticism, as the medical journalist Richard Smith makes clear in Prison Medical Care. (Smith, 1984) Smith considers the problem of the quality of prison medical officers when the thinking of integrating the prison medical service into the NHS. Prison medical officers argue that their work is specialised, but they are given little specialist training, and this training provided is not inspected by any of the medical Colleges. Smith argues that by comparison with general practice outside, the prison medical service is deficient, but he does not indicate how integration might improve the quality of care.

Smith's discussion is in marked contrast to the Introduction to his book written by Professor John Gunn. Gunn rejects the idea of abolishing the prison medical service because the NHS 'simply could not take over all its functions'. He points out that most prison medical officers are in fact NHS doctors working part-time in the prisons. Gunn suggests that what is needed is an improved administrative structure and more autonomy for prison doctors which could be achieved by establishing of a prison health authority. Gunn's view seems to turn Smith's conclusions on their head - the problem is not the people but the organisation.

The official, Prison Department, view is pitched at the level of accountability. In the 1981 Report on the work of the Prison Department, the argument is made that if the Prison Medical Service were to be incorporated into the NHS, it would not be possible to devise arrangements for centralised control and ministerial accountability. The Prison Department recognises that lack of freedom of choice on the part of prisoners is the central problem, but then states that the present system provides an essential safeguard for those in custody. (Home Office, 1982) The prisoner's constitutional rights are protected: the paradox is that his health may be at risk.

A further way of dealing with complaints is through the P.C.A.. This does not seem to have been explored anywhere in the literature. The

P.C.A. is able to investigate complaints relating to the Special Hospitals and hospitals run by the Ministry of Defence for members of the armed forces. (Stacey, 1979, p. 179) These include complaints on matters of clinical judgement outside the jurisdiction of the Health Service Commissioner. It is not clear why this mechanism could not be used in respect of health care complaints made by prisoners since prison doctors are directly employed by the Home Office.

Procedures of the European Convention on Human Rights

Many criticisms can be made of the European Convention on Human Rights, and it makes most sense to begin with the procedural difficulties. Not all of these criticisms are the fault of the Commission or the Court. Some relate more properly to the Council of Europe, which is responsible for funding and staffing.

The Commission, a part-time body, employs some 20 members of staff as a secretariat. (House of Lords Select Committee on the European Communities, 1978, para 28) These 20 people are responsible for the complaints of 200 million people living in 17 different countries. It is worth noting that the P.C.A. has a staff of 110, but only has to deal with 48 million potential clients. The Commission members who deal with the investigatory and resolution stages of the procedure are usually academics, legal advisers or judges in their country of origin, and have considerable constraints on the time to deal with alleged violations.

As the right of individual petition has been conferred on more people the Commission has to deal with more applications. The Commission decides on admissibility and the vast majority of cases fail at this stage. (Drzemczewski, 1978, p. 42) It is not clear how much this is due to the criteria of admissibility themselves, or to the poor preparation of applications. Legal aid becomes available only when cases have been accepted by the Commission. It is open to doubt how effective legal aid has been in the past. The rate is low because it is an average of legal aid rates in the member states and as these are generally low, this may serve to deter lawyers from acting. (House of Lords Select Committee on the European Communities, 1978, p. 57)

The procedures employed by the Commission are time consuming. The applicant and the defendant each have to provide statements of their arguments on three occasions. In the Golder case, for example, both written and oral arguments were presented when the Commission considered the application's admissibility, then again in front of the full Commission for an opinion as to the merits of the application, and again when the case was presented to the Court of Human Rights itself. To make matters worse, each party is asked to present a written response to the arguments advanced by the other party. In the Golder case no new information was added in either of the last two stages in the process, i.e. the Commission's decision on the merits of the case, and before the Court. (Hurwitz, 1980, p. 161)

In most of the British cases, the Commission has taken two years to decide. The time required to take the case right through to the European Court of Human Rights was six years for Golder and eleven years for Silver. The current record time taken between application and the termination of proceedings is 15 years. (Beddard, 1980, p. 167)

The prisoner who wishes to complain faces a series of formidable hurdles unless he can find a solicitor who will take on the case for its own sake. There are probably no more than a dozen such solicitors in England. The next hurdle is to discover whether there are any remedies in the domestic courts; but there are unlikely to be any law books in the prison library, and schemes to provide duty solicitors on request are patchy and uncertain. The next hurdle is that the complaint to the European Commission of Human Rights would have to be prepared without access to a copy of the Council of Europe booklet Bringing an Application before the European Court of Human Rights, although there is a copy of the Convention in each prison library. The next hurdle is that the applicant has to avoid all of the pitfalls on admissibility described in chapter 4. Failure could lead to automatic rejection, whatever the justice of the complaint. For a prisoner to overcome all these hurdles without adequate legal advice would take tremendous persistence and a remarkable degree of sheer luck in having the right kind of complaint at the right time.

There are indications that the European Commission of Human Rights is moving cautiously towards a consideration of the merits of complaints rather than emphasising technicalities of admissiblity, it is still open to the defending government to raise these questions in an attempt to defeat the case.

Interpreting the European Convention

The European Convention is constrained by its history. It contains only those rights considered important after the Second World War. The rights and freedoms were also limited by the need to reach agreement and ratification by the States involved. The drafting committee had to tread warily.

The task of interpreting the Convention has fallen on both the Commission and the Court. Both have been in the situation where precedent did not exist and had to be created but having at the same time to develop and sustain the confidence of the High Contracting Parties, who could opt out of accepting the compulsory jurisdiction of the Court and the right of individual petition. The Commission and the Court have been involved in politically sensitive debates because they are empowered to review practice and policy across Europe. The institutions have been put in the situation of having to decide from time to time whether to move beyond the accepted view of their functions and terms of reference.

All of these problems have been evident in prisoners' rights applications. The Commission has been very conservative most of the time; but in recent years it seems to have broken its own procedural rules to deal with the merits of an application. The Court has gone further, and interpreted the Convention to define new rights not included in the Convention.

The Commission has been criticised on the grounds that in order to be admissible a case may have to pass both a legal and a political test. Hurwitz has demonstrated that the procedural steps laid down in Articles 25, 26 and 27(i) are clearly defined. But some applications which have passed these procedural tests have been rejected on the grounds that they were either 'manifestly ill-founded' or 'abusive of the right of petition'. (Hurwitz, 1980, p. 149) These last two grounds allow the Commission the means of avoiding potentially sensitive issues.

An occasional willingness to cause embarrassment can be seen quite clearly in the development of the right of access to the courts that has been developing in Knechtl, Golder, and Silver. In Knechtl, the Commission seems to have broken its own rules by considering the merits of the case at the same time as deciding admissibility, rather than subsequently.

In the Golder case, the Court decided that prisoners had a right of access to the courts. When the same issue had first been raised in 1972, the Commission dismissed the application as manifestly ill-founded. The Silver case has raised similar issues, and the Court has again recognised prisoners' rights of access to the courts.

The significant turning point is the way the Court reached its decision in Golder. The decision represents an important change in the behaviour of the Court because it recognised that the decision was a ruling on matters normally within a state's domestic jurisdiction. Also the conclusion, that there was a right of access to the courts, was reached after drawing together a series of 'clues' scattered throughout the text of the Convention. At first sight this seems to run counter to the explicit wording of Article 1 which requires States to guarantee the rights and freedoms 'defined' in the Convention. Could a right be said to be defined if it is not even mentioned? In his dissenting opinion the Judge of British nationality, Sir Gerald Fitzmaurice, argued that whatever justification there might be for judicial legislation within national legal systems, there is litle or none in the field of inter-State treaties which are based on agreement between the parties. If there were gaps in the rights guaranteed, the remedy was the re-negotiation of the Convention, as the judges were not Convention-makers.

The process which led the Court to 'recognise and guarantee a right of access to the courts', makes sense if it is seen as interpreting a written constitution. The Convention is usually described as an international treaty, but the evidence is that the Court is actually following a constitutional approach. This view of the Golder case has been put forward by F.A. Mann, and it is perfectly clear that he disapproves of this type of judicial lawmaking in general, and for a prisoner's rights case, finds it even less acceptable. (Mann, 1978, pp. 523-4) If this view of the European Court's activities is correct it helps to account for some of the conflict between British law and the Convention.

It is necessary to return to the studies of prisoners and the European Convention on Human Rights which were mentioned earlier, Douglas and Jones, and Zellick. Douglas and Jones introduce their essay with the comment

> The European Convention itself was born out of the post-concentration camp desire to ensure that history was not repeated. It is perhaps ironic in view of this that conditions of detention are not of themselves within the ambit of the Convention, being examinable only in so far as they involve a breach of rights actually guaranteed by the Articles of the Convention. (Douglas and Jones, 1983, pp. 352)

It is open to debate whether the original draftsmen of the Convention felt that prisons and prisoners were outside the scope of the Convention in the sense that criminal offences reduced one's rights, or that the Convention actually provided sufficiently broad ranging provisions so as to cover prison conditions.

Douglas and Jones, and Zellick have suggested the use of the European Standard Minimum Rules for the Treatment of Prisoners. These Rules were adopted by the Committee of Ministers of the Council of Europe in 1973. The Resolution adopted in 1973 is not binding on a member state but Douglas and Jones have suggested that the Standard Minimum Rules provide detailed guidance for prison practice. It was noted in chapter 1 that the Chief Inspector of Prisons uses these Standard Minimum Rules as part of the inspection process.

There are problems with this approach. First, as Silvia Casale has argued there are ambiguities 'both as to the status of standards and their relationship to rights'. (Casale, 1984, p. 5) Should the standards have the force of law or simply be expressions of intentions. The standards tend to be worded vaguely, e.g., rule 9 states that accommodation 'shall meet all requirements of health'. There is no precision as to minimum levels of heating, nor is anything stated about the other extreme, the heat of summer. There is the problem of circularity as successive British governments have taken the view that the training of prison staff, the Prison Rules and Standing Orders reflect the European Standard Minimum Rules. (House of Commons Debates, 2 August 1978, col 231 WA) This is not too surprising as the Standard Minimum Rules are in fact an updated version of the United Nations Standard Minimum Rules for the Treatment of Prisoners, adopted in 1955, which were in turn influenced in many respect by the Prison Rules of 1949. (House of Commons Debates, 1 July 1982, cols 357-8 WA)

If the Convention is silent on the protection of prisoners, there have been occasional attempts by the Court of Human Rights to comment on penal sanctions generally. In Tyrer v. United Kingdom, a case concerning the judicial use of corporal punishment in the Isle of Man, the Court took the view that judicial corporal punishment was degrading and consequently violated Article 3 of the Convention. The Court argued that for a breach of Article 3 to occur the individual should have suffered humiliation as a result of the punishment which is imposed upon him.

> The Court must also recall that the Convention is a living instrument which .. must be interpreted in the light of present day conditions. In the case now before it the Court cannot but be influenced by the developments and commonly accepted standards in the penal policy of the member States of the Council of Europe.

Unfortunately this argument is virtually impossible to translate into the prison system. It is difficult to see how the treatment of Hilton (described in chapter 4) could have failed to meet the level of degrading treatment more recently considered to violate Article 3 of the Convention. The Commission took the view that ill treatment had to be deliberate for a violation to be proved. This was in spite of the fact that the Commission had suggested that overcrowding and understaffing had 'had their depressing and discouraging effect upon the applicant'. Dissenting members found it unacceptable that a prison system should reduce a prisoner to an 'animal-like' state. The main cause of was held to be 'the extremely repressive application of disciplinary measures'. Overcrowding and understaffing are artefacts of the prison system: they do not occur naturally.

This case highlights one of the fundamental flaws in the procedures to safeguard prisoners' rights. In spite of all of the provisions and safeguards, Hilton left prison in a far worse state than when he entered it. The prison system and the prisoner were sucked into a downward spiral of conflict and confrontation from which the most likely outcome was the destruction of the prisoner. It is disturbing that the prisoners' grievance mechanisms were not effective in de-escalating the confrontation. A majority of the European Commission of Human Rights could not accept that the consequences of unofficial action and official indifference could amount to degrading treatment.

Domestic law and the Convention

The relationship between the British courts and the European Convention on Human Rights has developed slowly, and contact has brought antagonism rather than understanding. Whenever representatives of the British government have been asked about the protection of civil or human rights they invariably reply in terms of a common law approach. A good example of this approach can be seen in the reply to a Parliamentary Question

> Mr Tebbitt asked the Secretary of State if he will list the basic rights of the citizen throughout the United Kingdom together with the statutes under which they are guaranteed.
> Dr Summerskill: there is no distinction in the law of this country between 'basic' and other rights, and many rights of the citizen are derived from common law rather than statute. (House of Commons Debates, 15 January 1976, col 196 WA)

The common law approach to rights is essentially negative, the citizen has the right to do whatever is not forbidden by other legislation. The European Convention on the other hand represents the positive approach to rights and enumerates the rights guaranteed to citizens; any limitations are clearly stated in the same document. Common law rights depend on liberty, and if liberty is removed then the individual's rights are reduced or removed. Inherent in the common law approach is the view that rights may be curtailed and reduced in a number of unspecified circumstances, of which imprisonment is one. In this sense, rights are dependent on status. In the European Convention rights do not depend on status: they are held to be inalienable.

There are other difficulties in addition to the conflict of perspectives. A fundamental rule of the British Constitution is that a treaty requires legislative incorporation for it to take effect in domestic law. (Jaconnelli, 1976, p. 228) The European Convention on Human Rights was ratified by Britain in 1953, but treaties are traditionally seen as agreements made by the Crown. [2] Signature by the Foreign Secretary created international obligations, but nothing has been done to secure the implementation of these obligations, and as Mann has pointed out, even where the terms of the Convention are currently being observed, nothing has been done to prevent the introduction of inconsistent legislation in the future. (Mann, 1978, p. 516) Drzemczewski makes the important point that implementing legislation was not considered necessary at the time of ratification because the government of the day assumed that domestic law conformed with the Convention. Successive governments have all taken the view that these rights and freedoms were already secured by domestic law.

English judges have not ignored the Convention completely. The judges have laid down a rule of statutory interpretation that legislation is presumed not to intend to violate international law. But this rule is limited. The Convention cannot be invoked judicially as a body of public policy. If this was to be done, it would then be possible for the courts to set aside a result obtained by the ordinary law of England without Parliamentary sanction, and that would be contrary to a firmly established principle of English constitutional law.

The relationship between the Convention and domestic interpretation has gone through several stages since 1974. The history of this relationship is also the history of Lord Denning's relationship with the

Convention. In R v. Miah, an action relating to the Immigration Act 1971. The European Convention was quoted as forbidding the enactment of retrospective legislation. In Birdi v. Secretary of State for Home Affairs, Lord Denning suggested that the courts could, and should, take the Convention into account when interpreting statutes: the Crown was bound by international law to give effect to its provisions, and all concerned with framing legislation since the Convention came into force must be assumed to have borne it in mind. Lord Denning suggested that an Act which did not conform might have to be held invalid, a view which he subsequently withdrew.

Later in 1975, Lord Denning gave judgment in R v. Secretary of State for the Home Department ex parte Bhajan Singh. Lord Denning repeated his statement that the courts should take the Convention into account when interpreting statutes. He added that those who administered and applied the law ought to have regard to the Convention in carrying out their duties. But he withdrew his suggestion that an Act might be declared invalid if it did not conform to the Convention, and said that in such circumstances, the Act would prevail. It was a situation which he hoped would never actually occur.

In 1976, the position of the Convention was further weakened in R v. Chief Immigration Officer, Heathrow Airport and Another, ex parte Salamat Bibi. Lord Denning said that the Convention was not part of our law, but that if there was any ambiguity in statutes, or uncertainty in the law, the courts would look to the Convention as an aid to interpretation. When Parliament passed an Act, or a minister framed rules, they must be assumed to have had regard to the provisions of the Convention. The position slipped again in Ahmad v. Inner London Education Authority. Lord Denning said that the Convention was not part of English law but the court did its best to see that its decisions were in conformity with it.

The European Convention slowly lost its importance in the thinking of Lord Denning, but there are still other judges who consider it to be of great importance. At the time Lord Denning was strategically placed as Master of the Rolls to hear all of the important appeal cases. In an assessment of Lord Denning's place in recent legal history, Claire Palley distinguishes between Lord Denning's achievement in developing remedies and grounds for relief in litigation against the state and public authorities, and his jaundiced views about certain categories of person whom he believed either behaved unlawfully, or badly, or were prone to do so. Amongst those who were thought to have received less than impartial treatment from Lord Denning were convicted prisoners. (Palley, 1984, pp. 251-366)

It was suggested above that the Convention is alien to the common law tradition, but this does not seem to be the complete picture. One frequent theme over the years is the difficulty posed by what was thought of as the vague wording of the Convention. Doubts were cast on the judges' ability even to make sense of the Articles if they were ever to become part of the domestic law. All of this kind of discussion conveniently ignored the central position of British lawyers in the drafting process, and the British insistence on clarity and precision of the definition of the Articles. The view now being circulated is that the Convention is a fine example of continental vagueness.

Remedies and enforcement

The discussion of the issues has concentrated so far on legal arguments. It is also necessary to look at the nature of the remedies available to prisoners, and at the effectiveness of litigation.

One feature is immediately apparent from the review of cases brought before the English courts: the rarity of civil remedies. The courts have effectively precluded the possibility of prisoners being awarded monetary damages. Lord Justice Goddard held in Arbon v. Anderson that breaches of the modern Prison Rules could not be the basis of action for 'breach of statutory duty'. The problem is that the phrase has two meanings - first, a general meaning of failing to comply with the duties specified in a statute; and second, there is the tort of 'breach of statutory duty'. A breach of the first type may be liable to judicial review while the latter would involve the payment of financial damages. Even if a money award were to be made against a member of the Prison Service, the Home Office would pay both the damages and the costs of the defence. All actions against prison governors and the members of boards of visitors have been paid for by the Prison Department.

More recently, plaintiffs who have sought judicial review of the activities of boards of visitors have asked for remedies in administrative law. At first, the application made by St Germain and others for an order of certiorari, was thought not to be available in such a case. Judges have largely discredited the notion of unfettered administrative discretion, on the grounds that powers must normally be exercised strictly in accordance with the purposes of the statute. (Zellick, 1980, p. 697) The Williams case however is an exception, as it was demonstrated that members of the control unit committee had exceeded the provisions of the rules.

Zellick has suggested that Arbon v. Anderson was not the best case to persuade the courts to intervene in prison administration. The plaintiffs were aliens making claims for damages in war-time for what the court thought to be simply a matter of inconvenience and slight discomfort to the plaintiffs. An administrative law remedy might, in Zellick's opinion, have been more successful. (Zellick, 1981, p. 606) This might not in fact have succeeded as the revolution in administrative law has only occurred in recent years.

Administrative law remedies are relevant only to the immediate case. It is left to the prison authorities to revise their procedures when the court sets aside a disciplinary decision, but it does not prevent the disciplinary case being re-heard. Any suspicion that the proceedings have not been fair can only be reviewed after a long and expensive High Court action. The extent of change in administrative procedures and practices after such decisions have been successfully challenged is unclear.

It needs to be stated clearly that the British government has been accused of violating the guarantee of the right of access to legal advice on three separate occasions (i.e. Knechtl, Golder, and Silver). In one of these instances (Golder) the Court itself has found a violation, and the British government has responded in a limited way. The Home Secretary has made changes either in the Prison Rules or in prison procedures as a result of these cases. Cohen and Taylor in their book Prison Secrets suggest that the Standing Orders which control day-to-day operations were changed to defeat both the letter and the spirit of the Golder decision. Cohen and Taylor suggested that access to lawyers was actually more restricted than previously. (Cohen and Taylor, 1979, pp. 42-8) This comment shows how quickly things have changed in this area. Cohen and Taylor's remarks were made before the series of decisions in the domestic courts which have had important effects on prisoners' access to the courts and to legal representation before boards of visitors when facing disciplinary charges.

The issue of compliance with the decisions of the European Commission and the Court of Human Rights is open to great uncertainty. Sir James Fawcett, who was then President of the Commission of Human Rights, said in evidence to a House of Lords Select Committee that the Court's judgments were not enforceable, and added that more than one judgment had not been implemented. (House of Lords Select Committee, 1978, p. 40) The Court of Human Rights usually makes declaratory judgments which state that actions violate the Convention. The Court does not specify what it considers to be acceptable practice or behaviour. The supervision of enforcement by the Committee of Ministers tends not to be too demanding and this puts the onus on to aggrieved citizens to test the status of any remedial action.

The legal status of prisoners

While there have been relatively few advances and fewer victories for prisoners when attempting to assert their rights, there has been a slow but significant change in the way prisoners are seen. This change can be found in the jurisprudence of both the European institutions and the English courts. The English courts have not taken the view that prisoners were 'slaves of the state', as did their American counterparts. Prisoners in England may not have had many legal rights but they have always had some, although the courts may have been reluctant to intervene in prison administration. The judges seem to have taken the view that once prisoners had been convicted by a demonstrably fair legal system, they should serve their sentences without troubling those in lawful authority over them with the threat of litigation. In their dicta, the judges have frequently referred to the impudence of the plaintiff. To their great surprise and obvious distaste, the judges have found meritorious arguments presented by apparently frivolous and vexatious litigants.

The Commission used to hold a doctrine of 'inherent limitations' which was applied to prisoners' applications. The wording of the Convention gives the impression that its provisions apply to everyone except when one of the explicitly stated restrictions applies. In fact, the Commission adopted a double standard when dealing with convicted prisoners. Until the early 1970s, the Commission was prepared to allow restrictions due to the inherent nature of imprisonment, and for this reason such restrictions did not have to be justified under any of the listed exceptions.

Jacobs condemned the doctrine of inherent limitations as both incorrect and unnecessary. The doctrine is incorrect because the application of special limitations to one class of persons is contrary to the whole idea of the Convention, which is intended to apply equally to all human beings. The wording of the Convention is quite specific: the word 'Everyone' is used throughout the text. Further the doctrine is unnecessary because the permitted exceptions allow wide scope for the control of prisoners and others. Jacobs also suggests that the drafters of the Convention had convicted prisoners in mind when doing their work, as Articles 3 and 4(3) specifically recognise and protect the prisoner. (Jacobs, 1975, pp. 199–200)

The Court of Human Rights took a firm stand on the inherent limitations doctrine in one of its judgments in 1971. The doctrine which now applies requires the state to justify any restriction on the rights guaranteed by the Convention. The change is from a blanket prohibition to individual control. In Golder, the British government tried to justify its control over prisoners' correspondence within the permitted exceptions as well as using the inherent limitations argument. The Court took the view that letters to legal advisers could not be brought within the scope of a ban designed to prevent crime and disorder. The implied threat to all prison administrations is clear – prisoners will have to be given reasoned decisions; but once reasons are given, debate, argument and discussion are sure to follow. The discretionary grant of privileges becomes liable to challenge, and the whole nature of the relationship between the prisoner and prison administration changes.

So far, this discussion of the changing status of prisoners has been derived exclusively from the European connection. There has been a parallel change in the English courts. In both St Germain and in Raymond v. Honey, it has been argued that although a convicted prisoner lost many of the rights of an ordinary citizen, the rights he retained always remained the proper concern of the courts. But the main question to be dealt with by the courts was that of the extent of the remaining rights. Counsel for the plaintiff (Raymond) quoted the judgment of Mr Justice Dickson of the Canadian Supreme Court in the Solosky case heard in 1979

A person confined to prison retains all of his civil rights, other than those expressly or impliedly taken from him in law.

When Raymond v. Honey was heard on appeal in the House of Lords, this statement of principle was quoted with approval by Lord Wilberforce. The decision was that the Prison Act and its Rules did not restrict the right of a prisoner to access to the courts. Lord Bridge of Harwich went further and said that he thought a citizen's right of access to the courts could only be removed by express enactment or by implication in an Act of Parliament. This view of prisoners' legal status has only been established since March 1982 and it remains to be seen how it will be applied in other cases.

Conclusions

Four points are of great importance. First, the central aspects of the daily lives of prisoners are still beyond the review of the courts and have been placed there by the actions of the courts themselves. Decisions on where each prisoner will spend his sentence and the extent of extra deprivations he will suffer e.g. overcrowding, will be unreviewable. Second, the conflicts between the British government and the prisoners in its gaols will continue to be heard by the institutions of the European Convention, and the Government may fail to appreciate how the Court is now interpreting the Convention. The Home Office seems to treat the Convention simply as a static piece of international law which is largely peripheral to its daily concerns. The Silver decision may have the greatest impact of all the cases brought either domestically or in Strasbourg; the Home Office may in the future be required to publish its Standing Orders in order to meet the requirement that actions should have foreseeable consequences and this will mean more information on which litigation and general disputes can be based.

Changes consequent on Silver relate to the third major conclusion from this discussion, that of the difficulty in enforcing the decisions made against prison administrators. A court decision made against either prison staff or boards of visitors is without personal impact. The only threat of a direct personal nature was that to Honey, the assistant prison governor, who was threatened with imprisonment for contempt of court. The court decided that this ironical sentence should not be given as the delay to Raymond's papers was a brief one. But the system of official payment of costs means that the cost of failing to respect the rights of prisoners is very slight to individuals in the Prison Service.

The fourth and final point is that of the very recent change in the judicial view of prisoners' legal status. The courts now seem to have changed their perspective from a negative one to a positive one. Until Raymond v. Honey, the courts said something like this – 'Show us the statute which gives the right to x'. The current situation before the English courts means that prisoners possess all of the rights of an ordinary citizen except those 'taken away expressly or by necessary implication'. This view of prisoners has been accepted by the House of Lords and therefore is binding on all the lower courts. This is perhaps the most significant symbolic change in the legal status of prisoners, although in practice its real effects are not likely to be very great.

Notes

[1] These Standard Minimum Rules were Resolution 73(5) of the Council of Ministers. They are reprinted in JUSTICE, 1983, Appendix 3.

[2] For a description of the processes of drafting and ratification in relation to the European Convention on Human Rights see Lester, 1984, pp. 49-55 and Drzemczewski, 1983.

6 The legal basis of prisoners' rights in the United States

When British readers look at American institutions of government they see strong similarities with the British equivalents. There has been an active interchange of ideas and the similarities are enhanced by a common language. This impression of similarity exists in both the legal and penal fields. Both legal systems share the common law, and have similar ideas about the functions of lawyers and judges. In the penal field, there has been an interchange of ideas and people since the early nineteenth century. But the apparent similarities mask fundamental differences. It may well be that the similarities are now merely a matter of assumptions about a common legal heritage.

Both Britain and America shared the same common law until the War of Independence. Since then the two legal systems have diverged increasingly. The first feature which distinguishes the American system of law and government is a written constitution. The Constitution spells out the rights of the citizen and places limits on the power of the government. The US Constitution is entrenched in the sense that it cannot be easily superseded and can be amended only as a result of special procedures. An Amendment to the Constitution may be proposed if it gains a two-thirds vote in both houses of Congress. The Amendment must then be ratified by the approval of the legislatures in three-quarters of the states within a specified time.

Article III of the Constitution gives to the Supreme Court the power to consider 'all cases, in Law and Equity, arising under this Constitution, the Laws of the United States....'. The power of the Supreme Court to exercise judicial review was established in 1803, and since that time the Court has had the power to void acts of Congress.

In spite of the emphasis on the common law, there has always been a much greater stress in the US on a written Constitution and a codified criminal and civil law. At a very practical level, this has meant that prisoners and others have been able to organise their own arguments for presentation to the courts without recourse to qualified legal advice.

Two concepts: the separation of powers and federalism, will occur frequently in the next two chapters. Put at their simplest, these two concepts can be seen as providing a horizontal and a vertical division in public life. (Gunther, 1964, p. 400) The Constitution divided the federal government into three branches - legislative, executive and judicial. Each of the three branches is constitutionally equal to and independent of the other two. The framers of the Constitution hoped in this way to prevent any single branch from becoming too powerful. The framers also attempted to prevent the consolidation of power by making these branches and officials responsive to different constituencies.

The vertical distribution of power between the federal government and the states is described by the concept of federalism. The US Constitution delegates power to the federal government, while the states have all the residual powers. The Constitution, especially in the first three articles, defines certain legislative, executive and judicial functions of the federal government; there are also implied and inherent powers which go to the federal government. The Constitution reserves to the states all of the powers not exclusively granted to the federal government nor denied in the Constitution to the states. Some powers may be exercised concurrently by the states and by the federal authorities, provided there is no conflict of responsibilities. The supremacy of the federal government is established in Article IV of the Constitution; all state and federal officials are sworn to uphold the Constitution. The federal government may exercise its full powers throughout the US and the states may not interfere with the constitutional activities of federal officials. Congress has had a great deal to say about the extent of state powers and ultimately the Supreme Court has to decide whether state governments' autonomy has been invaded, or whether the states have usurped the powers of federal government.

Americans live under two systems of law, that of the state in which they reside and that of the federal government. The organisation of law enforcement and prisons has been a power largely reserved to the states and this has meant the development of a wide range of sentencing systems and of penal institutions.

Before describing the prisoners' rights cases which have been decided in the American courts it is essential to provide some background information on the prison and court systems. This chapter ends with a discussion of cases which established prisoners' rights of access to the courts, and chapter 7 will be concerned with the more substantive litigation.

Conviction and imprisonment

Each state has its own criminal code, which covers more or less the same range of activities as the criminal law of England. At the same time, there is a federal criminal code which to some extent parallels the state codes but also includes offences across state boundaries or which are concerned with other federal interests such as taxation or counterfeiting. Over the years, the number of offences against the federal criminal code has increased, extending the jurisdiction of the federal authorities. Most offenders will however be charged with offences against the state code and be tried by state courts. Many of the states retain the distinction between felonies and misdemeanours.

Felonies are the more serious crimes and invariably carry sentences of one year or more in prison. Anyone convicted of a misdemeanour can be sentenced to imprisonment of up to one year, or such lesser penalty as allowed by the state penal code. The actual sentence for a felony will vary from state to state, as some states have indeterminate sentencing systems in which a minimum (one year) and a maximum period of imprisonment will be read out by the sentencing judge. In indeterminate systems, the range of the sentence will be specified in the penal code and the judge simply reads out the range appropriate to the offence for which the conviction has been obtained. The actual sentence will be determined at a later date by a parole board. Other states and the federal criminal code employ determinate sentencing systems in much the same way as the court system in England. By 1984, some 43 states had introduced mandatory prison sentences for people convicted of violent offences, 30 states for habitual offenders, 29 for narcotics offences, and 37 states impose such sentences for crimes committed by a person using a pistol. (New York Times, 28 August 1984) Four states have abandoned parole entirely in the drive to increase the courts' sentencing powers. (New York Times, 3 May 1982)

The population of state and federal prisons has increased dramatically in the last decade. The total number of sentenced prisoners in 1971 was 198,061. This figure rose to 242,750 in 1975, and had increased to 581,609 at the end of 1987. Of these totals, the number of federal prisoners has always been less than 30,000. It seems from these figures that not only have prison sentences been increasing in the last decade but the use of imprisonment has been increasing as well. In 1971, the rate of imprisonment was 96.4 per 100,000 of the population, by 1987 the rate was 228 per 100,000 of the population. (The comparable figure for England and Wales in 1987 was 94.1.)   There is a wide variation in the use of imprisonment between the states: in 1981 there were 39 prisoners per 100,000 of the population in New Hampshire while the comparable rate for North Carolina was 256, and the rate for the District of Columbia was 439. (Hacker, 1984, p. 229)

There are fifty different state prison systems, and the federal government has its own system. The range of institutions is difficult to imagine for people coming from countries with a unified prison service. The Federal Bureau of Prisons has its own prisons, ranging from minimum to maximum security conditions. Some house prisoners from several states, though the Federal Bureau can also lease space from state prisons to hold its prisoners. In the state prisons, the standard of life for prison inmates varies greatly from one state to another. The states in the north east tend to have prisons which are more easily recognisable to an English observer - high surrounding walls, single cellular confinement designed to be open to centralised surveillance. Elsewhere the prisons would not be so readily recognisable. In some of the southern states, the majority of the state's prisoners are held on prison farms, successors to the plantations of the nineteenth century. Prisoners on these farms have until the last decade been housed in racially segregated barracks under the supervision of fellow prisoners who had the power of life and death over them. These prison farms were designed to be self-supporting financially and prisoners worked in physically arduous manual labour - 'stoop labour' - in which the field worker stoops at the beginning of the row to be hoed and only stands upright several hundred yards further on. The range of conditions is considerable. The Federal Bureau of Prisons provides the best conditions, and the states of Arkansas and Alabama have generally been considered to have provided the worst.

The majority of the states have developed inmate grievance procedures of one sort or another. These will not be described in any detail as there as many variations as there are states. These mechanisms have been of secondary importance to the courts, and most were developed in response to litigation.

A British visitor is struck by the size of some of the prisons. Many American prisons are much larger than British prisons, with populations of two to three thousand. The California prisons are larger still, some holding as many as five thousand prisoners. The degree of specialisation of prisons also varies - some of the smaller and less populated states have only one prison for all prisoners, those awaiting trial as well as convicted men. The states of North Dakota, New Hampshire and Vermont had 295, 360 and 512 prisoners respectively in June 1981. (Hacker, 1984, p. 228) Other states have extremely sophisticated systems of classification, so their prisons vary from closed maximum security prisons to open, minimum security work camps. The states with the largest prison populations do not invariably have the most sophisticated system - Texas had 30,954 prisoners in June 1981, the vast majority of whom were kept in maximum security conditions. The states of California, New York and Florida each had over 20,000 prisoners in 1981. The New York Times reported that at the end of 1987 the nation's prison population was experiencing a net weekly increase of 750 prisoners.

Prisoners' rights litigation

The bulk of the prisoners' rights cases which have been decided have been concerned with the rights guaranteed by the US Constitution, and the litigation has taken place in the federal courts. In particular, prisoners have brought cases claiming violation of their rights protected by those Amendments to the Constitution usually called the Bill of Rights.

The First Amendment states

> Congress shall make no law respecting an establishment of religion, or prohibiting the free exercise thereof; or abridging the freedom of speech or of the press; or the right of people peaceably to assemble, and to petition the government for a redress of grievances.

Prisoners have used this Amendment to assert their rights in several areas e.g. religious and political beliefs and expression as well as correspondence with family, friends and the media.

The Eighth Amendment states

> Excessive bail shall not be required, nor excessive fines imposed, nor cruel and unusual punishment inflicted.

The phrase 'cruel and unusual punishment' was borrowed from the English Bill of Rights of 1689 and incorporated directly into the US Constitution. The concept is important as it has allowed for the development of standards which reflect contemporary views of what limitations should be placed on imprisonment.

The Fourteenth Amendment states

> All persons born or naturalised in the United States, and subject to the jurisdiction thereof, are citizens of the United States and of

the State in which they reside. No State shall make or enforce any law which shall abridge the privileges or impunities of citizens of the United States; nor shall any State deprive any person of life, liberty or property, without due process of law; nor deny to any person within its jurisdiction the equal protection of the laws.

The significant phrases relate to 'due process of law' and 'equal protection of laws' which have been used to outlaw discrimination against prisoners and to provide them with the safeguards of due process.

The federal court system

Prisoners' rights litigation is usually brought before the federal courts. There are three levels of federal courts - the District Courts, the Courts of Appeals and the Supreme Court. There are 94 federal district courts staffed by an authorised total of 515 judges. Among these are one district court for the District of Columbia, four in the Territories (i.e. Puerto Rico, Virgin Islands, the Canal Zone and Guam), and at least one in every state. With only one exception (the Yellowstone National Park), the boundaries of these courts do not cross state lines. In the more populous states, there are a number of district courts, each having jurisdiction over a part of the state. The number of district courts per state varies from one to four. (Rohde and Spaeth, 1976, p. 55)
    The district courts have original jurisdiction. They are trial courts and handle disputes between citizens of different states and violations of federal law, e.g. of civil rights, patent and copyright, immigration, bankruptcy and postal laws. Between 1910 and 1976, all suits which challenged the constitutionality of a statewide law, regulation or administrative practice had to be heard by a special three-judge district court from whose decision the losing party could appeal directly to the Supreme Court. (Fiss, 1978, p. 96) Any decision of the court in a suit brought against a state's prison system and its officials is binding only on those who are party to the dispute. A class action which may be brought by a logical class of claimants (e.g. all prisoners in a state prison system) is designed to be binding on the state prison administration generally. The district court's ruling will apply only to the state in which the district court is located, even if there are similarities between prison systems in different states. A ruling by a district court does not bind its fellow courts at that level; precedent is provided by a superior court only. (Glick, 1973, p. 299)
    The next level of jurisdiction is that of the US Courts of Appeals. The US and the Territories are divided geographically into eleven judicial circuits, each of which has a court of appeals. The District of Columbia Judicial Circuit covers only the Federal territory. All the other circuits are numbered, and contain between three and nine states, and between five and eighteen district courts. Each state or territory is wholly contained within a single circuit.
    Each court of appeals has from three to fifteen judges, but usually three judges hear a case. In 1978, the authorised total number of circuit judges was increased to 132. (Congressional Quarterly Almanac, 1978, p. 173) The jurisdiction of these courts is appellate only. The rulings of each court of appeals are binding on the district courts which comprise that circuit and it is quite possible for the circuits to arrive at different conclusions on similar topics.

At the zenith of the judicial hierarchy there is the US Supreme Court. Since 1869, the size of the Supreme Court has been set at eight associate justices and a Chief Justice. When a vacancy occurs on the Court, the President nominates a candidate and sends that name to the Senate. The Senate has to consider the candidate, and if a majority of the Senate support the nomination, the candidate is confirmed and fills the vacancy. The Supreme Court has both appellate and original jurisdiction. The Constitution specifies the original jurisdiction which is granted to all cases affecting ambassadors, other public ministers and consuls, and those in which a State shall be party. The Supreme Court has appellate jurisdiction over the federal courts, so appeals will be heard from the two lower levels.

Federally protected civil rights

How then do prisoners' rights cases actually arrive before the federal courts? Prisoners have rarely until recently been able to bring legal actions against the state by which they are incarcerated within the courts of that state. The states have constitutions which guarantee civil rights, but some have statutes which treat the convicted person as being civilly dead. The term civil death has been declared judicially 'to import a deprivation of all rights the exercise or enjoyment of which depends on some provision of positive law'. Prisoners may lose their rights under the state constitution following conviction, but they retain their rights guaranteed by the US Constitution or by federal statute law unless these are explicitly removed or suspended by the law under which they have been convicted.

The great majority of prisoners' rights cases are brought by using a section of the federal Civil Rights Act of 1871. This section is codified in the US Code as '42 USCS section 1983' and for brevity's sake is usually referred to simply as section 1983. The wording of section 1983 is

> Every person who, under colour of any statute, ordinance, regulation, custom, or usage, of any State or Territory, subjects, or causes to be subjected, any citizen of the United States or other person within the jurisdiction thereof to the deprivation of any rights, privileges, or immunities secured by the Constitution and laws, shall be liable to the party injured in an action at law, suit in equity, or other proper proceeding for redress.

This section was originally one of several Civil Rights Acts introduced after the Civil War both to guarantee the rights of newly-freed slaves and to cope with attempts in the southern states to prevent enfranchisement and to harass federal officials. The intention behind the Act was to allow people direct access to the federal courts when it was supposed that state courts would not be sympathetic to actions brought against state officials. For many years this Act was left unused, largely as a result of the narrow interpretation given to it by the Courts. Between 1871 and 1920 it appears to have been invoked in only 21 cases. (Emerson et al, 1967, p. 1447) The growth of the civil rights movement generally in the 1950s and 1960s revived this legislation and it has since become the main legal basis of prisoners' litigation.

Section 1983 of the Civil Rights Act has the great advantage that suit may be brought before bringing the case to the federal courts without having to exhaust the state remedies. The section also means that people

have a method of bringing an action against an official's abuse of his
position.

Litigation by prisoners

Two notable procedural features apply to civil rights litigation by
prisoners. The first involves the recognition that many prisoners will
be without funds to pay for legal advice; prisoners may petition the
courts to proceed in forma pauperis. The courts may authorise the
commencement of any suit or action without pre-payment of fees and
costs, or security by a person who makes an affidavit that he is unable
to pay such costs. The courts may then request an attorney to represent
any person unable to hire counsel. The courts may dismiss the case if
they find the allegation of poverty to be untrue, or if it is found that
the action is frivolous or malicious. (28 USCS section 1915) The
decision to allow the case to proceed in forma pauperis is in theory
made solely on the financial status of the plaintiff rather than on the
merits of the case. Plaintiffs do not have a constitutional right to
counsel, and a court appointed counsel has not in the past had any
guarantee of payment. The introduction of the Civil Rights Attorney's
Fees Awards Act of 1976 authorises the court to allow the prevailing
party a reasonable attorney's fee as part of the costs in a civil rights
action.
  The second feature of prisoners' litigation is the absence of
qualified legal advice. Many prisoners bring cases pro se (i.e. on their
own behalf). This has meant that many actions begin with the
presentation to the courts of petitions which are prepared by semi-
literate or illiterate prisoners who have little or no clear idea of
either the constitution or the law but who know or feel that they have
been the victim of some wrongful act, real or imagined. The Committee of
the Federal Judiciary under the chairmanship of Circuit Judge Aldisert
recommended the adoption of standard forms which would allow a simple
retelling of the alleged complaint in non-legal language. (Aldisert,
1980, p. 45) The federal judges have always been aware that important
issues may be concealed in poorly prepared complaints, and it has been
accepted that looser standards are required of pro se complaints than in
other cases, even to the extent that the judges may interpret the
complaint to find the complaint being made and its appropriate section
of the constitution.

Claims by federal prisoners

Prisoners held in federal prisons can also bring civil rights actions
against the Federal Bureau of Prisons and its personnel. Unlike state
prisoners who can proceed under section 1983, an inmate of a federal
prison may bring an action for damages and injunctive relief by a writ
of mandamus which orders a specified person to do or not to do certain
specified actions. Actions for damages may also be brought under the
Federal Tort Claims Act which allows federal officials to be sued for
damages for wrongful actions committed as a part of their official
duties. Prisoners who use this Act are required first to exhaust all of
the available administrative remedies. (Aldisert, 1980, pp. 42-3)

Class actions

A distinctive procedural feature of the American legal system is the
class action. The origins of the class action have been traced back to

English law, although it seems to have disappeared from English practice in the mid nineteenth century. (Anon, 1976, p. 1335; Yeazell, 1977, pp. 866-96) The Federal Rules of Civil Procedure allow the aggregation of instances of similar litigation. Aggregation has three basic advantages

1. class actions are useful in situations where an action regardless of its individual form either affects the interests of non-parties; or,
2. the class action provides an economical and convenient forum for disposing of similar lawsuits; or,
3. class suits provide a device for spreading the cost of litigation among numerous litigants.

Class suits are based on the theory that 'the representative parties must fairly and adequately protect the interests of the class'. (Federal Rules of Procedure 23a4) Class actions must raise a common question of fact or law which affects a large number of people. Some courts have added the requirement that claims have to show that the complaint is typical as well as common to the experience of members of the class.

Class actions are widely used in civil rights cases, and in the period 1973 to 1976, about 10% of all class actions commenced were prisoners' petitions. (Anon, 1976, p. 1325)

Forms of relief

In section 1983 cases, several forms of relief are available. The courts may award nominal, compensatory, or punitive damages and/or injunctive relief or declaratory judgments. Nominal damages are awarded in cases where it is possible to show that while a plaintiff had actually been deprived of a right, e.g. due process, it cannot be shown that an actual injury had resulted from this deprivation. Compensatory damages are available where it is possible to show that legal rights have been invaded, and where there is a federal right to sue for violation of those rights, e.g. injury to a prisoner while his hair was being cut forcibly just prior to release from custody. Punitive damages may be paid to deter or punish violations of constitutional rights e.g. where the defendant has acted wilfully and in gross disregard for the rights of the plaintiff, as in the case of an arrestee beaten up after arrest without a warrant. Injunctive relief allows the courts to exercise a broad discretion to control administrative processes but there is also the requirement on the judiciary to avoid interfering in areas best left to the expertise of prison officials. This type of injunction is designed to remedy the defects that are thought to infringe the constitutional rights of the prisoner-plaintiff. Injunctions are easier to enforce to prevent an action, as in the case of a court forbidding the use of a jail for the holding of pre-trial detainees, but are less effective when they require a course of positive action such as building a new prison. Finally, there are declaratory judgments which allow any court to declare the rights and other legal relations of interested parties whether or not any other kind of relief is being sought. (Sensenich, 1976, pp. 478-502) In prisoners' rights cases, declaratory injunctions have been sought in order to establish the rights that prisoners have been claiming. It is usual for injunctive relief and declaratory judgment to be sought simultaneously so that judges can order remedies to bring about a situation where the constitutional rights that have been violated may be protected.

There is one further strand to prisoners' rights ltigation which needs to be mentioned: the use of the writ of habeas corpus. In habeas corpus actions, the prisoner is claiming that his conviction was only obtained through the violation of his federally guaranteed constitutional rights at some stage in the process from arrest to conviction and that this can only be corrected by his release from custody. Confusion has crept into prisoners' rights litigation, as some prisoners have tried to bring claims which cross the boundaries between different kinds of procedure. While the writ of habeas corpus does not fall directly in the area of prisoners' civil rights, it is important to remember the writ's existence and its continued importance in the US when in England it is most likely to be used when a person is detained, for example, as an illegal immigrant or so that he may be deported, or because he is mentally ill. This use of habeas corpus is a challenge to the authority of the administrative order which led to the detention. (Wade, 1961, p. 540)

Access to the courts

Until the 1960s, prisoners had very little success in bringing actions aginst prison administrators. The rationale underlying the court decisions to keep prisoners out of the court has been to prevent them from harassing prison administrators by litigation. The courts were reluctant to review administrative decisions for fear of subverting the authority of prison officials, the discipline of prisons and the efforts of prison administrators to accomplish the objectives of the system entrusted to their care and management. (Anon, 1963, pp. 508-9)

The courts applied what has been called a 'hands-off' policy in relation to prisoners' rights. The justification of this policy has varied over time. The generally accepted view in the nineteenth century was that expressed by a Virginia state judge who wrote that prisoners had no more rights than slaves, and that prisoners were the slaves of the state. (Ruffin v. Commonwealth, 1871) The implication seems to be that the state had complete control over the prisoner and could do to him what it would; the prisoner has no claims on his master, the state.

Judicial non-intervention has also been justified on the grounds that prison conditions were outside the jurisdiction of the courts at either state or federal level. A typical example of this attitude was given by a Tenth Circuit Court of Appeals Judge in 1954

courts are without power to supervise prison administration, or to interfere with the ordinary prison rules or regulations. (Banning v. Looney, 1954)

Prisoners' litigation was rejected irrespective of the means used by litigants.

The Civil Rights Act had considerable potential as a basis for litigation, but this was not realised until the 1960s. In the intervening years, Civil Rights Act actions were unsuccessful, as the courts construed the rights claimed in a narrow way. The courts also declared that allegations involving brutal treatment, unwarranted solitary confinement, censorship of mail and other features of prison mismanagement involved considerations of federalism and stated that it was not the function of the federal courts to supervise state penal systems. State prisoners were told to seek relief in the state courts, and these courts would also deny relief on the grounds that it was not within their power to supervise prison administration. The courts also used another line of reasoning, by denying relief rather than jurisdiction. In these cases, the federal courts used the reasoning from habeas corpus cases which declared that nearly all of the deprivations inflicted on prisoners were matters of internal prison management, but no relief short of release from custody was available and release was not justified. (Anon, 1963, p. 518)

Tort actions were equally ineffective. The Federal Tort Claims Act was available only for claims of $10,000 or more, and tort action in the state courts was frequently prevented by the existence of statutes proclaiming the civil death of prisoners, thus precluding them from being party to litigation. Also, potential defendants in prison litigation were protected by doctrines of sovereign immunity and administrative discretion. (Anon, 1963, p. 513) The principle was established that the US government was not responsible for the actions of its officers if they were exercising some discretionary power, even though the act causing the damage was done negligently. (Schwartz and Wade, 1972, p. 195)

A good example of the 'hands-off' doctrine in action is provided by Siegel v. Ragen, which was heard by the Seventh Circuit Court of Appeals in 1950. This case involved the claims by prisoners that Ragen (the prison warden at Stateville Penitentiary, Illinois) had stolen prisoners' welfare funds; had transferred prisoners to other prisons, or had segregated them in isolation cells, which constituted an unusual punishment; and had closed down the law library used by prisoners to prepare their litigation. The tone employed by the judge was dismissive. He found that the rights claimed were not guaranteed by the US Constitution, and continued

> The Government of the United States is not concerned with, nor has it power to control or regulate the internal discipline of the penal institutions of its constituent states. All such powers are reserved to the individual states.

The plaintiffs were rebuked for not having used the Illinois state laws to obtain redress, or alternatively not having sought a public inquiry into the alleged mismanagement. The judge added that since 1827, the state laws of Illinois provided that conviction of felony led to loss of civil rights

> (the felon) has become an alien in his own country and worse, he can be restored only as a matter of grace (a pardon), while an alien may acquire citizenship as a matter of right.

The plaintiffs had stated no facts which would entitle them to relief under the federal Civil Rights Act.

The situation began to change in the 1960s, as the courts began to enforce the Civil Rights Act more rigorously. The US Supreme Court opened the way for prisoners' litigation in Monroe v. Pape (1961). The facts of the case concerned a search conducted by Chicago police officers. The important issue settled by the Supreme Court was that the Civil Rights Act could be applied to the actions of state officials when it was claimed that these officials had violated rights guaranteed by the due process clause of the Fourteenth Amendment.

The Supreme Court held that by enacting the Civil Rights Act, Congress had intended to give relief to parties deprived of constitutional rights, privileges and immunities by an official's abuse of his position. One of the purposes of the legislation was to provide a federal right in the federal courts, precisely because a right guaranteed by the Fourteenth Amendment might be denied by state agencies. Moreover, the federal remedy was independent of the state remedy, and need not be preceded by exhaustion of other remedies.

This new means of access to the federal courts was not immediately available to prisoners. In Cooper v. Pate (1963), Cooper, a Black Muslim, claimed that he had been prevented from practising his religious belief. Although one of the grounds used in the claim was the guarantee of equal protection of laws in the Fourteenth Amendment, other prisoners were able to have Bibles, while he was not allowed a Koran, this was rejected in favour of the argument that the discipline that had to be maintained in prisons was not under the supervision of the federal courts.

As the Federal Courts gradually accepted claims under the Civil Rights Act, the general issue of access to the courts was resolved by treating cases on their merits. From early in the 1970s, the Supreme Court has operated an 'open-door' policy. The question of access to the courts has undergone a change of emphasis. The principal issue in recent years concerns the effectiveness of prisoners' access to the courts. The Supreme Court has dealt with this issue on at least three separate occasions.

In Johnson v. Avery (1969), the Supreme Court heard of the situation where Johnson had violated a prison regulation prohibiting inmates from helping other inmates to prepare writs and other legal documents and was placed in solitary confinement as a punishment. The Supreme Court held that

> unless, and until, the state provided some reasonable alternative to assist inmates in the preparation of petitions....it could not validly enforce the prison regulation barring inmates for furnishing such assistance to other prisoners.

The Supreme Court had earlier refused to allow states to charge a fee for the filing of writs to avoid discriminating against the indigent. Prison 'writ writers' might be a menace to prison discipline, as the administrators had claimed, but it was not for the prison administrators to protect the courts. The reality of the prison regulation was that it prevented access to the courts by deprived prisoners. There were techniques potentially available which allowed prisoners to exercise their constitutional rights, such as legal advice from public defenders and law students, and until such an alternative was made available, prisoners could help each other.

The main issues in Wolff v. McDonnell (1974) are dealt with in chapter 7, but one is of importance here. Wolff claimed that the inmate legal assistance programme in the prison where he was detained did not meet constitutional standards, and that the regulations governing the reading of mail to and from attorneys were improper.

The US Supreme Court held that it was constitutionally permissible to require that mail from an attorney to a prisoner should be identified as such, and that as a protection against smuggling contraband, the prison authorities might open this mail in the prisoner's presence. A prisoner's lawyer might also be required to identify himself before he could claim special treatment of letters marked 'privileged'. The authorities were entitled to check that senders were actually members of the Bar. The issue of the adequacy of legal assistance was remanded to the district court for further inquiry, but the Supreme Court seemed to have implicitly accepted the extension of the Johnson v. Avery requirement to civil rights cases.

A more recent Supreme Court case on access to the courts makes

explicit and formalises the trend implicit in <u>Wolff</u> and
<u>Johnson</u> v. <u>Avery</u>. In <u>Bounds</u> v. <u>Smith</u> (1977), the Supreme Court
considered allegations that prisoners in the correctional facilities of
North Carolina were denied access to the courts in violation of their
Fourteenth Amendment rights by the state's failure to provide legal
research facilities. The district court had found in favour of the
prisoners, and approved a plan proposed by the state for the
establishment of several libraries across the state, though it held that
legal advice facilities need not be provided. The court of appeals had
affirmed the judgment and basic provisions.
The Supreme Court affirmed these decisions. The Opinion of the Court
was that the fundamental constitutional right of access to the courts
required state prison authorities to assist inmates in the preparation
of

> meaningful legal papers by providing prisoners with adequate law
> libraries or adequate assistance from persons trained in the law.

Prisoners' access to the courts had to be adequate, effective and
meaningful. The Supreme Court had consistently required states to make
positive provisions to assure access to the courts. Arguments about cost
were not acceptable when constitutional rights were involved. The
Supreme Court recognised the risk that trial judges might miss important
cases if the issues were not properly presented and argued.
There has been a sudden and relatively rapid thaw in the courts'
attitudes to prisoners. The 'hands-off' doctrine has been replaced by a
concern with effective access to the courts. The issue of access has
been transformed into a problem of quality. It is open to debate whether
this is a recognition of the procedural safeguards which have been
provided in other areas and to other groups of potential and actual
litigants, or whether it is in part a response to the growth in <u>pro se</u>
litigation, which is frequently of poor quality. The question of access
also leaves aside the issue of the outcome of substantive litigation in
other areas of prison life.

Conclusions

The American systems of courts and prisons which appear superficially to
be similar to their English counterparts are in reality quite different.
The scale of organisations in the US is much larger. Any attempt to
survey the entirety of all the state prisons' system would be extremely
difficult, as there are estimated to be at least 4,500 penal
establishments in the country. (<u>New York Times</u>, 5 January 1982) This
problem is not of great significance for the present study as prisoners'
rights litigation has been largely dealt with by the federal courts.
One feature of the organisation of the American legal system that does
cause difficulty is that it is not a unitary system. This means that
the only legal precedent which binds all federal courts is that deriving
from the Supreme Court. Development may be very uneven at the lowest
level, and there can be considerable variation across the country unless
and until an authoritative decision is made by the Supreme Court.
The American legal system has several features which are highly
relevant to prisoners' rights. The first and most important, is the
existence of a written constitution. This provides the basis on which
claims may be made - it is a document of great symbolic importance,
containing as it does the Bill of Rights. The Bill of Rights sets out

the limits on the relationship between the citizen and the state. The existence of this document has not always in fact meant that prisoners have been afforded the protections of the Constitution. The court were reluctant to interfere with the rights of the states to manage their own affairs.

This chapter has been concerned with only on substantive area of litigation - prisoners' access to the federal courts. Cases were reported which showed how the old doctrine of 'hands off' was overthrown in the late 1950s and early 1960s. The Supreme Court under Chief Justice Warren (in office from 1958 to 1968) has been described as having one characteristic common to its decisons

> a vigorous concern for, almost an obsession with, the values of equality. (Funston, 1977, p. 28)

In a long series of case the Supreme Court brought the protections of the Bill of Rights to bear on issues previously thought of as falling within the exclusive jurisdiction of the states. Constitutional safeguards were extended to groups assumed to have lost their rights through their own actions, or through their status as poor or immigrants. This approach was criticised because it was thought to imply that every socially perceived need should have a remedy, and that the Court was looking for implied rights rather than rights explicitly stated in the Constitution. The consequences of this change of attitude by the Supreme Court were important, because once the right of access to the federal courts had been recognised, a powerful weapon became available to prisoners.

The federal courts have also recognised that mere access to the courts is not enough and that procedural complexity will reduce the use made of the courts by the disadvantaged. Usually these groups are the poor and illiterate, those in greatest need of protection. Pro se litigation makes it possible for prisoners to bring their own actions without qualified legal advice. Prisoners without means can proceed in forma pauperis which removes the requirement of the pre-payment of court fees. The courts have gone beyond simple inquiries into access, and have tried to insure that this right is an effective one. Prisoners are able to consult lawyers, legal aides, and university law students. When the state does not provide these resources, it must provide a law library to enable prisoners to prepare their cases. The following chapter is concerned with the ways in which these rights and procedures have been used by prisoners.

7 Prisoners' rights litigation in the United States

The relative ease with which litigation may be brought in the federal courts has led to a rapid increase in the number of cases brought by prisoners, claiming that their constitutional rights have been violated in some way. The actual numbers will be described later, but it is important to indicate clearly at this stage that in the review of court decisions which follows, a certain amount of selection has been necessary. There have been many thousands of prisoners' rights cases, and there have been several hundred important decisions which have extended prisoners' rights in a wide range of aspects of prison life. The cases described below have been chosen to illustrate: (i) the types of issues brought before the courts; (ii) the types of judgments and decisions given by the courts; and (iii) the issues which are at the boundaries of the debate about the extent of prisoners' rights.

The majority of the cases discussed refer to convicted and sentenced prisoners. This usually means prisoners who are serving relatively long terms for felonies rather than people awaiting trial or those seving short periods of custody for misdemeanours in local jails. There are exceptions to this general rule when, for example, the Supreme Court has decided an issue which provides precedent for similar issues in another area of litigation; in Bell v. Wolfish the Supreme Court decided what constituted overcrowding in a case brought by pre-trial detainees (i.e. remand prisoners). The standard specified in Bell v. Wolfish provided the basis for subsequent cases brought by prisoners in state penitentiaries and prisons.

Attention will be paid in this chapter to cases heard by all three levels of federal courts on the following themes
- due process;
- cruel and unusual punishment;

- freedom of expression;
- freedom of religion;
- rights to medical care; and,
- right to privacy.

Due process

The due process clause of the Fourteenth Amendment provides an essential
starting point for any discussion of prisoners' rights litigation. The
requirement that the due process of law should be followed in any case
involving the deprivation of life, liberty or property is one which
applies to all citizens in their dealings with government agencies, and
it reaches its peak in the criminal courts. The rights of accused
persons at risk of losing life or liberty are many, and they are well
protected as a result of a string of Supreme Court decisions in the
1960s and 1970s. The 'due process revolution' as it has been called
reached into many areas of public life. (Graham, 1970) The requirements
of due process in a hearing before an administrative agency might
include

(1) The right to notice, including an adequate formulation of the
subjects and issues involved in the case;
(2) The right to present adversary evidence (both testimonial and
documentary) and argument;
(3) The right to rebut adverse evidence, through cross-examination
and other appropriate means;
(4) The right to appear with legal counsel;
(5) The right to have the decision based only upon evidence
introduced into the record of the hearing;
(6) The right to have a written record, which consists of a
transcript of the testimony and arguments, together with the
documentary evidence and all other papers filed in the proceeding.
(Schwartz and Wade, 1972, pp. 107-8)

The courts have had to decide which and how many of these rights should
be exercised by prisoners in their dealings with prison administrators.
The due process cases fall into two main areas - prison disciplinary
hearings, classification and transfer decisions.

Prison disciplinary hearings

In the 1970s there were three cases in which the Supreme Court
considered the extent of due process required in prison discipline
hearings. The most significant was Wolff v. McDonnell. In Wolff, the
Supreme Court was asked to consider whether the prison disciplinary
system of Nebraska prisons was constitutionally defective in that
prisoners were not given the protection of due process; and that they
could lose good-time (the equivalent of remission for good behaviour) as
a result of disciplinary decisions being entered in their records
although the hearings had not respected their due process rights. The
Supreme Court held that a prisoner does not lose all of the
constitutional protections of due process and although the prison
disciplinary hearings do not implicate the full list of due process
rights, such hearings must be governed by a mutual accommodation between
the needs of the institution and generally applicable constitutional
requirements. An adverse decision at a disciplinary hearing can involve

the loss of good-time, and this means that certain minimum due process requirements must be met. Advance notice of the discipline charges has to be provided in writing 24 hours before the hearing. There then has to be 'a written statement by the factfinders as to the evidence relied on and the reasons for the disciplinary action'. In these circumstances, inmates should be allowed to call witnesses and to present documentary evidence in their defence if this does not jeopardise institutional safety or legitimate correctional goals.

The Supreme Court held that inmates do not have the constitutional right to confront and cross-examine in discipline hearings, as these procedures are within the exercise of discretion of prison officials because of the possibility of serious disruption in the prison. Unlike persons accused of criminal offences, inmates do not have the right to retain legal counsel, although in some very serious cases, substitute counsel may be provided. The Supreme Court did not think that the disciplinary board was sufficiently impartial to satisfy the due process requirement, but did not make any specific recommendations The suggested procedures all seem to be designed to give the appearance of fairness to the disciplinary hearings, and to reduce the impression that it is simply an arm of the administration.

In Baxter v. Palmigiano (1976), the Supreme Court was asked to look again at the due process requirements of prison disciplinary hearings. The Supreme Court held that prison inmates do not have a due process right to counsel in prison disciplinary hearings, even when the charges involve conduct punishable as crime under state law. The Fifth Amendment to the Constitution, which forbids people being compelled to give evidence against themselves does not forbid the drawing of adverse inferences against a state prison inmate in disciplinary hearings. The Court re-affirmed the previous decision against a right to cross-examine and confront witnesses. In the case before them, some aspects of due process were required because the charges were of serious misconduct. In the main, the decisions in Wolff were left to stand.

The third Supreme Court case in this area is Hughes v. Rowe. The prisoner claimed that his due process rights had been violated in that disciplinary action had been taken against him for violation of the prison regulations. The prisoner had admitted that he had consumed an alcoholic drink with two other inmates; this admission was made at a discipline board hearing held two days after he had been charged with the discipline offence and placed in segregation. The Supreme Court granted a motion for certiorari requiring the lower courts to look again at the case. The Court stated its Opinion that although the allegations made by the petitioner about bias and procedural irregularities in the disciplinary hearing among other things were insufficient to require further proceedings in the district court, the allegation that he had been unnecessarily placed in solitary confinement should have required some response by the defendants. Although this case is not important in terms of the substantive area of legal rights which have been defined, its significance is in showing how the Supreme Court has a wide discretion, which it is prepared to use, to require the inferior courts to look seriously at the claims made by prisoners who have not had access to professional legal advice. The lower courts in this case had dismissed the claim, as they did not think that a constitutional violation had been demonstrated. The Supreme Court was insisting on a trial of the merits of the case, and a response from the government agency responsible.

The case of Johnson v. Anderson, decided in 1974, is important because it demonstrates quite clearly the wide scope given to prison administrators over prison discipline. The district court held that it was necessary to strike a balance between the inmates' rights and the state's legitimate interest in both the security of the prison and the rehabilitation of the prisoners. The due process clause requires notice of charges and the opportunity to rebut them before being placed in solitary confinement but when the prison authorities were faced with an emergency of this kind, it was necessary to act first and to hold hearings afterwards. The reasons of security were important and had to be acted upon to prevent further disruption. But the district court recognised that any substantial deprivation should require fairness of procedure, as there is always the risk of factual error. In this case, when the emergency had ended, it should then have been possible to hold a hearing. It was thought that these circumstances were unlikely to recur, so no injunctive relief was granted.

In 1981, the Seventh Circuit Court of Appeals was asked to consider whether a prisoner's due process rights had been violated when a disciplinary committee was not provided with exculpatory evidence, and the prisoner was not informed of the charges against him. These issues were heard in Chavis v. Rowe. The Court of Appeals decided that there had been a miscarriage of justice in that exculpatory evidence had not been disclosed to the disciplinary hearing. The prison officials could not claim immunity from damages, as they had not acted in good faith. On the contrary, they had not implemented the requirements established in Wolff v. McDonnell some two years previously, and they had suppressed evidence. The prison authorities had ignored their constitutional duty, and as a result Chavis had spent six months in segregation for an offence he did not commit.

The issue of the general lock-up of the whole prison population has also been considered judicially. In 1982, the Ninth Circuit Court of Appeals was asked to consider the claim in Pepperling v. Crist that a general lock-up while a search was conducted violated prisoners' constitutional rights, because it punished the innocent. The court rejected this claim on the ground that there was nothing to indicate that the lock-up was intended to be punitive. The court stated that another view might have been taken if the prisoners had been told that they would be locked up until someone confessed to have broken some disciplinary rule.

The issue of which due process requirements apply when prisoners are charged with criminal offences was decided in United States v. Gouveia et al. (1984). This case was a consolidated appeal concerning six inmates. Four were inmates of a federal prison at Lompoc in California and they were placed in administrative detention during the investigation of the murder of a fellow inmate which took 19 months.

The Supreme Court stated that rights to counsel were triggered only by the initiation of formal criminal proceedings even when the accused were already in custody. The reason for this decision was that precedent had established over a long period that a right to counsel attaches only at or after the initiation of adversary proceedings. This interpretation depends not only on the literal language of the Sixth Amendment which describes the rights of those accused of crimes. Counsel is there to provide aid at the trial, to help the defendant cope with the intricacies of the law and the advocacy of the public prosecutor. When the right to counsel has been extended to pre-trial hearings, this has been because these hearings have shared the characteristics of judicial proceedings. The extension of counsel to these hearings is designed to prevent the defendant's fate from being settled prematurely thus reducing a trial to a mere formality.

In 1985, the Supreme Court held that the due process clause did not require prison officials' reasons for denying the prisoner's request to call witnesses at a disciplinary hearing to be recorded in the administrative record. In Ponte v. Real the Supreme Court stated that a prisoner must be told why his request was being refused, but a written record is only one way of discharging the prison officials' duty of proving they had a legitimate reason for refusing to call the witnesses reuqested by the prisoner

Classification and transfers

Prisoners have asked the courts to consider the due process safeguards governing the systems of classification used by prison administrators and the related matters of transfers either to other types of prison or transfers to other institutions, e.g. mental hospitals. These cases can be seen as an extension of the issues raised by the cases involving prison discipline, as most of the classification and transfer cases are concerned with prisoners who are moved for disciplinary reasons.

In Clonce v. Richardson (1974), the district court was asked to consider the complaint of a prisoner who had been transferred involuntarily to a behaviour modification programme which it was argued involved a major change in the conditions of confinement. The district judge held that as there were major changes in the conditions of confinement, the prisoners were entitled to the minimum due process requirements set down in Wolff v. McDonnell. These due process requirements were still necessary, even though the Bureau of Prisons argued that the transfers were for the benefit of those being transferred. The test to be applied was that of the major change in conditions of confinement.

The Supreme Court has considered transfers on three occasions between 1976 and 1979. In the first of these cases, Meachum v. Fano, the Supreme Court was asked to consider the complaint of a prisoner who had appeared before a prison classification board after there had been nine serious fires in the prison in two-and-a-half months. The outcome of the board's deliberations was 30 days' segregation and transfer to another prison.

The Supreme Court quoted Wolff on the need for an adequate hearing of discipline charges. Then, in a departure from previous thinking, the question was raised as to whether the transfer infringed or implicated a 'liberty' interest within the meaning of the due process clause. A conviction for a criminal offence extinguished the prisoner's liberty to the extent that the State could confine him in any of its prisons. The possibility that life may be more agreeable in one prison rather than another does not of itself signify a 'liberty' interest when there is a transfer. If the Court decided that this case should be subject to judicial review, it would bring in a wide spectrum of discretionary decisions which traditionally have been the business of prison administrators. The Court was unwilling to require hearings before prisoners could be transferred to less pleasant conditions. This case could be distinguished from Wolff v. McDonnell, as the liberty interest in that case was protected by a state law; in the case now before the court a sentence of imprisonment under Massachussetts' state law did not specify the prison in which the sentence was to be served. Prison officials had a wide measure of discretion over the allocation of prisoners to different institutions, and this discretion was not limited to cases of serious misconduct. It was then stated in plain language that the due process clause does not impose a nationwide rule requiring hearings before transfers between prisons.

The third of the transfer cases was decided at the same time as Meachum v. Fano. This concerned the transfer of a prisoner from Attica prison in the aftermath of the riot of 1971. In Montayne v. Haymes, (1976) Haymes claimed that his rights to due process had been infringed, as he had been transferred from Attica to another prison without a hearing. The Supreme Court took the view that the due process clause did not by its own force require hearings whenever the prison authorities transferred a prisoner even when the transfer involved 'substantially burdensome consequences'. The Opinion of the Court was that the due process liberty interest was not infringed unless there existed some right or justifiable expectation rooted in state law to the effect that transfer could only take place for misbehaviour or upon the occurrence of some other specified events.

The third case considered by the Supreme Court in this period involved the transfer of a prisoner out of the prison system. In Vitek v. Jones (1979) the Supreme Court held that an involuntary transfer of a state prisoner to a state mental hospital without notice or a hearing did violate the due process clause of the Fourteenth Amendment. In Nebraska, the law authorises the transfer of prisoners when a designated physician finds that the prisoner 'suffers from a mental disease or defect' and 'cannot be given proper treatment' in prison. For the central part of the judgment, the Court concentrated on the prisoner's liberty interest and held that such an interest was present in this kind of case. A criminal conviction and prison sentence, Justice White wrote

> extinguish an individual's right to freedom from confinement for the term of the sentence, but they do not authorise the state to classify him as mentally ill and to subject him to involuntary psychiatric treatment without due process protections.

Involuntary transfer to a mental hospital was a stigmatising event and the prisoner was likely to be exposed to behaviour modification in the hospital.

The Supreme Court has started to retreat from the standards laid down in Wolff and Meachum. In the 1982 Term, the Supreme Court heard two cases which again raised due process issues. In Olim v. Wakinekona there was a challenge by Wakinekona to his transfer from Hawaii's state prison to Folsom prison in California. Wakinekona had been singled out as a troublemaker, and after a committee hearing the prison administration recommended that he be transferred to a maximum security prison on the mainland which would be better equipped to cope with him. Wakinekona alleged that the committee hearing had failed to comply with the due process clause because it broke one of the Hawaii prison regulations requiring that at least three members of the committee should not have been involved previously with the case. The Supreme Court took the view that Wakinekona had no liberty interest in remaining within any one state while in prison.

In Hewitt v. Helms the Supreme Court considered the constitutionality of the state of Pennsylvania's decision to place Aaron Helms in solitary confinement for administrative reasons. He had been placed in restrictive confinement after a prison riot in December 1978, and was charged with assaulting prison staff. The Supreme Court appled a two-step test to decide whether the due process requirement existed. The court looked first to the Constitution and then to state law to see whether Helms possessed a liberty interest. Justice Rehnquist, who gave the majority opinion, said that it was necessary to balance the prisoner's hardship against the prison officials' need for broad discretion to deal with the difficult task of administering prisons. It was concluded that there is no liberty interest inherent in the due process clause of the Fourteenth Amendment. There was, however, a liberty interest in Pennsylvania state law which sets out a list of substantive conditions to be followed before prisoners could be segregated. The second step was to determine what process was due to Helms. This involved a balancing of individual interests versus the general prison population's interests. The majority decided that the state had a greater interest in prison control than in preserving Helms' rights.

In his commentary on the 1982 Supreme Court Term, R.M. Cover has argued that these two decisions are remarkable for three reasons.
1. The analyses on which they are based begin from the presumption that prisoners' core constitutional rights are minimal. Their rights have been curtailed as a consequence of their own actions.
2. The balance has shifted toward governmental concerns.
3. The Supreme Court is strongly resistant to fettering administrative discretion, and gives little weight to maltreatment of certain prisoners. (Cover, 1983, pp. 108-9)

The Supreme Court managed to find the possibility of a liberty interest in a state law relating to solitary confinement, but not in transferring a prisoner 3,000 miles from his home.

Deprivation of property

In the 1980s the Supreme Court has twice dealt with problems raised by the loss or destruction of prisoners' property. In both of these cases, prisoners have argued that they had been deprived of property in violation of the due process requirement of the Fourteenth Amendment.

In Parratt v. Taylor (1981), the Supreme Court was asked to consider the matter of the unintentional loss of property. Taylor commenced an action against the Warden and the hobby manager of a Nebraska state prison in the district court, to recover the value of the hobby materials which he claimed had been lost through their negligence. Taylor alleged that he had been deprived of property without due process of law in violation of the Fourteenth Amendment. Taylor had chosen this route in preference to a tort action in the Nebraska state courts.

The Supreme Court accepted that in the best of all worlds this loss of property should not go without redress, but it was necessary to discover whether the complex interplay of Constitution, statutes and facts actually allowed this interpretation.

The language in which section 1983 is phrased does not limit its use solely to intentional deprivations of constitutional rights. The precedent established in Monroe v. Pape suggests that section 1983 affords a 'civil remedy' as opposed to a 'criminal' remedy for a deprivation of federally-protected rights. The issue of whether section 1983 applied here depended on the answers to two questions: first, whether the conduct complained of was committed by a person acting 'under colour of state law'; and second, whether the conduct deprived a person of rights, privileges or immunities secured by the Constitution or the laws of the US.

The Supreme Court rejected the claim as the deprivation was not one guaranteed by the Constitution and to have allowed the argument would have opened the doors to all alleged injuries which might have been inflicted by state officials by turning them all into violations of the

Fourteenth Amendment under section 1983.

In Hudson v. Palmer (1984), this issue of deprivation of property was taken further to include the intentional deprivation of a prisoner's property. Palmer, who was an inmate in a Virginia state prison, was subjected to a 'shakedown' search of his cell by Hudson and another officer. A ripped pillowcase was found and Palmer was subsequently charged with, and later found guilty of, destruction of state property.

The Supreme Court held that while Parratt was limited by its facts to negligent deprivations of property, it was evident that the reasoning applied equally well to intentional deprivations. The underlying rationale was that when deprivations of property were effected through the random and unauthorised conduct of a state employee, pre-deprivation procedures were simply impracticable, since the state could not know when such deprivations might occur. The Court could discern no logical distinction between negligent and intentional deprivations of property insofar as the practicability of pre-deprivation hearings was concerned. Indeed intentional acts are even more difficult to anticipate, because the individual concerned would try to avoid detection. The Court held that unauthorised intentional deprivations of prisoners' property do not violate the due process clause provided that adequate post-deprivation remedies are available.

These due process cases demonstrate that the courts at all levels are reluctant to impose the full range of due process requirements that go with a criminal trial on prison administration. Prison administrators are left wide discretion in relation to the control of the institution and its code of discipline. The closer the prisoner is to freedom in the community, the greater the protection provided by due process. There are several important features to note here: first, there is the problem of whether prisoners facing criminal charges for offences committed in prison have an opportunity to prepare an adequate defence to the charges. The appointment of counsel only to assist with the trial seems to bring into question the quality of the defence which might be mounted as damaging admissions might have been made during pre-trial detention in solitary confinement. Second, it seems from both Parratt and Palmer that prisoners do not have rights to property free from state interference. The Supreme Court left open the possibility of bringing a suit for deprivation of property only when this had happened as a result of an established state procedure, or when there was no adequate state remedy, but the term 'deprivation' was not defined and no guidance for the future was in fact given.

Cruel and unusual punishment

The Eighth Amendment, which forbids the imposition of cruel and unusual punishment, is borrowed directly from the English Bill of Rights of 1689. For many years, it was believed that this constitutional prohibition referred only to barbaric penalties used before Independence. In the twentieth century, the Eighth Amendment has been revived and expanded to cover less obviously cruel and unusual punishments such as prison overcrowding. Before considering the development of the concept it is necessary to see how the Amendment acquired its contemporary significance.

The proportionality of punishments

The first significant case to deal with the Eighth Amendment in this century is that of <u>Weems v. United States</u> (1910). Weems was disbursing officer for the Philippines Branch of the Coast Guard and Transportation of the US, and was indicted for falsifying records and a cashbook in his office in Manila. At this time, the Philippines were an American dependency. Weems was found guilty under a colonial law which provided a minimum punishment of twelve years and one day of imprisonment in chains at 'hard and painful' labour; certain additional penalties including deprivation of rights of parental authority, guardianship of person or property, participation in family council, marital authority, administration of property, or the right to dispose of one's own property, permanent loss of the right to vote, hold public office, receive retirement pay or honours, subjection to official surveillance for life, and a fine of 1250 pesos.

The case was brought to the US Supreme Court which took the view that the original intention of the English Bill of Rights was to inhibit excessive punishments. The Supreme Court decided that it had the power to set the sentence aside: the minimum sentence was repugnant to the Constitution, as it was so disproportionate to the offence.

In 1958 the Eighth Amendment was adapted further. In <u>Trop v. Dulles</u>, the Supreme Court was asked to consider the case of a man convicted of desertion from the US Army in wartime who had been deprived of his citizenship as part of the sentence of the court martial. The Supreme Court traced the origins of the Eighth Amendment back to the English Bill of Rights, and stated that the basis of the Amendment was nothing less than the dignity of man. The Court recognised that the Amendment had to draw its meaning from the evolving standards of decency that mark the progress of a maturing society. In this case, the punishment involved not a physical punishment, but the total destruction of the individual's status in organised society. The Court went on to say that this punishment was offensive to the cardinal principles for which the Constitution stands.

The significance of these cases is that they introduce very clearly a relative, evolving standard to be applied to the severity punishments. This development was of considerable importance in the prison conditions cases decided in the 1960s and 1970s.

The prison system cases

In <u>Holt v. Sarver</u> (1970), a district court in Arkansas heard an action brought by state prisoners to have declared unconstitutional the conditions and practices of the state prison system. The Arkansas prison system was based on a number of large prison farms. It was argued that the trusty system, the open barracks, conditions in isolation cells, and the absence of meaningful rehabilitation programmes were such that the confinement of persons in the system amounted to cruel and unusual punishment. The district court judge held that the conditions in the Arkansas prison system violated the Eighth Amendment. The judge said that the concept of cruel and unusual punishment is not limited to instances in which a particular inmate is subjected to a punishment directed at him as an individual.

> Confinement within a given institution may amount to cruel and unusual punishment where confinement is characterised by conditions and practices so bad as to be shocking to the conscience of reasonably civilised people.

The judge said that the distinguishing features of Arkansas penitentiary life must be considered together. All the features of the system exist in combination, and taken together, they have a cumulative impact on the inmates regardless of their status.

Arkansas prisons were run by trusties who had the power of life and death over other prisoners. Trusties also controlled numerous rackets which meant that prisoners had to pay for what they should have received as a matter of course. Prisoners slept in large dormitory barracks each containing more than a hundred men. Fights and assaults were frequent. There had been 17 stabbings in the 18 months before the case was brought to court; four of them fatal. Cells used to hold prisoners either for disciplinary offences or for their own protection were insanitary, filthy and overcrowded. The few facilities for rehabilitation available in the Arkansas system were the exclusive preserve of white prisoners. The totality of this situation led the judge to say that the conditions militated against reform and rehabilitation.

The judge gave declaratory relief to the extent of saying that, as then constituted, the Arkansas prison system was cruel and unusual punishment, and as such violated the constitution. The respondents were ordered to make a prompt and reasonable start towards eliminating these conditions. Unless the conditions were brought up to a level of constitutional tolerability, the prison farms could no longer be used for the confinement of prisoners. The court insisted on giving guidance to help the respondents. The court rejected out of hand any plan that would phase out the trusty system over time, it had to be abolished immediately. Prisoners should not be placed in positions of authority over other prisoners, and they should not intervene between prisoners and medical staff.

The court was involved with the Arkansas prison system throughout the 1970s. Holt v. Sarver was notable as the first case where the court threatened to close the entire prison system as an incentive to remedy constitutional defects. There were further sensations when bodies were discovered buried on some of the farms. Thomas Murton, who had been appointed as Corrections Commissioner to reform the whole system, was dismissed and threatened with criminal charges. (Mitford, 1974, pp. 43-5) A consent decree was agreed in 1978 but the whole state prison system has only slowly been brought up to date.

The next case of this kind occurred in 1976, when the state of Alabama was the defendant in Pugh v. Locke. District Court Judge Johnson held that conditions in the Alabama penal system constituted cruel and unusual punishment where they bore no reasonable relationship to legitimate institutional goals. Conditions as a whole created a situation where inmates were compelled to live in constant fear of violence, in imminent danger to their physical well being, and without any opportunity for rehabilitation. The Alabama State Board of Corrections was responsible for four large institutions for men, a centre for young men, six road camps, one pre-release and eight work release centres, with a total population in excess of 5,000. The four principal institutions were appallingly overcrowded: one had a design capacity of 632 but actually held over 1100.

The overcrowding was exacerbated by dormitory living. Bunk beds were packed so tightly together that there was no room between them. In these circumstances, both sanitation and security were impossible. The buildings were dilapidated, and overrun with flies, mosquitoes, cockroaches and other vermin. Personal cleanliness was impossible: the state supplied only razor blades (no razors) and soap, and all other materials were to be bought if the prisoners had any money. Prisoners were paid 25 cents per week. The conditions in which food was cooked and served were described as being equally unsanitary. Public health service officials who gave expert testimony stated that if the prisons had been within their jurisdiction, they would have closed them down as unfit for human habitation.

Judge Johnson said that the court had a clear duty to remedy the massive constitutional infirmities which plagued Alabama's prisons. He said that it was with great reluctance that the federal courts intervened in the day to day administration of the state penal systems; but in this case such intervention was completely justified. Normally the courts were asked to balance the valid goals of the prison authorities against the competing interests of the prisoners but in this instance the state had no valid purpose in allowing these conditions, so the usual considerations did not apply. A state, the Judge said, is not at liberty to afford its citizens only those constitutional rights which fit comfortably within its budget.

A Human Rights Committee for the Alabama Prison System was to be set up, independent of the Board of Corrections, to monitor the implementation of the proposed changes. The defendants had six months in which to bring forward a plan for overhauling the system with a timetable for its implementation. The Judge also retained jurisdiction over the case to supervise the implementation of reform plans.

In 1976, the Alabama Board of Corrections was back in court, and the court concluded that the Board was not making a serious effort to comply with its orders. The court ordered that control of the prisons be removed from the Board of Corrections and placed in the receivership control of the Governor. (Newman v. Alabama) It was only in January 1983 that the receivership was wound up after the court had decided that the major constitutional violations had finally been remedied. (New York Times, 14 January 1983)

In 1977, the District Court for Rhode Island was required to consider the totality of prison conditions in the state's prison in Palmigiano v. Garrahy. The Rhode Island state prison was built about a hundred years ago, and designed to contain 55 inmates. It was subsequently extended to hold about 420 in maximum security. The physical conditions of the prison were appalling. The various public health officials who gave expert testimony said that it was the filthiest prison they had encountered. It was unfit for human habitation according to any of the criteria they used. In the medium security section, prisoners held in isolation for their own protection, and those isolated for disciplinary reasons, and those being held before trial were held in three large, mixed dormitories, and violence and sexual assaults were rife.

The District Court Judge said that the prison demonstrated a comprehensive pattern of neglect which, together with overcrowding, had a cumulative impact on the prisoners. The prison was unfit for human habitation, and prisoners went in constant fear of violence. In these circumstances, rehabilitation was impossible. The Judge said that the responses he had been given made him doubt whether the prison officials were capable of dealing with the Herculean task of rebuilding the state's prison system.

The constitutional prohibition against cruel and unusual punishment was designed to protect the weak and powerless against the passions, or the reckless neglect, of the majority and its leaders. In this case, it was not a matter of making prison life more pleasant. The conditions found in the Rhode Island prison had shocked the court, and the court was convinced that they would have shocked the conscience of any reasonable citizen who had the opportunity to view them.

The Judge appointed a master to oversee and monitor the court's decree. The state was given 30 days in which to decide on the closure of the maximum security section and to find new accommodation for the pre-trial detainees. The Judge then listed the minimum standards for any new facilities and ordered that these be inspected by a range of professional bodies concerned with public health, education and vocational training, whose own standards would be applied. The Master and any staff or consultants that the Master needed to hire would be paid for by the state. The Judge specifically retained jurisdiction over the case so that any further action could be started without additional litigation.

These three cases demonstrate quite clearly the appalling conditions which have been found in some of America's prisons, and the way in which the judges have used the Eighth Amendment to outlaw these practices. It has not been necessary to demonstrate that any individual prisoner has been subject to the worst of the conditions that have been described: what the judges have done is to look at the cumulative effect of the prison conditions and to decide whether these conditions are acceptable to the contemporary conscience. Clearly they have found such conditions to be unacceptable. The judgments have gone into fairly considerable detail, especially in Pugh and Palmigiano. The judges have used their own initiative or they have been able to use both the testimony and ideas of the various expert witnesses who have been involved.

Solitary confinement

The prohibition against cruel and unusual punishment has been invoked in cases concerning the use of solitary confinement as punishment for prison disciplinary offences. An early instance of its use occurred in Johnson v. Anderson (1974). In this class action, the plaintiffs were held in six by ten foot cells which were described as being dry and clean. The heating system was the same as that supplying heat to the rest of the prison. Each cell had a flush toilet and wash basin. Prisoners in solitary confinement had fewer privileges than other prisoners, e.g. no visits, and no opportunity for exercise outside the cell. Solitary confinement had been condemned elsewhere (e.g. Holt v. Sarver) when it denied prisoners rudimentary hygiene, or it posed acute danger to health. In this case, while the conditions may have been unpleasant, they did not amount to cruel and unusual punishment under the tests used elsewhere. Nor could it be shown that the amount of time that the plaintiff was held in solitary was disproportionate to the offence. The court rejected Johnson's complaint.

Solitary confinement was considered by the Supreme Court in Hutto v. Finney. This case was a continuation of issues raised in Holt. In the initial court action, it was claimed that isolation in punitive solitary confinement violated Eighth Amendment rights. In Arkansas punitive solitary confinement was for an indeterminate period in a windowless eight by ten foot cell. 'Solitary confinement' was a misnomer: the cell was shared with up to eleven other prisoners. These cells had a water supply and a flush toilet, but its flushing mechanism was controlled from outside the cell. At night, the occupants of the cells were given mattresses to sleep on. These were given out randomly despite the fact that some prisoners suffered from infectious diseases such as hepatitis or VD.

The district court limited the number of men who could be confined in these cells, required that each should have his own bunk, specified that a new diet be provided, and limited the maximum isolation sentence to 30 days. The state challenged the 30 day limit on appeal in both the Court of Appeals and the Supreme Court. The Supreme Court affirmed the limit on the grounds that the court had given the state authorities repeated opportunities to remedy the situation of cruel and unusual punishment in the isolation cells, and that the time limit would reduce the overcrowding that was also the basis of complaint.

Prison overcrowding

In a parallel development, the concept of cruel and unusual punishment has been applied to prison overcrowding. In Pugh v. Locke, a standard emerged that prisoners ought to have at least 60 square feet of cell space. It was only a short step to using 60 square feet of cell space as a standard in its own right. Subsequently, multiple occupancy of cells has come to the courts.

The constitutional basis for all of the ensuing debate was set Bell v. Wolfish which relates to pre-trial detainees, but its principles provide precedent for prison litigation as well. Inmates of a federal pre-trial detention facility challenged among other things the practice of 'double bunking' inmates, i.e. assigning inmates to rooms originally intended for one person where single bunks had been replaced by doubles. The Supreme Court's reason for rejecting this claim was that the detainees were required to spend only seven or eight hours per day in their rooms, during most of which time they were asleep. This situation lasted only for 60 days, the maximum time for which detainees were held in the facility.

The decision reached in Wolfish was later extended in a case brought to the Supreme Court by state prisoners, Rhodes v. Chapman (1981). In this case, Ohio prisoners brought a civil rights action claiming that their Eighth Amendment rights had been violated. The district court held that conditions violated the prisoners' constitutional rights for the following reasons

1. inmates at the prison were serving long terms of imprisonment, which accentuated the problems of close confinement and overcrowding;
2. the prison housed 38% more inmates than it was designed to hold;
3. the court accepted several studies recommended that each inmate ought to have at least 50 to 55 square feet of living quarters, as compared with the 63 square feet in the double cells;
4. the court found that, at best, a double-celled inmate would spend most of his time in a shared cell; and
5. the prison had made double celling a practice, and it was not a temporary condition.

The Supreme Court rejected the complaints on appeal holding that the evidence did not support the district court's conclusion that double celling constituted cruel and unusual punishment. The Supreme Court added that the practice of double celling in modern prison buildings did not constitute cruel and unusual punishment since there was no evidence that the practice inflicted unnecessary or wanton pain, nor was it grossly disproportionate to the severity of the crimes which warranted imprisonment.

The issue of overcrowding has come back to the courts again in Ruiz v. Estelle (1982). This class action against the Texas Department of Corrections claimed that the totality of conditions amounted to cruel and unusual punishment. At the time of trial by the district court, the Texas Department of Corrections confined over 26,000 inmates, a figure which had increased to 33,000 by the time the case was appealed. The

Department of Corrections confined two to four inmates in cells measuring 45 square feet, originally designed for one occupant. Overcrowding was seen by the district court as exercising a malignant effect on all aspects of inmate life. The court distinguished the conditions from those in Rhodes, and ordered a reduction in the prison population and a minimum space standard. The Court of Appeals for the Fifth Circuit set aside these decisions on the grounds that the expense involved, approximately $300,000,000, could not be required of the state of Texas. Other less expensive changes might have the effect of reducing the effects now attributed to overcrowding, e.g. better supervision. This judgment was given on the basis that prisoners could bring further litigation a year later to see whether the improvements had had their designed effect. If not, an order would be made in relation to overcrowding.

There is currently a degree of uncertainty surrounding cruel and unusual punishment. All of the courts have been at pains to point out that they have not lost interest in prison conditions of the Holt and Pugh kind, but are less willing to specify detailed prison conditions. Even in Ruiz the court was not willing to order remedies which were not demonstrably required to protect constitutional rights; nor was it willing to intrude unduly on matters of state concern. In Rhodes, the Supreme Court stepped away from setting national standards. The federal government had been pledged to allocate $2 billion to state prison building programmes but this money was never allocated by the Reagan administration. The expense of prison reform has become an issue in the recessionary climate of the 1980s. These cases raise the question of effectiveness of litigation in improving prison conditions.

Freedom of expression

A rapidly expanding area of litigation concerns prisoners' freedom to express their views in correspondence with their families, friends and others, the opportunity to give interviews with the mass media, and the organisation of Unions to represent prisoners vis-a-vis the administration. Although these various issues appear disparate, they form a set of rights guaranteed by the First Amendment which states

> Congress shall make no law respecting an establishment of religion, or prohibiting the free exercise thereof; or abridging the freedom of speech or of the press; or the right of the people peaceably to assemble, and to petition the government for a redress of grievances.

Access to reading matter

The courts have considered whether prisoners have the right to receive books, newspapers and magazines. Much of the litigation has dealt with the right to receive books on religion. The courts' decisions on freedom of access to religious material have opened the way for other material. Prisoners' rights to receive ideas have been justified as a corollary of the right to express their ideas. The general right to freedom of expression under the First Amendment has been of considerable importance in the 1960s and 1970s. The courts were reluctant to impose any limit on freedom of expression as practised by the mass media and the public. The extension of the general right has carried over to prisoners.

In Fortune Society v. McGinnis (1970), a district court was asked to consider the right of inmates to receive the newsletter of a self-help society run by ex-offenders. The Fortune Society produced a newsletter which contained information on prison reform and rehabilitation schemes, as well as the Society's own activities. The court rejected the prison authority's ban on the newsletter saying 'censorship is utterly foreign to our way of life, it smacks of dictatorship'. But this freedom to receive ideas was not complete. The district court did allow some limitation on the First Amendment rights. Restrictions on prisoners' rights of access to ideas were permissible when prison security so demanded, or when there was a clear and present danger of a breach of prison discipline, or when there was some substantial interference with prison administration. The court would not allow censorship on the grounds that it was for the prisoner's own good or as part of punishment. It was not permissible to ban material that was critical of prison administration.

One of the very few exceptions to open access to material is to be found in Johnson v. Anderson (1974) mentioned earlier in relation to solitary confinement. Johnson and his fellow plaintiffs were refused access to books, magazines and periodicals when held in solitary confinement. The judge ruled that these rights were left in the main prison, because solitary confinement involved the deprivation of reading matter rather than the censorship of particular ideas. This deprivation was for a limited time. The prison authorities had a right to maintain order through the sanction of solitary confinement. A sentence of 15 days would involve a delay in receiving ideas. If the maximum time spent in solitary confinement was longer, then that would provide a more difficult question. The judge concluded that there was no violation of the First Amendment.

Interviews with the media

Contacts between prisoners and representatives of the mass media present special difficulties. The access guaranteed to the media in the US is far greater than anything found in Britain. The press investigations which led to the resignation of Richard Nixon provide a clear demonstration of both the power of the press and the absence of legitimate official controls.

The Supreme Court has twice considered the question of media access to named prisoners. Both of the cases were dealt with at the same time in 1974. In Saxbe v. Washington Post Co., the constitutionality of a Policy Statement issued by the Federal Bureau of Prisons was challenged. The Policy Statement prohibited interviews between reporters and individually designated prisoners in federal prisons other than minimum security facilities. The Supreme Court held that the prohibition did not abridge the freedom of the press, as the Policy Statement did not deny the press access to sources of information available to the public.

The second case, Pell v. Procunier was brought by inmates of prisons in California and journalists attacking the constitutionality of a state regulation banning interviews with individually designated prisoners.

The Supreme Court held that the prisoners' rights of access to the media were limited, as prisoners had other means of communication available to them, e.g. the mail, and visits by friends or families or attorneys or political representatives. When the Supreme Court turned to the media, it held that the prison authorities must have control. The media had a considerable degree of freedom to enter Californian prisons and to conduct random interviews; media access was greater than that afforded to the general public. The sole prohibition on the activities of the press was that of interviews with named inmates. The prohibition had been introduced in 1971 after a violent incident in which three members of staff and two inmates had been killed as a result of the notoriety achieved by inmates involved in press interviews. The restriction was legitimate, as the state had a right to maintain order and security in the prisons. There was no violation of any constitutional guarantee in this case, because the constitution did not guarantee the press special access to information.

More prisoners have an interest in controls over their correspondence through the post. Procunier v. Martinez (1974) originated in a class action brought by inmates of Californian prisons challenging the constitutionality of prison regulations on censorship of mail. The regulations authorised censorship of statements that 'unduly complain' or 'magnify grievances', express 'inflammatory, political, racial, or religious, or other views', and matters deemed 'defamatory or otherwise inappropriate'.

The Supreme Court held that the real test of censorship regulations was the infringement of the unabridged rights of the outside correspondent who sent or received the letter. The free correspondent's rights under the First Amendment were unaffected by the status of the other person. In the present case, the regulations were unconstitutional because they were broader than was demanded by legitimate governmental interests such as prison security and order, or prisoner rehabilitation. Prisoners' correspondence was also protected from censorship by the Fourteenth Amendment because uncensored communication was a 'liberty' interest that could only be restricted after due process of law. The wording used in the regulations of the California Department of Corrections was unacceptable, because it allowed officials to apply their own personal prejudices and opinions as standards for censorship.

The freedoms upheld in Procunier v. Martinez do not extend to correspondence with other prisoners or ex-prisoners. In Lawrence v. Davis (1975), a district court upheld a regulation made by the Virginia Department of Corrections allowing the seizure and retention of mail from ex-prisoners.

Prisoners' unions and political associations

Prisoners have brought a number of actions before the courts to establish rights to organise themselves. In Butler v. Preiser (1974) an action was brought to overturn a prohibition imposed by prison officials on the solicitation of funds from prisoners to pay for the defence costs of prisoners and ex-prisoners accused of criminal offences allegedly committed during the Attica prison uprising. The plaintiffs complained that this was an arbitrary intrusion upon rights of freedom of association. The behaviour of the prison officials against this fund was held to be both arbitrary and capricious. The plaintiffs were granted an injunction removing the official ban.

Attempts to unionise prisoners have been less successful. The most significant case is Jones v. North Carolina Prisoners' Labour Union Inc (1977). The Union brought an action challenging the regulations of the North Carolina Department of Corrections which prohibited prison inmates from soliciting other inmates to join a prisoners' union, barred all meetings of the Union, and refused to deliver packets of Union publications that had been mailed in bulk for redistribution.

The Supreme Court stated that they should give the deference appropriate to the decisions of the prison administrators. The administrators who had appeared before the court had testified that a prisoners' labour union was fraught with potential danger. The decision to restrict the prisoners' union was reasonable, and was consistent with the legitimate operational considerations of the prison.

Visits to prisoners

The final area covered by the First Amendment concerns visits to prisoners. In Argon v. Montayne (1975), prisoners brought an action challenging a practice by New York State prison officials barring visits from families and friends to prisoners who refused to shave as a matter of choice rather than as an aspect of religious belief. The district court granted a preliminary injunction, and ordered a trial to hear fully the merits of the case. The final outcome is not available, but the important feature is the judge's view that while the prisoners lost some rights to control their appearance, the real issue was whether prison officials could stop visits. The judge thought that this was probably unconstitutional, as the importance of visits was to be found in both the rights and needs of prisoners' families.

In Bribson v. Lane (1983) a prisoner claimed that his First Amendment rights had been violated by the prison authorities' refusal to allow visits by his girlfriend who was suspected of having played a role in the escape attempt of another prisoner. The district court held that it had never been clearly established that prisoners had an undisputed constitutional right to visits. Prisoners' rights were limited by either the status of being a prisoner or the legitimate penological objectives of the prison system. The authorities must be able to take steps to maintain order and to prevent escapes. It did not make any difference that the girlfriend had never been conclusively found guilty of the alleged conduct. This issue was within the proper discretion of the prison officials and there was no case here to show that this discretion had been abused.

The issues based on the First Amendment have not been decided in a uniform manner. The correspondence cases resulted in the removal of blanket restrictions on what may be written. The rationale, which is novel on this side of the Atlantic, is that prison censorship restricts the rights of the free party to the correspondence. On the other hand, the courts have been less liberal when dealing with prisoners attempting to organise themselves in opposition to the prison authorities. Control, order and discipline are more important than freedom of association.

Freedom of religion

The issue of freedom to practise one's religious belief preceded that of freedom to express non-religious views. The First Amendment has provided the basis for religious toleration in American society. The practice of various forms of Christianity in prisons has never been regarded as an infringement of the prohibition on the establishment of religion, forbidden by the same Amendment. The main cases which have come before the courts have concerned the right to practise other, less conventional, religions. There has traditionally been an assumption on the part of the courts that religious belief is an important step towards rehabilitation. The growth of the Black Muslim movement and its espousal of black supremacist and separatist views has led to some changes in the behaviour of the courts.

The cases brought by the Black Muslims raised a wide variety of issues which included the right to receive religious texts, to gather together to hold religious services, and to receive visits from their religious advisors. All of these rights and privileges have been granted to other religious groups. But in the case of the Black Muslims, there were aspects of their practices which were seen by administrators as being disruptive to prison life. Most American prisons have based their diet on pork, which has usually been the only meat in the diet and has provided the fat in which other foods were cooked. Muslim dietary law requires a pork-free diet. Other Muslim practices such as the month-long, day-time fast of Ramadan when food and drink can only be taken during the hours of darkness, have also been the cause of serious conflict with prison administrators.

In some of the early cases brought by Black Muslims the prisoners were forced to rely on arguments to prove unequal protection of the laws (in violation of the Fourteenth Amendment). They claimed that while other religious groups were protected by the law, protection was not extended to Black Muslims. The court required in Long v. Parker (1968) that it be shown that a Muslim weekly paper was basic religious literature essential to belief and understanding of the religion and that receipt of similar literature was permitted to other faiths. The court balanced this right against the need of the prison authorities to maintain discipline and security. In Walker v. Blackwell (1969), the court allowed certain of the rights requested by the Muslims, but refused them privileges in addition to those already granted to other religions. e.g. meals after dark during Ramadan, and religious broadcasting on the radio.

In Barnett v. Rodgers (1969), the Court of Appeals for the District of Columbia heard a suit brought by Black Muslim prisoners who argued that continued confinement where the food (pork) broke their religious dietary laws constituted cruel and unusual punishment. The Court of Appeals sent the case back to the district court for reconsideration as only a 'compelling state interest' was sufficient to justify restrictions on religious practice as religious freedoms were so important in American society. The burden has slowly shifted on to the state to demonstrate a 'compelling' security interest leading to restrictions on religious practices.

When the Court of Appeals for the Fourth Circuit heard Brown v. Peyton (1971), the state was required to demonstrate a paramount interest to justify a restriction on the freedom of religion. The state had to show convincingly that a paramount state interest required limitation of religious rights. Censorship of religious material had to be based on detailed evaluations of the material concerned, and any such censorship was reviewable by the courts. As to the matter of the censorship of Black Muslim publications, each issue would have been looked at and judged on its merits. Comparisons would also have to be made with those prison systems which allowed free access to these publications, to discover whether they had any effect on prison discipline and order.

Equal treatment of all religious groups was discussed by the Supreme Court in Cruz v. Beto (1972). The prisoner claimed a violation of his civil rights on the grounds that while prisoners who were members of other religious sects were allowed to use the prison chapel, he and other Buddhist prisoners were not; and that as a consequence of sharing Buddhist religious material with other prisoners, he was placed in solitary confinement. It was also claimed that Buddhist prisoners were prohibited from corresponding with their religious advisors, were not provided with free religious literature, and were denied good jobs and early parole. The Supreme Court returned the case and said that if these allegations were true, the state had violated both the First and Fourteenth Amendments by discriminating against the Buddhist religion through denying the plaintiff a reasonable opportunity of pursuing his faith comparable to that afforded fellow prisoners who adhered to conventional religious beliefs.

The Second Circuit Court of Appeals has been asked to consider more conventional issues of Jewish religious practice. In Kahane v. Carlson (1975) Kahane, an Orthodox Jewish rabbi, sought an order requiring provision of kosher food. The Court of Appeals held that the prison authorities would be required to provide a diet to maintain the prisoner in good health without violating the dietary laws, but the court could not order the provision of specific items of diet.

The question of dietary requirements and religious practice has been extended in Prushinowski v. Hambrich (1983). Prushinowski sought a writ of habeas corpus on the grounds that his health was suffering from the lack of an adequate diet. This resulted from official failure to provide him with the facilities and food in order that he could observe the strict dietary laws of his religion. The district court judge held that the Federal Bureau of Prisons had unintentionally violated its own regulations on special diets in this case, and had violated the prisoner's constitutional rights. Claims made on behalf of the Bureau of Prisons that allowing special food into its prisons would pose a security problem was rejected, as there was no evidence to demonstrate that smuggling had taken place in this way. No cost would be added to the Bureau of Prisons, as the Hasidic community had agreed to provide the food for Prushinowski.

There has been a distinction made by the courts on the basis of the courts' views of the religion being practised. The Black Muslim movement was quite alien to conventional religious practice, its dietary requirements were treated as being unusual despite the fact that there were some similarities with Jewish practice. The real issues were to do with the content of Black Muslim beliefs – an aggressive black separatism. Prison administrators saw Black Muslims as a threat to order and discipline, and a threat to administration because they were demanding different treatment from their fellow prisoners, destroying the uniformity of prison life.

Rights to medical care

There is a small but growing body of cases dealing with prisoners' rights to adequate medical treatment. The issue of the adequacy of medical care has already been mentioned in Holt v. Sarver, and Pugh v. Locke. But the question of medical treatment in its own right is more recent.

The district court in Newman v. Alabama (1972) held that

> the failure of the (Alabama) Board of Corrections to provide sufficient medical facilities and staff....constitutes a wilful and intentional violation of the rights of prisoners, guaranteed by the Eighth and Fourteenth Amendments.

The court ordered the state to implement the federal government's standards for Participation of Hospitals in the Medicare Programme.

In Freeman v. Lockhart (1974), Freeman claimed that he had been placed in special confinement with a man known to have TB, that he had

contracted the disease which settled in his eyes. The main claim was
that repeated attempts to see the prison physician were denied, and as a
result, the prisoner's vision was permanently damaged. The Court of
Appeals applied the principle established in Newman that deliberate
indifference to a prisoner's request for essential medical treatment was
sufficient to make a claim under section 1983 of the Civil Rights Act.

Whether failure to provide adequate medical treatment was the basis of
a civil rights action claim has been decided by the Supreme Court in
Estelle v. Gamble (1976). The prisoner claimed that the defendants had
violated the cruel and unusual punishment clause of the Eighth Amendment
by failing to provide adequate medical treatment after the prisoner had
sustained a back injury while performing prison work. The Supreme Court
accepted the argument that the failure to provide adequate medical care
constituted cruel and unusual punishment for two reasons. First, a
prisoner has to rely on the prison authorities to treat his medical
needs and if they fail to do so, these needs will not be met. Second,
indifference constituted the 'unnecessary and wanton infliction of pain'
when the medical needs were serious, which at worst could lead to a
lingering death. No one can suggest that this pain and suffering would
serve any penological purpose.

The issue of adequate medical care has occurred again in
Venus v. Goodman (1983). The district court awarded $4,500 in punitive
damages with costs because of the slight but permanent damage to a
finger. The indifference in this case was the delay in obtaining
treatment details from an outside hospital for two months in the face of
repeated demands for treatment. When a specialist was called in there
was an immediate operation performed to alleviate any further damage.

There have been attempts to establish a right to be free from
involuntary medical treatment. This issue was raised in
Peek v. Ciccone. The prisoner claimed that his constitutional right to
freedom from unusual punishment had been violated when he was forcibly
given an injection of a tranquilliser by a non-medically qualified
prison official after he had refused to take orally a tranquilliser
prescribed by a prison physician. The claim was dismissed on the grounds
that both the method of administration and the dosage had been
prescribed by the medical officer, and that the dosage was a reasonable
one and was a recognised part of the treatment of chronic schizophrenia.
The prisoner had not been treated cruelly, unusually, or in any way
unlawfully. The injection he had been given was not designed to punish
or to harm the prisoner. The right to refuse treatment may well be an
area of litigation that will develop in the future, although the impetus
formerly given by behaviour modification has largely disappeared.

The issues of the right to refuse treatment and the right to treatment
have spread slowly into the arena of prisoners' rights litigation from
the mental health field. Wyatt v. Stickney in 1971 established the
requirement that involuntary mental hospital patients have 'a
constitutional right to receive such individual treatment as will give
each of them a realistic opportunity to be cured or to improve his or
her mental condition'. Attempts to apply a right to rehabilitation in
prisons have been unsuccessful. In Pugh v. Lock the court ruled that a
prison system was not required to rehabilitate prisoners, but it could
not debilitate a prisoner's constitution or render him less able to re-
enter society successfully.

Right to privacy

In addition to question of due process and the destruction of prisoners' property, Hudson v. Palmer raised the issue of a right to privacy. Palmer based his claim on the Fourth Amendment which states

> The rights of the people to be secure in their persons, houses, papers, and effects, against unreasonable searches and seizures, shall not be violated, and no warrants shall issue, but upon probable cause, supported by oath or affirmation, particularly describing the place to be searched, and the persons or things to be seized.

The Supreme Court restated its insistence that prisoners be accorded those rights not fundamentally inconsistent with imprisonment itself or incompatible with the objectives of incarceration. The Supreme Court took the view that society was not prepared to recognise a prisoner's subjective expectation of privacy within his cell and accordingly the Fourth Amendment protection against unreasonable searches did not apply within the confines of the prison cell. The recognition of this right could not be reconciled with the concept of incarceration and the needs and objectives of penal institutions. The circumstances of imprisonment the balance has to struck in favour of institutional security.

This case has a number of disturbing implications, all of which were heralded by the Supreme Court's insistence that it respected prisoners' rights, a statement which almost invariably means that a new limitation is about to be imposed. The terse statement that society would not recognise the prisoner's expectation of privacy is too sweeping, as society might well distinguish between an absolute right and a more limited right.

The Supreme Court judgment places a higher duty on protecting prison staff and visitors than it does of prisoners. This may be a realistic view in the sense that prisoners may well attack each other because total surveillance is impossible, but it also re-inforces the view that because some prisoners are highly dangerous little can be done. This case is significant because the Supreme Court seems to be reacting to the crisis in the prisons (the doubling of the prison population and the high level of violence) by giving almost total deference to prison administrators. The Palmer decision is aimed primarily at satisfying the requirements of prison security, not of the Bill of Rights.

Under the notion of a right to privacy inmates of San Quentin prison in California brought a class action alleging that the prison policy and practice of allowing female staff to view them in states of partial or total nudity while dressing, showering, being strip searched, or using toilet facilites. The Ninth Circuit Court of Appeals rejected the claim on the grounds that the female staff were restricted in their contacts with inmates and the record showed that they had conducted themselves in a professional manner with respect and dignity. (Grummett v. Rushen, 1985)

Conclusions

The American prisoners' rights cases are distinctive for five main reasons. First, the conditions in which many prisoners have been kept even in the very recent past, appear closer to the nineteenth century than to the twentieth. The violence and neglect of the prison farms of Arkansas and Mississippi are particularly striking images. The overcrowding of entire state prison systems may appear less dramatic, but the effects may be as bad in the long term. While the courts have been concerned to improve conditions, state legislatures have been introducing mandatory prison sentences and early release has been abolished in some states. Changes in sentencing have increased the number of prisoners and the length of time spent in prison. The prison population of the US has doubled between 1970 and 1988. Prison building programmes to alleviate overcrowded or poor conditions are politically highly contentious while changes in sentencing powers respond to popular demands and do not appear to have cost implications. Second, the range of issues which have been brought before the federal courts has been extensive. The courts have consistently taken the view that the Constitution follows prisoners into the prison. Some rights survive a sentence of imprisonment better than others. Access to the courts is almost by definition one of the most sturdy. Other rights such as freedom of thought and freedom of expression also survive to a considerable extent.

Third, some of the judges seem to have a distinctive way of dealing with the rival claims of prisoners and prison administrators. There has been a small number of decisions which treated the prisoners as the moral equals of prison administrators. Judge Frankel's decision in Butler v. Preiser is perhaps the most extreme example. The judge refused to accept suggestions that coercion might be used by some prisoners against their fellows. At one level, the judge appears to be remarkably naive and lacking in knowledge of how prisons function that there is a great deal of interracial conflict reported within many American prisons. But at the same time, it can be argued that he was simply trying to apply a general notion of even-handed treatment to the two parties in a suit. The prison administration lost its case when its representatives appeared to be prepared to make up rules on the spot in the witness box.

Fourth, even though there are exceptions, the general attitude of federal judges seems to be that prisoners have lost most of their rights. Prisoners are given into the care of administrators who have to be allowed to get on with a very difficult job. The standards maintained by those prison administrators have to fall to low levels before the courts are prepared to intervene. There seems to be an increasing tendency for the Supreme Court to be sceptical of claims made by prisoners. Rights are being seen as alienable in the sense that full rights apply only to citizens who are both law-abiding and free. If any individual breaks the law, then he will lose some rights and that loss will be his own fault.

Fifth, the sheer amount of litigation that has been completed is staggering. The procedures by which civil rights actions may be brought are relatively simple - a letter to the court may be sufficient. The volume of litigation has led to complaints that the federal court system can no longer cope and various solutions have been suggested.

Many issues have been left unresolved. At the end of all of the litigation there remains a series of questions which examine the links between litigation and prison conditions. The most basic, and most difficult to answer, is whether prisoners' lives have improved compared with 20 or 30 years ago. It is to issues of this type that attention must now turn.

8 Issues and trends in the United States

The vast number of prisoners' petitions to the courts in the US, more than 11,000 in the year ending June 1979, means that the American situation is much more complex than the British. (Jacobs, 1980, p. 439) There is variation between the states; the differences between their prison systems are enormous, ranging from the mega-prisons of California to the state prison farms of the south. The organisation of the federal courts means that the regional courts of appeals circuits can be moving in different directions, giving the Supreme Court the task of reconciling differences. It is important to look in more detail at some of the historical and political circumstances of the decisions described above and the dramatic recent changes in court decisions in a relatively short time.

Prisoners' rights litigation in the US has to be seen in its own context for several reasons. First, the changes are more than a series of disparate court decisions on cases brought by prisoners. There are good reasons for thinking of a prisoners' rights movement with a degree of organisation, continuity and direction. This movement has developed rapidly into new areas of litigation. There have been attacks on the constitutionality of the entire prison systems of 46 states. (Gottfredson and McConville, 1988, p. 3) This litigation has had two major kinds of consequences on individual prisoners, and on the prison regime as a whole.

Prisoners as a minority group

The history of prisoners' rights in the US is a relatively short one. The approach which began with <u>Monroe v. Pape</u> in 1961 coincided with changes in the status of other groups. The 1950s and the 1960s saw action by American blacks to achieve their civil rights. The federal courts acted on cases brought by blacks who had been discriminated against by state officials. The real watershed was when the Supreme Court rejected the argument on 'separate but equal' education, suits were brought which outlawed racial segregation in law schools, universities and then in commercial premises such as restaurants. Marches and sit-ins in southern cities were greeted with police repression and the imprisonment of demonstrators. This gave some blacks their first contact with the prison systems.

In the late 1960s and 1970s, various other minority groups have pressed their claims to equal treatment, e.g. the poor, the mentally ill, and Indians. Some of the groups' identities overlap, and their success varies. Prisoners have seen themselves, and have come to be seen, as one of these minorities. It is important to recognise that while groups such as prisoners might claim moral rights, they have actually established legal rights. The extension of legal rights to prisoners is significant in that they are clearly a stigmatised group who can easily be seen as undeserving of decent treatment, let alone equal treatment.

Alvin Bronstein, the Executive Director of the National Prison Project of the American Civil Liberties Union (ACLU), has argued that the prisoners' rights movement grew directly out of the civil rights and civil liberties movements. (Bronstein, 1980, p. 23) These movements used the courts to challenge legal barriers to racial equality in American society.

The composition of prison populations changed in the 1950s especially in the northern and western states. Until the 1950s the bulk of the population of state prisons had been white. In that decade, there was a considerable amount of internal migration of blacks from the southern states, and then more recently there have been waves of Puerto Rican, Cuban and Chicano immigration to various parts of the country. The racial pattern has changed so that whites are in a minority in the prisons in many states. (Huff, 1980, p. 53)

In the 1960s and 1970s, prisoners who were mainly black and poor identified themselves with other 'victimised minorities'. The radicalisation and politicisation of blacks in the 1960s produced vocal and articulate descriptions of prison life and its consequences for blacks. The letters written by George Jackson, one of the anti-heroes of the early 1970s, turned the conventional image of the Californian prison system on its head. Jackson describes the rehabilitation programme in the following terms

It is the function of the uniform to hold a man here. This means they do the key work, the searching, beating, killing. The individual with the tie and shirt (i.e. the Care and Treatment staff) (really another type of uniform) determines what we'll eat, what bullshit academic and make-work programs we'll have. He presides over the silly group therapy games that always end in fights or switch contests. Oh, and he also makes out board reports.

These two types of cops have been vying for control of the joints ever since the counsellor breed came on the grounds. (Jackson, 1971, p. 189)

The publicity surrounding Jackson's death (he was shot by guards in 1971) and the bloody assault on rioting prisoners in Attica Prison in upstate New York, helped to bring the prisons to public attention for the first time in many years. [1] The politicisation of crime meant that for the first time prisoners saw themselves as victims of a system of political control, and this led to links with other radical groups.

While prisoners have pressed their claims harder, the judiciary also become more responsive. New generations of federal judges have changed their views and have accepted prisoners' demands for legal rights. The Supreme Court might lead the way, but the daily work of the federal courts takes place at district court level. It is essential to recognise that while the Supreme Court Justices are presidential appointees, the district court judges are dependent on senatorial patronage and influence. (New York Times, 19 February and 30 September 1980) This difference suggests that the federal district court judges would tend to be more conservative than Supreme Court Justices. In practice, some of the most far-reaching decisions by judges might be thought of as being the more conservative. The scope of the decisions, e.g. that relating to Alabama, is somewhat surprising given the southern tendency to take a narrow view of civil rights. Individual judges seem to have their own clear views on what is acceptable by way of prison conditions. An additional gloss of respectability may be given by the interest taken by the American Bar Association (ABA). But whatever their political views, many federal district court judges have accepted the legitimacy of prisoners' claims.

In the 1960s, the situation of prisoners changed as one element in a wider social change. Not only did the prisoners' rights movement acquire a common legitimacy of the wider movement but it also gained skills for some prisoners in how to work their own way through the legal system. In addition professional advocates were able and willing to take up the cause of prisoners' rights. Berkman has argued that the public interest in prisons was slight until judges began to comment on the desperate conditions in the prisons, then people took more notice. (Berkman, 1979, p. 50) The media also responded, which in turn increased public awareness of prisons.

Pressure groups and activists

The Black Muslims, were by common agreement among prison observers, the most important agents of change. (Jacobs, 1980, p. 434; Huff, 1980, pp. 53-6) The movement appealed to black youths brought up in the urban ghettoes. The experiences of black youths, first with the police and the courts, and later with the prisons, highlighted the difference between the rhetoric of racial equality and the reality of discrimination. Muslim policy called for non-violent tactics of protest and legal challenge. The conventional self-image of prisoner, as a criminal, was less frequently accepted by them. Black prisoners began to reject this traditional view and to see themselves as political prisoners, their imprisonment was the result of a political process. The Black Muslims brought black prisoners together through raising racial consciousness and the politicisation of imprisonment. (Jacobs, 1980, p. 433)

Converts took on the various religious practices of Islam, demanding to have their food specially prepared, to pray daily at the prescribed times, and to observe religious festivals; all extremely effective ways of disrupting the prison regime while exploiting ideas about freedom of religion. Prison authorities across America responded by rejecting requests for recognition of changes in religious affiliation and freedom to practise their new religion. The Black Muslims were demanding rights and freedoms that were inconsistent with traditional definitions of imprisonment, and required an entirely new relationship between prison guards and prisoners. (Huff, 1980, p. 56)

The Black Muslims were successful in their litigation for two reasons: first, the issues were raised at the most appropriate time; and second, the issues were likely to appeal to the federal judiciary. (Jacobs, 1977, pp. 60-70) The civil rights movement was was arguing for the equal protection of laws and this was regarded as a legitimate demand. Freedom of religion is basic to the US Constitution whose First Amendment states

Congress shall make no law respecting an establishment of religion, or prohibiting the free exercise thereof....

The Supreme Court has consistently held that the word 'no' is an absolute and total ban on abridgements. The federal courts became actively involved in the prisons for the first time, and presentations of prisoners' grievances in constitutional terms have kept them there.

The impact of the Black Muslims can best be seen by concentrating on Statesville Penitentiary in Illinois which produced some of the most important cases, e.g. Cooper v. Pate. The Muslims were relatively few in numbers, about one hundred in a prison population of over three thousand. They were, however, the best organised and most cohesive group to exist for any length of time. The prison authorities responded to the Muslims' activities by putting them in solitary confinement as troublemakers. Attempts to use the courts to gain freedom of religion were met by administrative repression. The Black Muslims stood up to the pressure put on them; and eventually, when the courts responded by upholding their claims, their example showed other groups of prisoners what could be achieved.

The development of a legal profession specialising in civil rights cases also helped the prisoners' rights movement. Jacobs suggests that there are large numbers of lawyers who make a speciality of this kind of litigation. (Jacobs, 1980, pp. 437-40) Several of the leading lawyers were involved in the civil rights movement of the 1960s, and moved on to prisoners' rights. The involvement of many lawyers in this kind of litigation is limited as most prisoners will not be able to pay fees the few private lawyers prepared to act are highly selective in their choice of cases, and only take those most likely to succeed. (Bergensen and Hoerger, 1974, p. 780)

The small number of lawyers who are involved are neither organisationally weak nor professionally isolated. The ABA created a Commission on Correctional Facilities and Services in 1970 to advocate correctional reform located in Washington DC. (Jacobs, 1980, p. 438) In 1977, the ABA published a draft of standards relating to the legal status of prisoners. (ABA, 1977) In addition, no less than 24 state Bar Associations had correctional committees in 1974.

An extensive network of local organisations existed to provide legal services for prisoners. Some are funded by the Office of Economic Opportunity (established under civil rights legislation in the 1960s) whose Legal Services National Research and Technical Assistance Centres were set up to cope with the legal problems of the poor. In other places legal service organisations have developed in different ways, e.g. a programme was established in the federal penitentiary at Leavensworth, Kansas began with members of the University of Kansas Law School providing legal assistance to prisoners. (Bullock, 1980) As the scheme developed a federal grant was obtained which attracted matching funding from the state legislature. The fund pays salaries for public defenders and the expenses of appointed counsel.

Finally, there is the National Prisons Project. The National Prison Project is a publicly-funded offshoot of the ACLU, and it has concentrated on litigation and lobbying in relation to prisons and jails. This organisation, based in Washington DC, employs only seven full-time lawyers, but carries on litigation across the whole country. In many instances, the cases are begun with the support of a local ACLU chapter. The National Prison Project also coordinates the services of a body of expert witnesses, including ex-prison officials who will attend trials. (Jacobs, 1980, p. 440)

The impact of legislation

The dominant impression of prisoners' rights litigation is that success has always depended heavily on judicial attitudes. Changes in judicial interpretation brought about the boom in litigation. New federal legislation may have an effect in the future.

The litigation of the early 1960s concentrated on establishing violations of prisoners' rights guaranteed either by the US Constitution or through federally guaranteed statutory rights. The way was opened to prisoners through the resurrection of the Federal Civil Rights Act of 1871. This Act enables a prisoner to bring an action in tort seeking to strike down oppressive prison rules and practices as well as to claim punitive damages when his constitutional rights have been violated.

Two pieces of legislation enacted more recently gave further procedural assistance to prisoners – the Civil Rights Attorney's Fees Awards Act of 1976, and the Civil Rights of Institutionalised Persons Act of 1980. The Attorney's Fees Awards Act was enacted to secure qualified counsel for plaintiffs in civil rights actions. The Act allows the court to award the successful party a reasonable attorney's fee. There are difficulties, as the Act does not empower the courts to appoint counsel in general or a specialist in particular to work for what is, in fact, a fee paid out of any award made by the court. There is the additional problem of defining who is the successful party. The court must consider whether the party has accomplished the objectives of the litigation rather than win a full trial on the merits of the case. (Leeke, 1980, p. 117)

The Civil Rights of Institutionalised Persons Act of 1980 empowers the US Attorney-General to initiate or to intervene in civil actions brought to redress systematic deprivations of constitutional and federal statutory rights of persons residing in state institutions. (US Code Congressional and Administrative News, 1980, p. 1937) The Justice Department had acted either as amicus curiae or plaintiff-intervenor in suits brought in relation to institutions housing the mentally ill, the mentally retarded, the chronically physically ill, juvenile delinquents, prisoners and neglected children. An amicus curiae brief allows the federal government to represent third party interests in suits brought between an institutional inmate and the administration of the institution. Many states faced with a suit assisted by the Attorney-General voluntarily upgraded conditions, or revised laws to comply with previously announced constitutional safeguards.

The impetus behind the Civil Rights of Institutionalised Persons Act derived largely from the belief that the Justice Department should be actively involved in the process of securing decent living conditions for people in the country's institutions. Some of the conditions revealed in cases such as Gates v. Collier were 'so base, inhumane and barbaric' as 'to shock the conscience of any right thinking person'. The ACLU hailed the new legislation as 'the first civil rights victory of the 1980s'. (New York Times, 29 February 1980) The Act can be seen as redressing the balance of power available in what has usually been an unequal contest in the past.

The new Act was used in 1983, when Attorney-General Smith initiated an action under the cruel and unusual punishment prohibition of the Eighth Amendment in respect of two prisons in Hawaii. The state governor and four state officials were named as defendants. The decision to sue came after state officials refused to allow the Department of Justice access to its prisons. (New York Times, 6 March 1983) This use of the Civil Rights of Institutionalised Persons Act was all the more remarkable as it happened under a Republican administration fiercely opposed to federal intervention.

The more recent history of the Civil Rights of Institutionalised Persons Act has not been free from controversy. In June 1984, a dispute broke out between the Department of Justice and a federal district court judge over the Department's use of its powers under the Act. Critics, including the ACLU, said that the Department of Justice was taking a 'states' rights view', i.e. leaving a wide discretion to the state officials in deciding how they wished to administer affairs in their state. The Director stated that the federal government should not be involved in overseeing a state's enforcement of its own law, but should be concerned with constitutional issues. (New York Times, 11 June 1984)

The worst fears of the ACLU were not in fact confirmed. Although the Reagan administration believed in the federal government staying out of civil rights actions, the Rights of Institutionalised Persons Act has not become a dead letter.

Problems of access to the courts

The bulk of American prisoners' rights litigation is filed pro se. A standard recommended form is available, with instructions on how to complete it; complainants are asked to recount the facts of the case rather than legal arguments or statutes. If completed properly, the pro forma should contain all the information necessary to bring a civil rights action. The question of whether the plaintiff should be allowed to proceed in forma pauperis, is based on the financial status of the plaintiff, rather than on the merits of the claim. Counsel can be appointed to help the preparation and presentation of the case as if the prisoner had hired a lawyer in the ordinary way.

The courts have developed various methods of screening to deal with the flood of petitions. Decisions about the merits and the financial status of the plaintiff are rarely made by judges: most are in fact made by magistrates and law clerks. (Turner, 1979, p. 620) Applications can be rejected on a variety of grounds, including lack of merit or the frivolous or malicious nature of the complaint. If the petition survives this hurdle, it is then for the petitioner to begin an action. Failure to prosecute a case is a further ground for dismissal. Prisoners rarely have the knowledge or resources to conduct a pre-trial discovery of evidence and law to move towards trial. Of the many that start out, few of these petitions are tried on their merits. To make matters worse, court staff may be biased against pro se cases the belief that pro se petitions will only be made when the petitioner has discussed the case with a lawyer who has rejected it as worthless. (Bergesen and Hoerger, 1974, p. 778)

Relatively few of these cases can be settled by negotiation between the parties. The opponents are prisoners presenting their own cases and state's attorneys, and they are not likely to reach agreement. In most civil litigation there is a resolution reached at the door of the court, but in prisoners' cases a full hearing is the norm. (Turner, 1979, p. 637)

Prisoners' rights litigation in the US is complicated by the organisation of the federal courts. The courts of appeals can be divided on issues. For example, the Third, Fifth, Sixth, Ninth and Tenth Circuits have held that the due process requirement does not apply to parole applications. The remaining circuits have taken the opposite view. (Bronstein, 1980, p. 38) Until an issue is taken to the Supreme Court, precedent will depend on where the prisoner is geographically located.

There is a distinction between the kinds of decisions made at different levels in the courts. The Supreme Court has dealt primarily with narrow procedural issues, while the lower courts have begun to look at wider issues which concern the totality of prison conditions and attempt to remedy the broad constitutional defects in state prison systems. (Bronstein, 1980, p. 39)

Problems of judicial intervention

Prisoners' rights litigation is but one source of the conflict over the interpretation of the US Constitution. There are two polar positions in this debate which John Ely has termed 'interpretivism' and 'non-interpretivism'. (Ely, 1980, p. 1) Interpretivism insists that the judge may only enforce those constitutional requirements that are fairly drawn from the text of the Constitution itself. Non-interpretivism allows judges to range beyond the wording of the Constitution to apply fundamental values imputed to open-ended constitutional provisions such as the need for due process of law or the prohibition of cruel and unusual punishment. The complaint is that non-interpretivism allows judges to impose their own values under the guise of enforcing constitutional limitations, while interpretivism fails to respond to new situations. (Benedict, 1981, p. 70)

Prisoners' rights litigation has been attacked by interpretivists, as it benefited from the 'due process revolution' of the Supreme Court under Chief Justice Warren. (Huff, 1980, p. 51) In a series of decisions in the 1960s, the Supreme Court made it a requirement (binding on all the states) that suspects should be informed of their rights when arrested (Miranda), that juveniles should be represented when liable to custody (Gault), and that indigent accused should have legal representation at trial (Gideon). Judicial decisions affected the situation of groups which had previously been powerless, and this activism carried across into the prisons.

Two related issues have acted as a brake on judicial activity. The 'separation of powers' and 'federalism' are issues which stem from American constitutional and political traditions. Prison administration is an executive action, and if prisoners have grievances about the conditions of their custody, these should be resolved within the institution. It is argued that judges do not have sufficient knowledge of institutional administration to cope with these issues, or that piecemeal litigation is not an effective way of dealing with the complex problems of penal policy-making. The main problem with this argument for restraint is that these professional deficiencies and constitutional constraints have not prevented the judiciary from regulating government intervention in other areas, for example, business and trade. A more radical explanation of this unwillingness to intervene is the fear of undermining prison discipline. (Glick, 1973, p. 284)

The other constitutional issue is federalism. The United States of America is a union of states which has a federal government over and above the states. The power of the states to control the daily lives of their citizens through the criminal law and the prisons is one of great sensitivity and is jealously guarded. Involvement by the federal judiciary in these areas is seen as unwarranted interference in the lawful activities of state government. The judiciary is restrained by the respect due to states' rights. In prisoners' rights litigation, state's attorneys-general are not slow to remind the federal judges that the state should be allowed to correct any abuses in its own system. (Bergesen and Hoerger, 1974, pp. 781-2)

By the 1960s the federal courts came to the view that the states were actually abusing prisoners' rights rather than allowing complaints to be aired. The judges' reluctance was overcome by their recognition that there were no effective state remedies. More recently the prisoners' rights litigation has brought a great development of internal grievance mechanisms. New members have been appointed to the Supreme Court largely because they hold this view. Recent Supreme Court decisions in (Rhodes v. Chapman for example) are designed to avoid imposing national standards with their attendant costs on the states.

The problems of enforcement

Constitutional issues are equally important when the discussion turns to enforcement. The enforcement of many court decisions has led to problems for the courts, the prison authorities and for prisoners themselves. The number of decisions and their scope need to be treated as issues in their own right.

The doctrine of the separation of powers means that the courts are dependent on the other branches of government for enforcement of decisions. If force is needed, federal marshalls responsible to the President must exercise it, and although the President is obliged by the Constitution to see that the laws are executed faithfully, presidents have frequently chosen to ignore Supreme Court rulings or to delay their implementation.

The court's decisions in many cases required considerable changes in the organisation, staffing and resources of state prison systems. These cases have implications for the allocation and expenditure of the state's funds, which means that the federal courts actually intervene directly in the administration and government of the state. The potential for conflict over the issue of federalism is clear.

In Gates v. Collier, the judicial decision meant that the Mississippi prison authorities were required among other things to build a prison which did not violate the constitutional rights of its inmates. The emergency building programme alone was budgeted at $1 million. The money was actually provided by a federal agency, the Law Enforcement Assistance Administration, which reduced some of the conflict.

The bulk of the literature on prisoners' rights litigation does not look at the consequences of change over time. Jacobs' case study of Stateville Penitentiary, Illinois is a notable exception to this trend. Jacobs is primarily concerned with plotting the changing integration of the prison with the larger society, and in showing how these changes are reflected in the changing patterns of authority within the prison. (Jacobs, 1977)

When the Cooper case came to court, the administration claimed that any concession, no matter how slight, would lead to chaos. The court ordered partial relief, and allowed the Muslims access to the Koran and their religious advisers. The later years of the decade saw an increasing level of violence between groups of prisoners and against guards.

The prison began to change in the early 1970s. New senior staff were appointed who introduced a concern for the respect, dignity and status of prisoners. In 1971 the federal court of appeals insisted that prison rules should be stated formally and made available to prisoners. But a gap began to develop between formalised rules and working procedures. The rules were simply not followed. More prisoners were held in solitary confinement than ever before. The courts could only demand that official decisions were reasoned and reasonable, but they could not affect the substance of low visibility decisions made by basic grade staff. The prison administrators evaded the clear meaning, if not the letter, of court decisions. The prison had become a legal battleground. In 1969 there were 66 suits brought, a figure that doubled by 1971 and remained at that number at the time Jacobs was writing.

Jacobs makes an important point in arguing that the greatest impact of the court decisions on the prison came from the legal process

> The administrators don't like being sued, hate going to court, and fear personal liability. They feel that attorneys and inmates harass them with lawsuits and incessant demands for depositions and interrogations. (Jacobs, 1977, p. 118)

The proliferation of prisoners' rights litigation generated a continuous flow of attorneys into the prison. The presence of lawyers who are continually asking for records and who question the reasons for rules and decisions provides in effect a system of independent inspection. Jacobs suggests that this had had a profound effect on day to day administration.

There have been several attempts to collate the results of the different methods that have been employed to increase compliance with court orders. (National Association of Attorneys-General, 1980, Nathan, 1979 and Anon, 1977) The conclusions that have been reached are two-fold. First, the establishment of a monitor of some kind has meant that while the monitor's existence 'did not cause additional compliance it forced the defendants to maintain the level of compliance they had achieved, effectively preventing any 'back sliding''. (Nathan, 1979, pp. 444-5) Monetary damages have rarely been awarded, as this is not a method that can be used to effect change within the prison system and that is the real objective. (National Association of Attorneys-General, 1980, p. 42)

Litigation and institutional reform

Prisoners' rights litigation is not an end in itself. It may be initiated to reduce or remove the effects of a prison system on one individual, but ultimately it has implications for some broader change. There is a great deal of controversy about the impact of prisoners' rights litigation on institutional change.

Prison officials have argued vociferously that all of the litigation and the court orders have increased pressure on already overstretched staff and their limited budgets. (Jacobs, 1980, p. 430) The head of one institution for young men estimated that 20% of his time was spent either in court or preparing for court appearances. (New York Times, 1 June 1980) The argument is also made that the judges cannot see that these civil rights demands conceal a deadly struggle for control over the prisons. Prison administrators have been horrified to find that judges have become actively involved in the oversight of administrative decisions. The pessimism of professional prison administrators has a mirror image in the response by prisoners' rights activists, who treat every unfavourable ruling as a total defeat, demonstrating in their view that the courts have gone back to the 'hands-off' doctrine. (Woodbury, 1982, p. 746)

At an impressionistic level, arguments for a pessimistic view do predominate. Much of the debate about the effectiveness of prisoners' rights litigation has to be at a rhetorical level because there is no adequate methodology as yet to investigate the effects of litigation on the prison as an organisation, nor is there any organisational research designed to report the effects of litigation on different prisons.

The optimists' case hinges on two features which stem from the way that litigation has opened up the prisons. The first is that judicial review has constrained the power of the states to remove, limit or suspend the rights of offenders. (Thomas, 1980, p. 245) John Conrad suggests that there has been a transition from absolute to limited authority in the prisons. (Conrad, 1977, p. 17) Slowly, litigation has made the prison administration more responsive to the needs of prisoners, and less completely dominated by the needs of the staff.

The second is that the chance of doing irreparable damage to prisoners, either intentionally or unintentionally, is slowly being reduced as a result of the litigation. Prisons are being forced to become correctional facilities. (Thomas, 1980, p. 255)

The case for the pessimists is more highly elaborated and consists of the following main points

1. When judges come to decide what ought to be done to improve prison conditions, their standards are both highly subjective and highly flexible so that administrators can rarely anticipate what represents constitutionally acceptable conditions. (Robbins, 1978, p. 554)

2. Neither judges nor legal activists have any real idea of how prisons work as organisations. Few have wanted the long-term contact with prisons and prisoners that would perhaps achieve lasting change. (Thomas, 1980, p. 250)

3. The adversarial nature of court procedure means that prison administrators are forced to defend policies and practices with which they as individuals may be dissatisfied.

4. The real task of implementing the courts' judgments falls to those people who were on the losing side and it is perhaps too much to expect that they comply with enthusiasm.

5. Reforms inevitably require additional financial resources, and state legislatures may be reluctant to make the money available. (Anon, 1977, p. 434) In Alabama, for example, $45 million was required in 1981 for new prison buildings, and state expenditure on prisons had nearly tripled in two years. (New York Times, 16 May 1981) The cost implications of Ruiz v. Estelle in Texas were estimated to be $300 million.

6. Judicial decisions on prison reform may actually have damaging consequences. Charles Thomas, who has worked for many years in US

prisons, has argued that in prisoners' rights litigation the objective has been to change the balance of power, but the real effect has been an increase in the levels of tension and violence. (Thomas, 1980, p. 250) John Conrad has also argued that discipline among the guards deteriorated as a result of litigation. (Conrad, 1977, p. 16)

7. Prison administrators have become skilled in implementing those sections of judicial decisions which increase security. Lipman has argued that administrators dealt only with the defects which would remove judicial oversight as quickly as possible. (Lipman, 1974, p. 724)

The optimistic and pessimistic views on the prospects for reform are both impressionistic and judgemental. There has been little systematic evaluation. The limited amount of evaluative work which has been done falls into two basic categories: first, a legal evaluation of the effectiveness of court orders; and second, criteria for evaluating reforms. (Anon, 1981; Eisenberg and Yeazell, 1980; Fletcher, 1982; Starr, 1981) It is to the second of these that attention must now turn.

Jacobs argues that the underlying reason for the discrepancies claimed to exist between the optimistic and pessimistic camps is the absence of a methodology for identifying the impacts of litigation, and the absence of criteria for judging their importance. (Jacobs, 1980)

He suggests that some of the important effects of the prisoners' rights movement include the organisation of prisoners, the mobilisation of citizen and interest groups, legislative and administrative budget making and lawmaking, and the setting of professional standards of prison management. These effects are in addition to the redistribution of power within the prisons. This approach emphasises the open nature of the prison, and stresses those features which may contribute to continuing change, a momentum of pressure for reform. Jacobs also identifies a number of secondary changes which have their origins in prisoners' rights' litigation. One example of such changes is the introduction of a new generation of administrators.

Huff and Alpert echoed many of Jacobs' concerns but they add several important considerations. They argue that evaluation cannot make progress until there is a larger sample of cases to allow the formulation of a general theory of decree implementation and its impact on social institutions. (Huff and Alpert, 1982) Four basic issues could provide part of the research agenda

(1) What factors contribute to compliance or non-compliance with court-ordered reform?
(2) What are the unanticipated consequences of such reform within the organisational context?
(3) What impact does court-ordered reform have on employees, the management, and the clients (in this case, prisoners and the public)?
(4) What strategies are used by organisations to facilitate or to impede compliance? (Huff and Alpert, 1982, p. 118) (emphasis in original)

It is proposed that evaluation research should be of the 'summative' type as opposed to 'formative'; that is, research designed to produce an assessment of effectiveness after the completion of the project or programme. Huff and Alpert recognise that research in this context would provide methodological and ethical problems. It is suggested that theoretical frameworks could be provided by complex organisational theory and systems theory to tackle the sorts of issues mentioned above.

Conclusions

The prisoners' rights cases have brought virtually every state in the Union before the federal courts to defend some aspect or another of its prison system against the charge that it violates the constitutional rights of its inmates. Prison administrators have been required to describe why they have organised their institutions in a particular way. But it is difficult to assess how much any one individual prisoner's life may have been changed by all this litigation. The prisoners' rights cases do not seem to have reduced the considerable variations in prison conditions between the states. States which had progressive and enlightened systems before the prisoners' rights movement began still have equally enlightened systems.

The prisoners' rights cases have been important because they have taken the federal judiciary into new areas of responsibility, where they had little skill and knowledge to start from. Major constitutional issues have been raised, and while the more senior members of the judiciary have been reluctant to extend prisoners' rights as quickly as have the lower courts, the whole issue has been taken extremely seriously. The federal judiciary has organised conferences and committees to co-ordinate its practice and standards.

The prisoners' rights movement has gained wide support. Concern with the prisons has not remained a peripheral social and political issue. Prisoners' rights cases have attracted money and support from a wide variety of individuals and institutions. Lawyers have contested cases, and citizens groups have lobbied their legislatures. The mass media have dealt with the issues as a matter of public importance. Despite considerable resistance, much of it covert, the prisoners' rights movement has achieved a legitimacy that has never been achieved in Britain. In some ways, this political point may ultimately be of more importance than the decisions reached by the courts. The prisoners' rights litigation has been a means of moving the problems of the penal system back into the political arena, where the question of the nature and purpose of imprisonment really belongs.

Note

[1] A total of 46 people were killed when the riot was finally suppressed; the public was outraged because the New York state troopers killed members of the staff held as hostages as well as prisoners (Wicker, 1976).

9 England and the United States: comparison and contrast

One of the main themes of this book has been the ways in which two prison and legal systems cope with the idea of prisoners' rights. The starting point in each case was a description of the organisation of the legal system and the mechanisms by which litigation may be brought and enforced. In the course of description and evaluation it has become clear that there are both similarities and differences and it is now necessary to make more direct comparisons.

The process of making comparisons involves many of the well-known difficulties inherent in the comparative analysis of social institutions: one of the reasons often given for studying other countries is to discover what lessons may be learned for one's own country. In the case of prisoners' rights, this process has already been started in an unsystematic way. A number of commentators on and critics of the English penal system have made implicit and explicit connections between the two countries. The development of prisoners' rights in the US is held up as an example for possible adoption in England. Sometimes this is explicit, but more frequently, the approach is simply to describe what the Americans do to deal with some penal problem: the message is that something similar should be done in Britain. The simplistic view referred to in the Introduction was current in the late 1960s and early 1970s: the 'lesson' was seen as glaringly obvious, and the only real issue was that of the speed in attaining the goal of the full, American-style, judicialisation of prisoners' rights. That view might have been acceptable as part of a political manifesto, but it ignores both the past and the present; it simply assumes that Britain is a smaller version of America. Now it is important to see which rights and safeguards have developed in each country.

The major difficulty in any comparative study is that of deciding which characteristics or dimensions should be used as the basis for comparisons. The classical formulation of this has been stated many times - for example Martin Rein writes 'What is needed in social policy is not so much good tools but good questions'. (Rein, 1970, p. x) Unfortunately, he does not tell us what characteristics a good question should have, but the 'goodness' of a question is usually to be evaluated on a post-hoc basis: it is held to be good because it provided a feature which fitted into the investigator's view of what the similarities and differences ought to be in the field under study. In her study on comparative method, Joan Higgins has suggested that this work stems from nine different orientations. The approaches range from concentration on groups in need, through general policy areas such as medical care, to concepts and issues. Higgins concludes that it is difficult to draw conclusions as to the relative effectiveness of various approaches, but she suggests that a contribution of both description and explanation is necessary. (Higgins, 1981, pp. 20-5)

A number of basic differences between England and America make comparison more difficult. First, America has a written constitution to which prisoners can apply, while England does not. This difference between positive and negative approaches to rights creates the difficulty even of knowing what should be considered as constituting rights in the English system. Second, there is the problem that the English prison system is influenced both by English domestic law and by its obligations under the European Convention on Human Rights, while American citizens do not have access to a similar supra-national source of rights and freedoms.

The differences do in fact suggest a common basis for comparison and analysis. The European Convention on Human Rights provides a bridge between the English and American approaches to rights. The European Convention is a written statement of a number of rights which can be compared with the US Constitution. This use of the European Convention as the basis for comparison allows a number of other questions to be asked

1. which rights have been upheld in all three jurisdictions;
2. are there claims which are not recognised in any of the three jurisdictions?
3. are some jurisdictions silent on some claims to rights;
4. are some issues not litigated in some jurisdictions?

It is important at this stage to remember that the word 'rights' is not entirely unproblematic.

It is possible to make some fairly detailed comparisons of judicially recognised claims by using this strategy, although one point needs to be made before doing so. The American material tends to concentrate on decisions made by the Supreme Court. This reflects the fact that the federal courts are only unitary at the highest level, i.e. the Supreme Court. At the lowest level of the federal system, the district courts, there can be considerable variation, and this will continue unless and until an authoritative decision is made by the Supreme Court.

Rights claimed in England and the US

The material to be discussed in the main part of this chapter falls into seven sub-sections

1. rights appealed to in all three jurisdictions, under the European Convention on Human Rights, in English domestic law and under the

US Constitution;
2. rights appealed to under the European Convention on Human Rights and in English domestic law;
3. rights appealed to under the European Convention on Human Rights and under the US Constitution;
4. rights appealed to under the European Convention on Human Rights alone;
5. rights appealed to in English domestic law and under the US Constitution;
6. rights appealed to under the US Constitution alone; and,
7. rights appealed to in English domestic law alone.

Rights claimed under the European Convention on Human Rights, in English domestic law and under the US Constitution

The principal rights claimed from all three sources concern notions of inhuman and degrading treatment, slavery or involuntary servitude, access to the courts and jurisdiction over prison matters, freedom of correspondence, freedom of religion, and rights to property.

Article 3 of the European Convention on Human Rights has been interpreted in a strict way. Only one claim made by a prisoner (Hilton) in the English penal system has been admitted by the Commission and this led eventually to a friendly settlement. The Commission has rejected arguments which have relied on either a single blow allegedly struck by a prison officer, or the loss of privileges or restrictions resulting from a prisoner's classification or categorisation. The one remaining case concerned the deterioration of a prisoner through alleged threats of violence from staff and prisoners.

There are three points to be made about the cases brought under the American Constitution. First, there have been a large number of cases which have claimed that the prohibition on cruel and unusual punishment had been violated. Second, the US courts have accepted arguments extending the meaning of the Eighth Amendment so that the totality of prison conditions can amount to cruel and unusual punishment. This Amendment has been used to bring the neglect of prisoners' medical needs to the attention of the courts. The US Supreme Court has set standards relating to overcrowding and the use of solitary confinement. Ultimately, the Eighth Amendment is concerned with the dignity of man.

The one English domestic case reported is noteworthy because the English interpretation of the prohibition on cruel and unusual punishment found in the Bill of Rights of 1689 differs from the American. The phrase 'cruel and unusual' has to be understood conjunctively and it is unlikely that prison conditions would fall within this meaning. The sorts of issues raised in the American courts have never been discussed in England, because similar conditions have not existed. Violence by prison staff could be dealt with through criminal charges of assault, but charges of this kind are difficult to prove, as was seen after the Hull prison riot.

The dignity of man is an important symbol which can be used to control what can legitimately be done to convicted offenders. There is no similar notion available explicitly in the European Convention on Human Rights. Both the Preamble and the Articles are stated in a more prosaic manner, and there does not seem to have been any clear notion of human dignity in the discussions of the European Commission or the Court of Human Rights. There is a paradox here, in that the prison conditions described in the totality of prison condition cases and that relating to solitary confinement refer to conditions which are a little reminiscent of English prisons in the late eighteenth century. The prohibitions in the US Constitution did not prevent these appalling conditions occurring in the first place, but they have provided some subsequent relief.

The one attempt to invoke Article 4, which prohibits slavery and servitude, was always doomed to failure as one of the permitted exceptions is labour done in the course of lawful detention. The same is true of the US Constitution. Involuntary work has been a recognised part of imprisonment. Work has been an important feature of imprisonment in England: it is a matter of choice for prisoners awaiting trial on remand. For the majority, work has been seen variously as a means of rehabilitation, a way of filling time, or a contribution to the running costs of the prison.

The European Court of Human Rights has been diligent in safeguarding prisoners' rights of access to the courts and to legal advice. The English courts have been rather slower to move in the same direction but have now done so. Broadly similar rights are available from the two sources. The American federal courts led for many years in guaranteeing prisoners access to the courts to test their claims in relation to the US Constitution. Prisoners in the US may be limited in terms of the nature of the litigation they can bring. English prisoners have not been limited in this way, as the right to sue is no longer lost as a consequence of conviction. The English judges have produced rights of access to the courts and to legal advice out of the common law.

The rules of natural justice have been elaborated to produce a list of guidelines in relation to prison disciplinary hearings held by boards of visitors. English law appears to give better protections to prisoners than is found under the US Constitution. English law now permits legal representation for prisoners facing 'grave' and 'especially grave' charges against prison discipline. In the US prisoners may be accompanied by a 'friend' when facing serious discipline charges, but the friend does not have to be a lawyer. Otherwise the substance of prisoners' rights when facing discipline charges are broadly similar in the two countries. Prisoners may present a defence, and are to be allowed to call witnesses and present documentary evidence, and the prison authorities are required to bring to notice exculpatory evidence. In neither country do prisoners have the right to cross-examine witnesses. The English boards of visitors are enjoined to be helpful towards the prisoner in the sense of giving him every opportunity to present an adequate defence.

The requirements of natural justice and due process do not apply so rigorously when the discipline charges are less serious. The English system divides discipline between the prison governor and the board of visitors, with the boards dealing with the more serious offences. The English courts used to hold that the disciplinary actions of the governor were outside the scope of judicial review, and this meant that most discipline hearings were subject only to the internal grievance mechanisms. There never seems to have been this judicially decided barrier in any of the American cases. The courts on both sides of the Atlantic recognise that the maintenance of order in the prisons is a difficult task, and that extending all of the rights of a criminal trial to prison discipline would place additional burdens on the staff. The American courts explicitly recognise a conflict between safety and due process, and allow the staff a discretion whether to allow witnesses to be called or evidence presented. This degree of discretion may present two risks - it may be too wide or it may be too narrow. Prison officials could use the vagueness of wording to limit the opportunities for a defence to be presented. The English courts have not given this potential loophole to prison administrators, and the decision of the European Court of Human Rights that boards of visitors' discipline hearings are covered by the same conditions as a criminal trial when the charges are serious (criminal as well as discipline offences) is a means of ensuring fairness.

Until the advent of the individual right of petition, prisoners in the English prisons had very limited rights in respect of correspondence with the outside world. The Prison Rules gave the Home Secretary the power to impose general and/or particular restrictions on correspondence. There has been no domestic remedy available to challenge the Home Secretary's discretion in this area until 1983, the House of Lords held that interference with letters and documents initiating court proceedings was a contempt of court. A series of cases brought to Strasbourg by prisoners in English prisons has led to the virtual collapse of the old system of censorship. The new Standing Order 5 has been made publicly available. Prisoners may complain about prison conditions as soon as a complaint has been registered internally. Prisoners are now able to correspond with their legal advisers all of which was simply unthinkable before 1980.

The First Amendment has been interpreted as meaning that absolutely no restrictions can be placed on freedom of expression. The attitude to prisoners' correspondence is rather startling at first sight because it is the person outside the prison who is seen as the victim of prison censorship. The free citizen cannot be deprived of his/her rights to communicate freely or to be the recipient of uncensored correspondence.

Both the European Commission of Human Rights and US district courts have been asked to decide whether visits fall within the terms of Article 8 and the First Amendment respectively. Both have been reluctant to accept prisoners' claims on these points. Both systems recognise that visits are secondary to the requirements of prison administrators. The European Commission has rejected the argument that the requirement to wear prison uniform violates this Article of the Convention.

Two features are immediately apparent in a comparison of rights relating to freedom of religion. First, there is an established religion in England, something the US Constitution specifically. Second, that there has been no use of Article 9 by prisoners in English prisons. In the US, a number of prisoners claimed that they were being discriminated against because of their religious beliefs. They argued that members of a faith or sect have not been given the same freedoms to pursue their religious beliefs as members of other faiths. This argument has been made by members of fringe religious groups such as the Black Muslims.

The experience in English prisons has been that religious beliefs and practices have usually been tolerated, and special diets have been made available for those whose religions demanded them. There have therefore been no parallel cases in England. The requirement that a prisoner must declare his religious belief on reception is not immutable. Prisoners may apply to the board of visitors to have that record amended, and the board 'may give directions accordingly upon being satisfied that the application is made in good faith'.

There is one recent exception to this apparently acceptable record of English prisons, and that concerns Rastafarianism. Rastafarians have been the objects of discrimination in the sense that until 1984 it is alleged that they were regarded by some prison medical officers as being psychotic because of their beliefs. It is not clear what happened to individual Rastafarians as a result of this view taken by medical staff.

When it comes to the protection of property, the stage has been reached when the European Convention on Human Rights provides an apparent right which has not been the basis of any claim by any prisoner in the English prison system.   In contrast to the US Constitution the right to property is relegated to a Protocol, while the right to life and liberty is accorded a higher priority in the Convention.   The deprivation of liberty is provided with a series of safeguards in Articles 5, 6 and 7.   The American Constitution links all three in the Fourteenth Amendment.

The US Supreme Court has rejected two claims when prisoners' property has been either lost or destroyed.   In both <u>Parratt</u> and <u>Hudson</u>, the Supreme Court held that the due process clause could only be invoked if there was no other remedy available, e.g. in state law.   The Court did not define an 'adequate' remedy, nor did it comment on the behaviour of prison staff who intentionally destroy prisoners' property – an abuse of power that the Fourteenth Amendment seems to be designed to prevent.

In English prison law, the one attempt <u>(Becker)</u> to claim damages for the loss (unlawful detention) of a prisoner's property ended with a rejection of the claim and a side-stepping of the real issues.   In England, this precedent denies the kind of remedy which the US Supreme Court said prevented similar American claims from being constitutional violations.   Lord Denning's diatribe against disgruntled prisoners allowed the issue to be closed without any consideration of how prisoners' property was to be treated, and left the prisoner with no remedy if property was either lost or destroyed.

European Convention and English domestic law

There is only one issue which has occurred so far under both the European Convention and in English domestic law and that concerns the right to marry.

In 1981, the European Commission of Human Rights held that because English domestic law would not allow marriages to take place in prisons, and the Home Secretary would not allow the prisoner to be released temporarily for a marriage ceremony, Article 12 of the Convention had been violated.   The British government subsequently introduced legislation allowing prisoners to be married in prison. There are no American federal cases relating to marriage because there is no equivalent right to marriage or to found a family guaranteed by the US Constitution.   It is possible that this issue has been raised under state laws.

European Convention and US Constitution

Two broad areas of rights which are established by both the European Convention on Human Rights and the US Constitution. The first is concerned with freedom of expression and the second concerns rights of assembly and the formation of associations.

For many years, prisons were designed and organised to make sure that the prisoner was cut off from the outside world, and limited in his opportunity to express his views within the prison.   The isolation of prisons has been reduced in more recent times and newspapers and fictional books are almost universally available in English prisons. Prisoners have access to radios and televisions, although only long-term prisoners are allowed to have their own radios.   The only censorship of television programmes is that imposed by having 'lights out' at a fixed time. Books and periodicals may be ordered, but are subject to censorship by the prison authorities. The European Commission of Human Rights has accepted as admissible one complaint from an English prisoner that restrictions placed on access to periodicals, and has yet to decide on the merits of the case.

But the restrictions on prisoners' freedom to express their own views have been greater. In England, the system of censoring prisoners' mail has severely limited their ability to correspond with other people, especially if their correspondence was concerned with complaints or was intended for publication. Prisoners had to submit any notes on their prison experiences for scrutiny before they were released at the end of the sentence. In fact, this type of censorship did not always work, nor was it always applied, prison memoirs have been published while the prisoner was still in prison. (Boyle, 1977) Some of these restrictions have been lifted after the Silver case.

All of this is in marked contrast to the US, where the First Amendment has been interpreted to allow very considerable freedom both to prisoners or correspondents and to the media. Prisoners can use the media to ventilate complaints about their situation, but the media do not have the right to interview named prisoners. There is a different official view of freedom of information which tends to open up prison administration in a way that is totally alien to the English tradition of the Official Secrets Acts.

The Americans have also taken the idea of freedom of expression further than in Europe by including 'a prisoner's personal appearance as part of his legitimate right to expression'. This right is not a complete one as the prison authorities can require prisoners to shave off beards. Although attitudes and practices have changed in the last ten years or so, there are still important restrictions on prisoners' ability to express themselves publicly.

The one claim made to the European Commission of Human Rights by a prisoner that his right to freedom of association had been violated led to a declaration that the claim was inadmissible. The Commission had decided that Article 11 is concerned with the freedom to form or be affiliated with a group or organisation pursuing particular aims.   It is concerned essentially with the right to take ollective action. The history of PROP, the one attempt in England to form a prisoners' union, was characterised by official rejection and decline into relative obscurity.   Such an organisation would fall within the Commission's definition of 'association', and would present a difficult issue for government, as the exceptions to this freedom listed in Article 11(2) do not appear immediately to rule out this kind of organisation.

The rationale used by the US Supreme Court in Jones v. North Carolina Prisoners' Labour Union Inc. was that the prison authority's refusal to allow prisoners to join or form a union, and among other things banning all meetings was reasonable and consistent with the legitimate operational code of the prison. The Supreme Court rejected arguments in favour of a constitutional right to freedom of assembly, and took the view that the opinions of prison administrators should be given precedence.   If prison administrators thought that a prisoners' union would cause security and other problems, then they could legitimately ban such an organisation.

The issue raised in Butler v. Preiser, the right to take up a collection for a prisoners' defence fund, was concerned with the apparent capriciousness of administrative decision-making.   The prison administrators could not provide a clear and consistent set of reasons for allowing some forms of fund raising, and for banning this one.

Prison administrators and judges have been particularly loath to contemplate prisoners' unions.   Even when unions are considered to be legitimate organisations, there are certain kinds of bodies which style themselves unions which are seen as being illegitimate, e.g. the Claimants' Union.   Prisoners are not perceived as being the kind of people to be allowed to engage in collective action.   One function of imprisonment is to place the prisoner in a position of subordination to the staff and ultimately to society, and anything which challenges that operating assumption will be unacceptable.   At least, that is the message for public consumption; the reality of the prison being open to low visibility negotiations between staff and informal inmate leaders is kept concealed behind the official version of events and processes.

European Convention on Human Rights only

One issue which has been the subject of litigation under the European Convention on Human Rights alone: the right to an education.   The European Commission of Human Rights declared inadmissible the only complaint brought by a prisoner under this Article which appears in the First Protocol of the European Convention on Human Rights.   Precedent in the European Court of Human Rights does not require a State to provide particular kinds of education, this Article of the Protocol merely guarantees the right of citizens in principle, to avail themselves of the means of instruction existing at a given time.
In the US, the right to education has not been an issue in its own right as it is not a federally protected right.   The right to education has been important in litigation concerning racial discrimination.   The absence of vocational training has been the subject of adverse comment in some of the prison system cases, e.g. Holt v. Sarver.
At this point, the European Convention runs out of applications in the context of prisoners' rights.   There are, however, still a number of issues which have been considered judicially in the courts in England and the US.

English domestic law and the US Constitution

The cases which occur in both English domestic law and under the US Constitution are concerned with procedural rights and fairness in decision-making.   The problem of fairness relates to decisions on transfers to other prisons or to mental hospitals.
The American concern with the requirements of the due process of law is strongest when the decisions approximate to the criminal trial.   In the US, the issue of transferring prisoners to state mental hospitals has been treated as an important matter.   The change of public status from 'criminal' to 'mentally ill' carries a number of additional disabilities including stigma and restrictions on release which cannot be applied lightly.   In England, by contrast, there seem to be no means of reviewing decisions about transfers from prison to mental hospitals.
The American courts revert quickly to ideas about safety and order in prisons as the question of liberty declines.   Prisoners can be placed in solitary confinement for administrative reasons, they can be transferred from one prison to another within the same state, and they can be transferred thousands of miles to a prison in another state if they are thought to be troublemakers, without any due process requirements.   The Supreme Court has taken the view that conviction for criminal offences means that prisoners lose any legal interest in how they are then dealt with by the prison authorities.   They have been

sentenced to imprisonment, and that gives a clear mandate to prison administrators to decide where and how they will be imprisoned so as to preserve order and prevent disorder.

US Constitution only

There have been a small number of claims which appear in one country only. The claim to a right to privacy in the prisoner's cell was, in fact, dismissed by the US Supreme Court. The claim was based on the right to privacy which stems from the Fourth Amendment. By contrast, there is no general right to privacy in English law, and what protection there is is piecemeal. What is meant by privacy in English law usually is concerned with intrusion by the media and various branches of authority. Search and seizure is usually covered by discussions of police powers, and there would be no basis in the Police and Criminal Evidence Act 1984 for a claim by prisoners.

English domestic law only

The common law duty of care which the English courts require of the prison authorities has provided some safeguards for prisoners. The prison authorities have a duty of care towards prisoners working in prison workshops. Prisoners have been less successful when they have asked the prison authorities to protect them from their fellows. There is no right in the US Constitution which provides similar safeguards.

Common features in England and the US

It is relatively easy to point to differences in both approaches to prisoners' rights and the content of rights between the two countries; looking for common features is more difficult. The principal similarity seems to be at the level of judicial attitudes to prisoners' claims.

It is useful to look at judicial attitudes in two time periods, up to 1979 and after. Until 1979, the American federal courts were prepared to consider claims made by prisoners, and the Supreme Court in particular took a strong lead in guaranteeing prisoners their rights under the Constitution. The main claims to rights upheld were those relating to due process. The federal courts extended rights of access to prisoners that were provided to other minority groups in American society. In this period, the English courts expressed a great reluctance to consider claims made by prisoners, and until the St Germain decision, prisoners had few judicially recognised rights after conviction. This marked contrast between the two countries was what gave such force to the arguments of writers like Cohen and Fitzgerald who held up the American example of how a prisoners' rights movement in England should develop. What these critics could not have foreseen was how the curve of judgments about prisoners' rights in favour of prisoners in the US would begin to flatten in the early 1980s while in England decisions in favour of prisoners began to increase dramatically.

The courts on both sides of the Atlantic now take the view that the rights of prisoners are not lost at the prison gates, and that prisoners do have legally enforceable rights; but it is also the case in both countries that this statement still does not tell the prisoner which rights he retains on entry into prison. The boundaries are constantly being tested when prisoners ask the courts to recognise new claims or new arguments are made to try old causes. What has happened in England and the US is that the courts have been willing to grant procedural rather than substantive rights to prisoners. At first these rights were simply those of access to the courts, but slowly rights to legal advice and representation have been recognised. The courts have also been prepared to grant rights in areas of activity which most closely resemble the courts themselves. Prison discipline hearings have gradually been surrounded by procedural safeguards for the prisoner defendant. There is no longer the judicial attitude that this is some form of private justice beyond the usual rules.

The concentration on procedural justice has been to the exclusion of substantive justice. Both the English and American judiciary have been reluctant to interfere in the administrative and managerial aspects of prison life, though the American courts have been prepared to say that some prison conditions are shocking to the conscience of reasonably civilised people. The conditions in which prisoners live, and the decisions made about their conditions, are seen as being managerial issues which fall within the proper sphere of prison administrators.

Prison administrators are regarded as being experts on a wide variety of topics, especially those relating to security and safety. This claimed expertise has allowed the judiciary to reject claims made by prisoners. The judges are able to allude to the potential problems of safety or disorder which would surely follow if the prisoner's claim was accepted. Statements about the risks of disorder are rarely accompanied by a critical evaluation of what the risk in fact consists. There is an ever present problem that the failure to recognise prisoners' rights, and the accompanying sense of injustice, will actually cause greater problems.

The one line of public policy running through prisoners' rights litigation then is the prison administrators' 'right to manage'. The 'right' is rarely the subject of open discussion but it is frequently described in dicta. The content seems to fluctuate over time, and it seems that a less expansive view is now being held in England. In the US, there seems to be evidence of a range of attitudes. The Supreme Court is more concerned with prison administration than with prisoners' rights, while the inferior courts seem more prepared to challenge the opinions of prison administrators, so much so that 46 state prison systems are currently under judicial supervision in respect of overcrowding. The consequence of this split between the levels of the judiciary is that there are few nationally applicable standards.

This leads on to the second common feature, the gap between rights on paper and rights in practice. One of the constant concerns of this study has been that of how prisoners' rights work in practice. The impression gained after a review of the various grievance mechanisms, official safeguards, pressure groups, ombudsmen, legal precedents and the activities of the European Commission and Court of Human Rights is that prisoners in English prisons have considerable protection against injustices and the abuse of power. There seems to be protection in depth, with alternatives available from simple requests to staff in the governor grades through to challenges of national legislation before the European Court of Human Rights. American prisoners do not have the same range of safeguards, but there have been other compensatory advantages such as the greater availability and interest of lawyers.

But it is equally clear that some issues cannot be dealt with by any of the grievance procedures; some jurisdictions may overlap but many are so restricted that they have very little effect. These problems would not be so serious if the prison population was declining: but the prison populations of both England and the US are increasing and sentences are getting longer.

The opportunities for conflict between prisoners and prison staff are increasing as sentences get longer and there is a risk that prisoners will be seen as legitimate objects for punishment because of the offences that they have committed. This means that prison administrators have to find some means of controlling both the level and nature of conflict. One possible mechanism to reduce tensions is to institutionalise conflict through formal grievance mechanisms such as the courts. The inconvenience of having to prepare a defence in a prisoner's rights case may be less significant in the long run than having to rebuild a prison after a riot.

This study is largely a record of the reluctance of prison staff and administrators to accept the changes forced on them by the courts. In England, the Home Office seems to have had an obsession with keeping lawyers out of prisons, and has attempted to prevent convicted prisoners from corresponding with them. Resistance was so strong that in the late 1970s it extended to non-cooperation with the experimental scheme to help prisoners prepare their defences before boards of visitors. Ten years later prisoners facing the more serious discipline charges may be legally represented and governors' disciplinary hearings are liable to judicial review. Many of the rights which now exist have been wrung from reluctant administrators and officials. But slowly these restrictions have been challenged and some of the prohibitions have been lifted. Opposition to change was so strong that the changes forced on the system are much more far-reaching than the changes which could have been carried out internally.

Similar stories can be told of conditions in the US where officials have resisted the enforcement of judicial decrees and unacceptable practices have persisted until further litigation has challenged official inactivity. In the US, the resistance was so marked that the courts eventually adopted the strategy of appointing special masters (i.e. court officials) to supervise the enforcement of remedies. Masters have become full-time overseers of programmes of prison rebuilding and reorganisation.

Even when there are these outsiders who exist exclusively to ensure official compliance with court orders, there are still problems in putting rights and safeguards into effect. The master cannot tackle the low-visibility abuses and injustices which may take place anywhere in the institution at any time of the day or night. The real problem of prisoners' rights has not changed since the first prison regulations were drawn up in the late eighteenth century, how are prison staff to be required or compelled to act in a lawful manner? This is a question of legal obligation - getting the staff to behave in accordance with both the law and common standards of decency in respect of a group of people of whom they may be afraid: who cannot be counted upon to reciprocate any generous gesture and yet over whom they have a considerable degree of power.

Where are prisoners' rights better protected?

Some evaluation has to be made at the end of a comparison of where prisoners' rights are better protected, or where prison standards are subject to better safeguards. It is immediately apparent is that there are wide differences both within and between the prison systems of the two countries. The range is greater in the US than in England, the best are better and the worst tend to be worse than anything found in England. The conditions described in the state prison systems of Arkansas, Alabama and Rhode Island in the 1960s have few equivalents in England: on the other hand some of the modern federal prisons provide standards which are equal to or better than some of the new prisons built in England.

The reason for mentioning the state of prison buildings and the methods of organisation is that the physical conditions in which prisoners live represent the most basic aspect of prisoners' rights. If the physical environment is unhealthy or dangerous, other rights hardly matter.   The prison system cases brought under the Eighth Amendment brought prison conditions into the twentieth century.

American prisons have been beset by political intervention in their administration and the view that prisons should not be a cost to the state.   Prisons have become the scene of racial segregation, racial discrimination and interracial violence.   This appears to have been much less true in England because the problem has been on a smaller scale but the information that is available shows a disturbing trend, for example in 1986 18% of those serving sentences of four years or more in English prisons were black. (NACRO, 1986, p. 20) However, there is widespread suspicion of the racially discriminatory attitudes and behaviour of some prison staff.

Prisoners' rights of access to the courts seem to be equal in England and the US. One advantage that English prisoners have is that they may have access to a wider range of rights, as they can bring actions not available to their American counterparts who may be limited to federally protected constitutional rights.   The courts in both countries have been prepared to extend a long list of procedural protections to prisoners facing more serious discipline offences, although only English prisoners seem to have some external participation in the prison discipline process.   Prisoners in both countries are equally bereft of rights when it comes to transfers to other prisons for disciplinary reasons, although the consequences may be worse for American prisoners, e.g. Wakinekona, a Hawaiian, was transferred 3,000 miles to California. On the other hand, there are more procedural safeguards governing transfers to mental hospitals for prisoners in America.

But while procedural rights offer an increasing level of protection in both countries, the position with regard to substantive rights leaves much to be desired.   In practice, the greater range of non-judicial safeguards in England means that prisoners in England are in a better position than their American counterparts.

Why have judges in both countries concentrated so largely on procedural issues while being comparatively neglectful of the major issues of substantive justice?   The reasons are fairly evident.   The judiciary in both countries are reluctant to become involved in discussions of the very contentious area of the theories of punishment; and they are unwilling to state the purposes of imprisonment.   Theories are remote from the daily lives of prisoners, and likely to remain so, except in Arkansas, Alabama and Rhode Island, where the judges have at least made some attempt to say what day-to-day conditions ought to look like.   The judiciary in England and the rest of the US have been unwilling to close the gap between theory and practice. Further, an involvement in moral and theoretical issues could lead to public disagreements between members of the bench which would provide arguments for further litigation.   Legal disputes which are kept at a strictly practical level can always be resolved in such a way as to uphold prison administrations.   Finally, decisions on substantive issues would carry

constitutional hazards, since they might be seen by government in either
country as judicial interference in the political process.

At first sight, the protections provided for prisoners in the two
countries look like patchwork quilts.   In reality, they are more like
string vests.   Prisoners and their problems can all too easily fall
through the holes.

Bibliography

Anon, (1963), 'Beyond the Ken of the Courts: a critique of judicial refusal to review the complaints of convicts', Yale Law Journal, vol. 72 no. 3, January.

Anon, (1976), 'Developments in the Law - Class Actions', Harvard Law Review, vol. 89 no. 7, May.

Anon, (1977), 'Implementation Problems in Institutional Reform Litigation', Harvard Law Review, vol. 91 no. 2, December.

Anon, (1981) 'Complex Enforcement: unconstitutional prison conditions', Harvard Law Review, vol. 94 no. 3, January

Advisory Council on the Penal System, (1968), The Regime for Long-Term Imprisonment, London, HMSO.

Advisory Council on the Penal System, (1978), Sentences of Imprisonment - a review of maximum penalties, London, HMSO.

Akester, K., (1988), 'Boards of Visitors and the Law', Prison Report, February issue, No 2.

Aldisert, R.J. (Chairman), (1980), Recommended Procedures for Handling Prisoners' Rights Cases in the Federal Courts, Washington DC, Federal Judicial Center.

American Bar Association, (1977), ABA Criminal Justice Standards Relating to the Legal Status of Prisoners, Boston, Little, Brown and Co..

American Friends Service Committee, (1971), Struggle for Justice, New York, Hill and Wang.

Anderson, Sir Norman, (1978), Law, Liberty and Justice, London, Stevens.

Beaven, A., (1980), 'Prisoners' Access', Law Quarterly Review, vol 95.

Beddard, R., (1980), Human Rights and Europe, London, Sweet and Maxwell.

Benedict, M.L., (1981), 'To Secure These Rights: rights, democracy, and judicial review in the Anglo-American constitutional heritage', Ohio

State Law Journal, vol. 42 no. 3.

Bergesen, B.E. and Hoerger, W.G., (1974), 'Judicial Misconceptions and the "Hidden Agenda" in Prisoners' Rights Litigation', Santa Clara Lawyer, vol. 14 no. 4, Summer.

Berkman, R., (1979), Opening the Gates: the rise of the prisoners' rights movement, Lexington, Mass., and Toronto, Lexington Books.

Birkinshaw, P., (1981), 'The Control Unit Regime: law and order in prison', Howard Journal, vol. XX.

Birkinshaw, P., (1982), 'New Rules on Prisoners' Correspondence', LAG Bulletin, July.

Borrie, G., (1976), 'The Membership of Boards of Visitors of Penal Establishments', Criminal Law Review.

Bottoms, A.E., and Preston, R.H. (eds),The Coming Penal Crisis: a criminological and theological exploration, Edinburgh, Scottish Academic Press.

Boyle, J., (1977), A Sense of Freedom, London, Pan.

British Institute of Human Rights, (1975), Detention: minimum standards of treatment, Chichester, Barry Rose.

Bronstein, A.J., (1980), 'Prisoners' Rights: a history', in Alpert, G.P. (ed), Legal Rights of Prisoners, Beverly Hills and Londn, Sage Publications.

Brownlie, I. (ed), (1971), Basic Documents on Human Rights, Oxford, Clarendon Press

Bullock, T., (1980), 'Legal Rights of Prisoners: a view from the bench', in Alpert, G.P. (ed), Legal Rights of Prisoners, Beverly Hills and London, Sage Publications.

Carlen, P., (1980), 'Radical Criminology, Penal Poloitics and the Rule of Law', in Carlen, P. and Collison, M. (eds), Radical Issues in Criminology, Oxford, Martin Robertson.

Casale, S., (1984), Minimum Standards for Prison Establishments, London, NACRO.

Clemmer, D., (1940), The Prison Community, New York, Holt, Rinehart and Winston, reprinted 1958.

Coggan, G., and Walker, M., (1982), Frightened for My Life – an account of deaths in British prisons, London, Fontana.

Cohen S. and Taylor, L., (1972), Psychological Survival – the experience of long-term imprisonment, Harmondsworth, Penguin.

Cohen, S. and Taylor, L., (1979), Prison Secrets, London, NCCL and RAP.

Cohen, S., (1975), 'A Futuristic Scenario for the Prison System', in Basaglia, F. (ed), The Crimes of Peace, Turin, Einaudi.

Committee of Inquiry into the United Kingdom Prison Services, (1979), (Chairman: Mr Justice May), Report, Cmnd. 7673, London, HMSO.

Conrad, J.P., (1977), 'Citizens and Criminals', Law and Psychology Review, vol. 3.

Corwin, E.S., (1958), The Constitution and What It Means Today, Princeton University Press,

Cover, R.M., (1983) 'Foreword: Nomos and Narrative, The Supreme Court 1982 Term', Harvard Law Review, vol. 97 no. 1, November.

Cox, B., (1975), Civil Liberties in Britain, Harmondsworth, Penguin.

Cranston, M., (1973), What Are Human Rights?, London, Bodley Head.

Cressey, D.R. (ed), (1961), The Prison: studies in institutional organization and change, Holt, Rinehart and Winston.

Ditchfield, J. and Austin, C., (1986), Grievance Procedures in Prisons: a study of prisoners' applications and petitions, London, HMSO.

Drzemczewski, A., (1978), 'The European Commission of Human Rights and Inadmissible Applications Against the United Kingdom', European Law Review, vol. 3 no. 1.

Drzemczewski, A., (1983), European Human Rights Conventions in Domestic Law: a comparative study, Oxford, Clarendon Press.

Dyson, K.H.F., (1980), The State Tradition in Western Europe - a study of an idea and and institution, Oxford, Basil Blackwell.

Eisenberg, T. and Yeazell, S.C., (1980), 'The Ordinary and Extraordinary in Institutional Litigation', Harvard Law Review, vol. 93 no. 3, January.

Ely, J., (1980), Democracy and Distrust: a theory of judicial review, Harvard, Harvard University Press.

Emerson, T.I. et al, (1967), Political and Civil Rights in the United States volume II, Boston, Little, Brown and Co..

Emery, C.T. and Smythe, B., (1986), Judicial Review, London, Sweet and Maxwell.

English, P., (1973), 'Prisoners' Rights: quis custodiet ipsos custodies?' in Bridge, J.W., Lasok, D., Perrott D.L., and Plender, R.O., (eds), Fundamental Rights, London, Sweet and Maxwell, 1973.

Expenditure Committee, (1977), Fifteenth Report of the Select Committee on Expenditure, The Reduction of Pressure on the Prison Population, London, HMSO, Cmnd 5375.

Feinberg, J., (1973), Social Philosophy, Englewood Cliffs N.J., Prentice-Hall.

Fiss, O.M., (1978), The Civil Rights Injunction, Bloomington, Indiana University Press.

Fitzgerald, M., (1977), Prisoners in Revolt, Harmondsworth, Penguin.

Fitzgerald, M. and Sim, J., (1978), British Prisons, Oxford, Basil Blackwell.

Fletcher, W.A., (1982), 'The Discretionary Constitution: institutional remedies and judicial legitimacy', Yale Law Journal, vol. 91 no. 4, March.

Fogel, D., (1975), '...We Are The Living Proof...', Cincinnatti, Anderson Publishing Co..

Foreign Office, (1953), Convention for the Protection of Human Rights and Fundamental Freedoms, Cmnd 8969, London, HMSO, Treaty Series No. 71.

Fox, Sir Lionel, (1952), The English Prison and Borstal System, London, Routledge and Kegan Paul.

Funston, R.Y., (1977), Constitutional Counter-Revolution? The Warren Court and the Burger Court: judicial policy making in modern America, Cambridge, Mass., Schenkman.

Galtung, J., (1961), 'Prison: the organization of dilemma', in Cressey, D.R. (ed), The Prison, New York, Holt, Rinehart and Winston.

Glaser, D. and Stratton, J.R., (1961) 'Measuring Inmate Change in Prison' in Cressey, D.R. (ed) , The Prison, New York, Holt, Rinehart and Winston.

Glick, B., (1973), 'Change Through the Courts', in Wright, E.O. (ed), The Politics of Punishment, a critical analysis of prisons in America, New York, Harper and Rowe.

Gottfriedson, S.D. and McConville, S. (eds), (1988), America's Correctional Crisis: prison populations and public policy, London, Greenwood Press.

Graham, F.P., (1970), The Due Process Revolution - the Warren Court's Impact on Criminal Law, New York, Hayden Books.

Gregory, R., and Hutchesson, P., (1977), The Parliamentary Ombudsman - a study in the control of administrative action, London, Allen and Unwin.

Gunther, G., (1964), Cases and Materials on Constitutional Law, St Paul, Foundation Press, Tenth Edition.

Hacker, E.A. (ed)., (1984), U.S. - a statistical portrait of the American people, Harmondsworth, Penguin Books.

Hailsham, Lord, (1983), Hamlyn Revisited - The British Legal System Today, London, Stevens.

Halsbury's Laws of England, (1982), vol. 37, London, Butterworths, Fourth Edition.

Hawkins, G., (1976), The Prison: policy and practice, Chicago, Chicago University Press.

Higgins, J., (1981), States of Welfare: comparative analysis in social policy, Oxford, Basil Blackwell.

Hobbes, Thomas, (1651), Leviathan, Harmondsworth, Penguin edition.

Home Office, (1951), Report of a Committee to Review Punishments in Prisons, Borstal Institutions, Approved Schools and Remand Homes, London, HMSO, Cmd 8256.

Home Office, (1973), Annual Report of the Work of the Prison Department for 1972, Cmnd 5375, London, HMSO.

Home Office, (1975), (Chairman: Mr T.G. Weiler), Report of the Working Party on Adjudication Procedures in Prisons, London, HMSO.

Home Office, (1979), Inquiry into the United Kingdom Prison Services, Volume 1, London, HMSO.

Home Office, (1982), Report of HM Chief Inspector of Prisons for England and Wales, 1981, Cmnd 8532, London, HMSO.

Home Office, (1983), Report of HM Chief Inspector of Prisons, 1982, HC 260, London, HMSO.

Home Office, (1985), Report of the Committee on the Prison Disciplinary System, Cmnd 9641, London, HMSO.

Home Office, (1986), The Prison Disciplinary System in England and Wales, Cmnd 9920, London, HMSO.

Home Office, (1987), A Review of Prisoners' Complaints, Report by HM Chief Inspector of Prisons, London, Home Office.

Horowitz, D.L., (1977), The Jurocracy: government lawyers, agency programmes and judicial decisions, Lexington, Mass., and Toronto, Lexington Books.

House of Lords Select Committee on the European Communities, (1978), Human Rights, 71st Report, HL 362, London, HMSO.

Howard League, (1983), Annual Report 1982/3, London, Howard League.

Howard League, (1982), A prospectus - an integrated approach to criminal justice and penal reform, London, Howard League.

Huff, C.R., (1980), 'The Discovery of Prisoners' Rights: a sociological analysis', in Alpert, G.P. (ed), Legal Rights of Prisoners, Beverly Hills and London, Sage Publications.

Huff C.R., and Alpert, G.P., (1982), 'Organisational Compliance with Court-Ordered Reform: the need for evluation research', in Monash, M. (ed), Implementing Criminal Justice Policies, Beverly Hills and London, Sage Publications.

Hurwitz, L., (1981), The State as Defendant - governmental accountability and the redress of individual grievances, London, Aldwych Press.

Jackson, P., (1979), Natural Justice, London, Sweet and Maxwell.

Jackson, G., (1971), Soledad Brother - the Prison Letters of George Jackson, Harmondsworth, Penguin.

Jacobs, F.G., (1975), The European Convention of Human Rights, Oxford, Clarendon Press.

Jacobs, J.B., (1977), Stateville: the penitentiary in mass society, Chicago, University of Chicago Press.

Jacobs, J.B., (1980), 'The History and Impact of the Prisoners' Rights Movement', in Morris, N. and Tonry, M. (eds), Crime and Justice: an annual review of research, volume II, Chicago, University of Chicago Press.

Jaconelli, J., (1976), 'The European Convention on Human Rights - the text of a British bill of rights', Public Law.

Jenkins, I., (1980), Social Order and the Limits of Law: a theoretical essay, Princeton, NJ, Princeton University Press.

Joyce, J.A., (1978), The New Politics of Human Rights, London, Macmillan.

JUSTICE, (1961), The Citizen and the Administration. The Redress of Grievances, Stevens.

JUSTICE, (1977), (Chairman: David Widdicombe, Q.C.), Our Fettered Ombudsman, London, JUSTICE.

JUSTICE (1983), (Chairman: Sir Brian Mackenna), Justice in Prison, London, JUSTICE.

JUSTICE - ALL SOULS, (1981), Review of Administrative Law in the United Kingdom - Discussion Paper, London, JUSTICE.

JUSTICE, The Howard League for Penal Reform, and NACRO, (1975), (Chairman: The Rt. Hon. the Earl Jellicoe), Boards of Visitors of Penal Establishments, Chichester, Barry Rose.

King, R.D. and Elliott, K., (1977), Albany: birth of a prison - end of an era, London, Routledge and Kegan Paul.

King, R. and Morgan, R., (1976), A Taste of Prison: custodial conditions for trial and remand prisons, London, Routledge and Kegan Paul.

King, R.D., Morgan, R., Martin, J.P. and Thomas, J.E., (1980), The Future of the Prison System, Aldershot, Gower.

Kleinig, J., (1978), 'Human Rights, Legal Rights and Social Change' in Kamenka, E. and Tay, A. (eds), Human Rights, London, Edward Arnold.

Leeke, W.D., (1980), 'The Negotiated Settlement: prisoners' rights in action', in Alpert, G.P. (ed), Legal Rights of Prisoners, Beverly Hills and London, Sage Publications.

Leigh, D., (1980), 'Down Comes a Prison Portculis', The Guardian, 10 April.

Lester, A., (1983), 'Why Deny Us These Rights?', The Times, 16 November.

Lester, A., (1984), 'Fundamental Rights: The United Kingdom Isolated', Public Law, Spring.

Lipman, D.M., (1974), 'Mississippi's Prison Experience', Mississippi Law Journal, vol. 45, no. 3, June.

Lloyd, D., (1979), The Idea of Law, Harmondsworth, Penguin, 1979.

Locke, John, (1690), Of Civil Government, Dent, Everyman edition, 1924.

Lord Chancellor's Department, (1983), The Government Response to the Report of the Royal Commission on Legal Services, Cmnd. 9077, London, HMSO.

McConville, S.D.M., (1981), A History of English Prison Administration, Volume 1, 1750-1877, London, Routledge and Kegan Paul.

Maguire, M., and Vagg, J., (1983), 'Who are the Prison Watchdogs? - The Membership and Appointment of Boards of Visitors, Criminal Law Review.

Maguire, M. and Vagg, J., (1984), The 'Watchdog' Role of Boards of Visitors, London, Home Office.

Mann, F.A., (1978), 'Britain's Bill of Rights', Law Quarterly Review, vol. 94, October.

Marin, B., (1983), Inside Justice: a comparative analysis of practices and procedures for the determination of offences against prison discipline in prisons of Britain and the United States, London, Associated Universities Press.

Martin, J.P., (1974), 'Justice in Prisons', New Society, 28 March.

Martin, J.P., (1980a), 'Jellicoe and After - Boards of Visitors into the Eighties', Howard Journal, vol. XIX no. 2.

Martin, J.P., (1980b), 'Maintaining standards: who guards the guards', in King, R.D., et al, The Future of the Prison System, Farnborough, Gower.

Mathiesen, T., (1965), The Defences of the Weak: a sociological study of a Norwegian correctional institution, London, Tavistock.

Mathiesen, T., (1974), The Politics of Abolition, Oxford, Martin Robertson.

McCleery, R.H., (1961), 'Authoritarianism and the Belief Systems of Incorrigibles' in Cressey, D.R., The Prison, New York, Holt, Rinehart and Winston.

Mitford, J., (1974), The American Prison Business, London, Allen and Unwin, originally Kind and Usual Punishment: the American prison business, New York, Knopf.

Morgan, R., (1982), 'Inspecting Prisons', Political Quarterly, vol. 5,

Morgan, R., (1984), 'Just Visiting - to what purpose', The Times, 7 April.

Morgan, R., (1985), 'Her Majesty's Inspectorate of Prisons' in Maguire, J.M., Vagg, J. and Morgan, R. (eds), Accountability and Prisons - opening up a closed world, London, Tavistock.

Morris, T. and P., (1963), Pentonville: a sociological study of an English prison, London, Routledge and Kegan Paul.

Nathan, V.M., (1979), 'The Use of Masters in Institutional Reform Litigation', Toledo Law Review, vol. 10, Winter.

National Association of Attorneys General, (1980), Implementation of Remedies in Prison Condition Suits, Raleigh, N., Carolina.

NACRO, (1984), NACRO News Digest No 28, London, NACRO, March.

NACRO, (1986), Black People and the Criminal Justice System, London, NACRO.

Palley, C., (1984), 'Lord Denning and Human Rights', in Jowell, J.L. and McAuslan, J.P.W.B. (eds), Lord Denning: the Judge and the Law, London, Sweet and Maxwell.

Parliamentary Commissioner for Administration, (1968), Annual Report for 1968, London, HMSO.

Powell, L.J., (1982), 'Are the Federal Courts Becoming Bureaucracies?', American Bar Association Journal, November.

Prescott, John, M.P., (1976), 'Hull Prison Riot, August 31 to September 3, 1976. Submissions, observations and recommendations of Mr John Prescott, M.P., Hull East', Unpublished report dated 21 December.

Rein, M., (1970), Social Policy: issues of choice and change, New York, Random House.

Richardson, G., (1984), 'Time to Take Prisoners' Rights Seriously', Journal of Law and Society, vol 11, no 1, Spring.

Robbins, I.P., (1978), 'Federalism, State Prison Reform, and Evolving Standards of Human Decency', Kansas Law Review, vol. 26, no. 4.

Rohde, D.W., and Spaeth, H.J., (1976), Supreme Court Decision-Making, San Francisco, W.H. Freeman.

Rose, G., (1961), The Struggle for Penal Reform, London, Stevens.

Royal Commission on Legal Services, (1979), (Chairman: Sir Henry Benson), Final Report - volume 1, Cmnd. 7648, London, HMSO.

Ryan, M., (1978), The Acceptable Pressure Group - inequality in the penal lobby, Saxon House.

Schrag, C., (1961), 'Some Foundations for a Theory of Corrections', in Cressey, D.R. (ed), The Prison, New York, Holt, Rinehart and Winston.

Schwartz, B., and Wade, H.W.R., (1972), Legal Control of Government, London, Oxford University Press.

Sensenich, I.J., (1979), Compendium of the Law on Prisoners' Rights, Washington D.C., Federal Judicial Center.

Smith, D.E., Austin, C., and Ditchfield, J., (1981), Board of Visitor Adjudications, Home Office, Research Unit, Paper 3.

Smith, R., (1984), Prison Medical Care, London, Britsh Medical Association.

Stacey, F., (1973), A New Bill of Rights for Britain, Newton Abbott, David and Charles.

Stacey, F., (1979), Ombudsmen Compared, Oxford, Clarendon Press.

Starr, M., (1981), 'Accommodation and Accountability: a strategy for judicial enforcement of institutional reform decrees', Alabama Law Review, vol. 32 no. 2, Winter.

Stevens, R., (1979), Law and Politics: the House of Lords as a judicial body, 1800-1976, London, Weidenfeld and Nicholson.

Stockdale, E., (1983), 'A Short History of Prison Inspection in England', British Journal of Criminology, vol. 23 no. 3, July.

Sykes, G., (1958), The Society of Captives, Princeton, NJ, Princeton University Press.

Taylor, L., (1980), 'Bringing Power to Particular Account: Peter Rajah and the Hull Board of Visitors' in Carlen, P., and Collison, M. (eds), Radical Issues in Criminology, Oxford, Basil Blackwell.

Taylor, S., (1981), 'Public Interest Jobs having Fewer Law Students, New York Times, 25 November.

Tettenborn, A.M., (1980), 'Prisoners' Rights', Public Law, Spring.

Thomas, C.W., (1980), 'The Impotence of Correctional Law' in Alpert, G.P. (ed), Legal Rights of Prisoners, Beverly Hills and London, Sage Publications.

Thomas, J.E., (1975), 'Special Units in British Prisons' in Jones, K. (ed), The Yearbook of Social Policy in Britain, 1974, London, Routledge and Kegan Paul.

Turner, W.B., (1979), 'When Prisoners Sue: a study of prisoner section 1983 suits in the federal courts', Harvard Law Review, vol. 92 no. 3, January.

von Hirsch, A., (1976), Doing Justice: the choice of punishment, New York, Hill and Wang.

Wade, H.W.R., (1961), Administrative Law, Oxford, Clarendon Press, Fifth edition.

Walker, D.M., (1980), Oxford Companion to the Law, Oxford, Clarendon Press.

Walker, N.D., (1972), Sentencing in a Rational Society, Harmondsworth, Penguin.

Walker, N.D., (1980), Punishment, Danger and Stigma: the morality of criminal justice, Oxford, Basil Blackwell.

Wallington, P. (ed), (1984), Civil Liberties 1984, Oxford, Martin Robertson.

Wener, G., (1983), A Legitimate Grievance: a report on the role of the ombudsman in the prison system, London, Prison Reform Trust.

Wheeler, S., (1961), 'Role Conflict in Correctional Communities', in Cressey, D.R. (ed), The Prison, New York, Holt, Rinehart and Winston.

Wicker, T., (1976), A Time to Die, London, Bodley Head.

Wilkins, L.T., 'Directions for Corrections', Proceedings of the American Philiosophical Society, vol 118.

Woodbury, E.G., (1982), 'Prison Overcrowding and Rhodes v. Chapman: double-celling by what standards?', Boston College Law Review, vol. xxxii no. 3, May.

Wright, M., (1982), Making Good - prisons, punishment and beyond, London, Burnett Books.

Yardley, D.C.M., (1981), Principles of Administrative Law, London, Butterworths.

Yeazell, S.C., (1977), 'Group Litigation and Social Context: toward a history of the class action', Columbia Law Review, vol. 77 no. 6, October.

Young, J., (1979), 'Left Idealism, Reformism and Beyond: from the new criminology to Marxism', in Fine, B. et al (eds), Capitalism and the Rule of Law: from deviancy theory to Marxism, London, Hutchinson.

Zellick, G., (1971), 'Prisoners' Rights in England', University of Toronto Law Journal, vol. 24(4).

Zellick, G., (1976), 'Why Prisoners should have an ombudsman of their own', The Times, 4 October.

Zellick, G., (1977), 'Legal Services for Convicted Prisoners', Howard Journal, vol. XVI no. 2.

Zellick, G., (1978), 'The Prison (Amendment) Rules', LAG Bulletin, June.

Zellick, G., (1980), 'Is Remission Enforceable?', Criminal Law Review,

Zellick, G., (1981), 'The Prison Rules and the Courts', Criminal Law Review.

Zellick, G,. (1983), 'Justice and Accountability in Prisons', in NACRO, A Prison System for the 80s and Beyond, The Noel-Buxton Lectures 1982-3, London, NACRO.

Index